The Democratic Enlightenment

The Democratic Enlightenment

By DONALD H. MEYER

Capricorn Books, New York

G. P. PUTNAM'S SONS, NEW YORK

SBN: 399-11686-9

Library of Congress Cataloging in Publication Data

Meyer, Donald Harvey, 1935-
  The democratic enlightenment.

  Bibliography.
  Includes index.
  1. United States—Intellectual life—18th century.
  2. Enlightenment. I. Title.
E163.M48   1975   973   75-15752

Contents

Preface

AMERICA was itself an experiment in an "age of experiments," as Benjamin Franklin called the eighteenth century. What made the American Enlightenment unique has less to do with the ideas Americans actually contributed to the world than with the practical use they made of ideas, particularly during their Revolutionary period. America served European intellectuals as an example and even an inspiration of ideas at work, theories put into practice. The American counterpart of the French *philosophe* was not the irreverent, witty, and forever critical intellectual, battling the powers of church and state in the name of reason and humanity. He was the self-taught tradesman seeking education along with fame and fortune, the preacher or lawyer curious to know more about the "New Learning," and the republican statesman laboring to establish a new nation. Ask any college student about the American Enlightenment, and, provided you receive any answer at all, you will probably be told of the Declaration of Independence or perhaps of the Constitution—official documents that, even if one contains the slogans of revolution, are rightly treated not as theoretical platforms but as cornerstones of American politics and government. In Europe the Enlightenment meant the appeal for a more tolerable life. In America it meant the good life. The Americans did not merely raise the cry for liberty: America became, in James Madison's phrase, the "workshop for liberty."

The American situation was such that we could put into practice many of the things the *philosophes* preached. In no position to afford being merely theoretical or speculative, the Americans were realistic, pragmatic, and because American society was less rigidly structured than most European societies were, the intellectual life and the common life tended to merge. The intellectual, far from being at the periphery of power, as was frequently the case abroad, was both a part of his society and often a respected leader of it. The Constitution begins with the phrase "We the People." In America the people were never a semifictitious horde to be uplifted, liberated, patronized, and feared. They were we.

All this has been said before. The main questions with which this study is concerned are: How did this merger of the intellectual and the common lives come about? More important: What have been the consequences of this remarkable state of affairs for American intellectual history? If the eighteenth century was truly an age of experiments, and if the Americans represented their age by performing one of its greatest experiments, what does this imply about the American experience? We could say that the Enlightenment became an American institution. If this is the case, what have been the results of making an inquisitive, liberating, intellectually adventurous frame of mind into a national institution?

Introduction

A PROVINCIAL ENLIGHTENMENT

I

IN 1803, in his *Brief Retrospect of the Eighteenth Century*, Samuel Miller observed that the history of American culture is "short and simple." He added ruefully: "the history of poverty is usually neither very various, nor very interesting." Measured by European standards, the American accomplishment looked meager indeed. Nevertheless, Miller insisted, anyone who remembers "the origin and progress of the settlements which now form the United States"—a nation still under thirty years old—may well entertain a "more respectful" opinion of America's intellectual achievement. Surveying American intellectual history in the eighteenth century, Miller concluded that the Americans were most successful in their production of "*theological* and *political* works, and those intended for the use of *schools*." It was in the pulpit, the public forum, and the schoolroom that the American intellectual most conspicuously distinguished himself.[1]

For Americans living in the eighteenth century, Western civilization ended relatively few miles west of anyplace along the Eastern Seaboard, and the center of that civilization lay some three thousand ocean miles eastward. As far as the intellectual culture of the Americans is concerned, it is true that ideas are one of the most easily imported commodities, and that communications between Boston, say, and London were probably not much worse than those between London and Edinburgh. Still, even though ideas are easily transported, libraries, art masterpieces, scientific apparatus—the facilities of culture—are not. Many things that eighteenth-century Europeans could take for granted—universities, organizations for the transmission of knowledge, a wealthy patron class, bustling cosmopolitan life in thriving urban centers, leisure—the Americans either did without, created, or improvised. All this did not preclude the intellectual life in America. It meant, rather, that for eighteenth-century Americans the intellectual life must also be the practical life. So, when Miller spoke of the American contribution to culture as consisting chiefly of theological, political, and academic works, he was describing a people for whom the life of the mind reflected the practical concerns of a newly founded society.

During the course of the eighteenth century, the Americans went through a startling transformation. Not only did they "become literary," as Miller put it, but they grew enormously in both wealth and population and, eventually declaring their independence of Great Britain, became the first new nation of the modern world. They established themselves as a Federal republic, and thereby opened a new era in the political history of the Western world. In the midst of all this, the Americans had to muster the intellectual resources not only to understand and cope with their changing circumstances, but also to explain their emerging national policy to the world and to give themselves a cultural identity as a people. Just as their intellectual life expressed practical concerns, the Americans' day-to-day life was informed by their intellectual response to the dominant ideas of their age.

What was that age like? The modern historian would probably not significantly revise Samuel Miller's description of the eighteenth century. Above all, he said, it was an age of "free inquiry," of searching, critical investigation of all things, including all authority. Further, it was an age of "science"—of social and psychological as well as natural science. It was an age of printing, books, and of the man of letters, an age of "unprecedented diffusion of knowledge" but often of "superficial learning." It was an age of infidel speculation and of Christian reaction.[2] Miller's is an extremely perceptive assessment of what Immanuel Kant, in 1784, called the "age of enlightenment," a term that historians have applied to the eighteenth century ever since.

Usually the Enlightenment is identified as a period of significant intellectual activity and conflict extending from the late seventeenth century through the coming of the French Revolution, and reaching a highpoint in the mid-eighteenth century with the publication of its greatest works. It was in the 1750's, for example, that Rousseau published his first work, *Discourse on the Sciences and Arts* (1751), and which saw the publication of the first volume of the *Encyclopedia*, edited by Diderot and d'Alembert (1751), Voltaire's *Essay on Manners* (1754) and *Candide* (1759), and Condillac's *Treatise on Sensations* (1754). Although the Enlightenment is often associated with a small group of French thinkers and polemicists known as the *philosophes*, the movement extends beyond France and is best regarded as an international phenomenon, the philosophe (without italics) being a cosmopolitan and not just a national figure.[3] At this point the problem is complicated by the fact that, properly speaking, there was not one Enlightenment but many. That is, the Enlightenment took different forms from country to country—Enlightened London being quite different from Enlightened Paris or even Edinburgh. And to say how far the Enlightenment extended beyond the London or Paris city limits presents all kinds of further problems. Naturally, when we leave Europe and turn to Colonial America all these problems are compounded. It has even been suggested that it is wrong to speak of an American Enlightenment at all.[4] Before turning to the American Enlightenment, however, the first problem is to determine what that significant intellectual activity and conflict is that distinguishes the Enlightenment from other periods of thought. How, in other words, are we to define "the Enlightenment"?

The phrase that comes most readily to mind is "Age of Reason." Such an easy definition, however, presents many difficulties, partly because of the various meanings that can be attached to the word "reason." For example, if by "reason" one means a deductive system that starts with certain first principles and proceeds logically to construct grand theories about the nature of God and the destiny of man, then we would have to say that the eighteenth century was quite the opposite of an age of reason. The most influential and important thinkers of the Enlightenment were very much the enemies of traditional rationalism and of what they called metaphysics, and frequently insisted on the limitations of man's rational powers. Indeed, eighteenth-century thinkers put great emphasis on the emotions (variously called the "sentiments," "affections," and "passions"), which were said to provide the driving energy in human affairs. Furthermore, we have the individual testimony of no less an American philosophe than Benjamin Franklin that man is a "rational animal" mainly in the sense that he can usually find a reason for doing whatever he really has a mind to. As if to lay the matter to rest once and for all, there is the emphatic testimony of another Enlightened American, John Adams, who declared in 1805:

> I am willing you should call this the Age of Frivolity . . . and would not object if you had named it the Age of Folly, Vice, Frenzy, Fury, Brutality, Daemons, Buonaparte, Tom Paine, the Age of the Burning Brand and Bottomless Pit: or anything but the Age of Reason.

Clearly, no simple identification of the Enlightenment as the Age of Reason will do.

At its very center the Enlightenment represents the philosophical assimilation of the scientific revolution of the sixteenth and seventeenth centuries. It is the effort, more specifically, to apply the techniques and assumptions of the scientific revolution to the study of man, including man's mind, and to the study of society. This meant that matters of the deepest concern—involving questions about human nature, for instance, morality and religion, and law and sovereignty—were to be raised with new urgency, and investigated from new angles and with new expectations. More than this, all the fundamental philosophical assumptions on which human knowledge had rested for centuries, including assumptions about the nature of knowledge itself, were to be subjected to searching public examination. Kant had this in mind when he announced: "Our age is the age of criticism, to which everything must be subjected." As an age of criticism, in contrast with the long centuries of faith and authority that constituted what the philosophers liked to call the Dark Ages, the Enlightenment is properly considered part of a wider historical development, and not entirely separate from the periods immediately preceding and following it. It is to be seen as an important stage in the emergence of the modern mentality.

To say this is not to imply that we may simply absorb the Enlightenment into a broader movement, and thus escape further responsibility for defining it. The Enlightenment is unique in spite of its wider ramifications and relationships. It is useful, at this point, to introduce a necessary distinction between the assumptions, methods, and habits of thought that may properly be described as Enlightened and the implications that these assumptions and methods had for future generations. In other words, we must distinguish between the shared assumptions of the age and the hidden logic of these assumptions.

We may easily set forth the assumptions of the Enlightenment. They include the things most textbooks recite. There was, above all, a new faith in science, inspired particularly by Isaac Newton's grand synthesis of terrestrial and celestial physics in his *Mathematical Principles of Natural Philosophy* (1686). Increasingly, the natural sciences provided the model for a rational explanation, for the natural sciences discovered the laws governing the world about us. Science employed the method of observation and experiment, so the adoption of science as the model for rational explanation implied the systematic testing of all things in the arena of human experience. "This is the age of experiments," Franklin announced toward the end of his *Autobiography,* and few of his contemporaries would have disagreed. Since "experiments" most conveniently test natural phenomena, the Enlightenment is rightly associated with a heightened interest in the natural world, including, significantly, human nature. Correspondingly, what could not be tested—claims to knowledge based on supernatural revelation, sheer authority, or abstruse speculation—increasingly came under suspicion; in the course of the eighteenth century we observe a growing impatience with mystery and "metaphysics."

Faith in science meant new hope for man. In the first place, science fostered the belief that this is an intelligible world, a world that may be understood through the determined application of the human mind. The dark corners of existence seemed both less numerous and less ominous. Second, scientific knowledge is a hard-won acquisition in which man may take justifiable pride; it is not received as a gift from some superhuman source, but is the publicly verifiable result of observations and experiments that—in theory, at least—anyone may repeat. Third, when science is applied to man himself, it is possible to comprehend the laws by which human existence is governed. Man then becomes capable of understanding himself as never before and, by understanding himself, of determining how he ought to live in order to realize his highest potential. Fourth, when applied to society, science enables man to understand and ultimately to design his social environment, engineering social institutions to serve his needs. Finally, scientific knowledge, applied to technology, allows man for the first time to conquer his earthly destiny and improve his moral and material estate beyond all imagination.

The thinkers of the Enlightenment recognized man's weaknesses and limitations, to be sure. Moreover, science itself had its darker side, threatening to dehumanize man in the very act of studying him, by reducing him to the status of a mere cog in the great world-machine of which he was considered a part. But the prevailing note was one of optimism. Because of science, one could now examine the human prospect more confidently than was ever before possible.

At this point we should note that throughout the eighteenth century it was possible, indeed common, for thoughtful persons to accept the ruling assumptions of the Enlightenment—to be committed to its scientism, its spirit of criticism, and its humanism—and still remain attached to traditional beliefs and authorities. For example, in spite of the distrust of mystery, one might remain a devout Christian, committed to the truths of Scripture, including the miracles reported in the New Testament. Human thought is seldom as logical and consistent as historians of ideas would like it to be. An eighteenth-century thinker might honestly consider himself possessed of a critical mind, yet—without being entirely aware of it—set aside certain cherished beliefs, refusing to examine them too closely, either because they seemed to be beyond any doubt or because they were too precious to be subjected to the indignities of searching cross-examination. To accept the basic premises of eighteenth-century thought, to be Enlightened, in other words, was not necessarily to be modern, as we understand the term today. In the eighteenth century, many a thinking person was informed and receptive to new ideas without being thoroughly modern.

Thus we arrive at the important distinction between the *assumptions* of the Enlightenment and the *hidden logic*—the historical implications—of those assumptions. Although always dangerous, it is also useful and perhaps unavoidable for the historian to "read history backwards" now and then, to examine the future of an idea in order fully to understand its importance at any particular time. We have already traced the Enlightenment back to the scientific revolution. Now, by pursuing it *forward* into the nineteenth and twentieth centuries, we are able to observe three modern developments that have their roots in the eighteenth century and that constitute the logical flowering of Enlightenment thinking. Let us call these developments secularism, naturalism, and positivism.

Secularism, in the broadest sense, is a concern for the things of this world and a general loss of interest in the fundamental truths of religion. This definition is perhaps too broad; and its critics are right when they point to statistics on church membership, not to mention popular enthusiasm for exorcism, gurus, faith-healers, pentacostalism, oriental mysticism, and visitations from beyond, to substantiate their contention that the modern age is no less interested in religion than any other. A narrower understanding of secularism seems in order. If we look at the intellectual world, for example, it is undeniable that modern thinkers are far more this-worldly in their writings than were their counterparts in the theological environment of a few centuries ago. Not only are a great many intellectuals indifferent about, for instance, whether there is or is not a god, but they are no longer even expected seriously to consider such a question. What is lacking today above all is a basic theological consensus, a shared metaphysic and mythology about the significance of life and the meaning of the universe. Many today have firm beliefs, but—despite the solemn words of some politicians and church leaders—we no longer share a common faith. And the intellectual community—if indeed it still *is* a community—has renounced metaphysical allegiances, and so no longer officially establishes the legitimacy of our beliefs. The prominent marks of secularism, then, are prevailing intellectual indifference to what are usually considered ultimate questions, and a loss of cultural consensus on how these questions should be answered.

Naturalism is the belief that the natural world is the real world. What is unnatural—or supernatural—is unreal. Naturalism is the implicit, if not explicit, denial of (or the denial of the meaningfulness in discussing) the existence of a transcendent, supernatural, or ultimate "reality." A naturalistic explanation of something treats the universe as a self-contained system of matter in motion: No attempt is made to look out beyond that system to account for what happens within it. Naturalism is simply the conviction that everything is subject to a naturalistic explanation.

Positivism, finally, is a limiting of the kinds of things we may rationally discuss. That is, it limits rational inquiry (except in mathematics and symbolic logic) to the results of observation and experiment and the legitimate inferences drawn from these. (The nature of "legitimate" inference remains, of course, debatable—but with increasingly less room for such debate.) Taking the method of experimental science as its model, positivism represents metaphysical modesty—a determined self-restraint when it comes to handling questions to which no empirically verifiable answers may be given.

Secularism, naturalism, and positivism are at the center of modern philosophical thinking: for some, setting the limits to be observed in philosophical discourse; for others, setting up an intellectual barricade to be breached in the struggle for Truth. Representing the direction Western thought has taken since the seventeenth century, secularism, naturalism, and positivism are the offspring of the scientific revolution and the collapse of traditional intellectual authorities. They take their precise philosophical form in the period we know as the Enlightenment.

Again, it is important to make the point clearly that, in the eighteenth century, it was possible for a thinking person to be committed to the general assumptions that we have associated with the Enlightenment—confidence in science as the model for a rational explanation, a critical and experimental approach to all questions, great interest in man and his world—and still reject or remain entirely unaware of the implications of these assumptions, namely, secularism, naturalism, and positivism. But the struggle had begun. The strenuous, sometimes torturous, efforts of so many eighteenth-century writers to reconcile their religious faith with their scientific philosophy reveals the conflict that rages at the center of Enlightenment thinking, the conflict between older beliefs and values that could not be denied and new methods and assumptions that could not be ignored. Even among those philosophes—like Diderot and Voltaire—who had liberated themselves from their inherited faith, the struggle between tradition and innovation, belief and criticism, is evident, though more with respect to moral values than religious faith.

In this connection, David Hume—the brilliant Scottish philosopher who drew out the full implications of Lockean empiricism—is a unique and interesting case. More than any other eighteenth-century thinker, Hume was aware both of the assumptions of the Enlightenment and of their secularistic, naturalistic, and positivistic implications. More than anyone of his generation, Hume appreciated both the strengths and the limitations of the new "experimental method" when, in his *Treatise of Human Nature* (1739), he resolutely applied it to "moral subjects." More than any other thinker of his age, with the exception of Kant, he understood the gap that separates our beliefs about things from the actual nature of those things, our "ideas" from the "realities" they are supposed to represent; and he understood the gap that separates facts and values, the "is" and the "ought," science and morality. All this makes Hume a central, but not a representative, Enlightenment figure.[5] Understandably, most other thinkers lacked the combination of genius, persistence, and daring that Hume possessed. For most, it was possible to rejoice in the ideas and experiments that Hume referred to as the "new scene of thought" without admitting that these ideas were ultimately to prove subversive to the moral and religious tradition that had lasted for centuries. This admission would have to wait until the nineteenth century, when the Darwinian revolution made the wider cultural implications of science alarmingly apparent to all reflective people.

Intellectually, then, at the center of the Enlightenment were the new scientific philosophy and the (unappreciated but potent and corrosive) implications of that philosophy. The Enlightenment, however, involves more than ideas. Set against the background of fundamental social and institutional change—the collapse of the late-medieval corporate society or what was often called the feudal system, the waning of the authority of the church, the rise of capitalism and of an energetic and increasingly self-conscious and literate middle class—the Enlightenment represents a peculiar style that sets it apart from both the century that precedes it and that which follows it.

To speak of the style of a period is to refer to those unique qualities of imagination, taste, and behavior that distinguish it from others. For instance, one usually associates the Enlightenment with a tone that is partisan, aggressive, polemical, questioning, abrasive—whatever its actual accomplishments might be. The Enlightenment was an age of political rhetoric and moral defiance as well as an age of experiments and reason: Its demands at times seemed anything but reasonable to those who worried about the stability of the social order. This distinctive tone characterizes an age in which are combined, on the one hand, the rising hopes and expectations of a generation that glimpses entirely new possibilities for human fulfillment, and, on the other hand, a growing frustration with a waning system of authority that had not yet lost its coercive powers. The partisan spirit of the Enlightenment reflects the irritating juxtaposition of new hopes and old restrictions.

The style of the Enlightenment is distinguished, above all, by a new consciousness. The concern with knowledge, the critical spirit, and the frequently polemical and partisan temper of the philosophes all fit in well with this new perception of things. Social evils that had, until the eighteenth century, remained below the threshold of society's consciousness were now noticed and condemned as unjust and inhumane: religious persecution, the brutal treatment of criminals (along with flexible definitions of criminal behavior), the use of torture—all received their share of exposure and denunciation. In a broader sense, the idea of natural rights—though its roots go far back in history—indicates the presence of a new responsiveness to human needs and aspirations, a new sensibility regarding human misery, and the growing belief that something can and should be done to change human life for the better. In part, one can explain the eighteenth-century concern with benevolence and kindness with reference to this new consciousness. Certainly, if the eighteenth century is to be praised for nothing else, it must be praised for having given rise to a tradition that is—despite monstrous and grotesque setbacks—still with us: a tradition of human decency and (though it sounds strange to say it) of awareness of the evil of suffering.

The eighteenth-century world in which the United States of America was born was morally and intellectually a fiercely exciting one. It marked Western culture's coming of age—a dawning of philosophical maturity, a struggle for moral autonomy, an awakening of political consciousness. And America was very much a part of that world. As one of Europe's most promising cultural provinces, America—for perhaps the first and last time in its history—was integrally related to the intellectual culture of the larger, transatlantic civilization.

II

"Colonists became colonials," Howard Mumford Jones observes, "colonials became provincials."[6] The distinction between a colonial and a provincial is important, for the latter has a cultural identity that the former lacks. Roughly, we may say that a colonial is identified in relation to a mother country mainly in political and economic terms, while a provincial is identified in relation to a center of civilization and defined in cultural terms. In the eighteenth century the adjective (and noun) "provincial" was often used to denote lack of sophistication and refinement. In his *Dictionary of the English Language* (1755), Dr. Samuel Johnson defined "provincial" as "rude" and "unpolished." Thus used, the term suggests pretension to some refinement or, at least, commitment to the standards of a cultural center by which one's own society is appropriately judged. It would have been preposterous to describe the first settlers at Jamestown as "rude" and "unpolished." But one might say that about the "first civilized American," Benjamin Franklin. The colonial Americans had to rise to the level of cultural provinciality. By the middle of the eighteenth century they had reached that level.

America's cultural provinciality expressed itself particularly in an awareness of inadequate resources, a feeling of dependence, and a willingness to improvise. The lack of resources was painful. One thinks of the famous example of the young artist, John Singleton Copley, complaining to Benjamin West of the lack of paintings to study in the Colonies, or of Franklin's lifelong interest in books—books *per se,* as physical objects, indispensable cultural tools. Throughout most of the eighteenth century the American provincials were dependent on England particularly for their books and for most of the other implements of culture, including everything from precision tools and scientific apparatus to literary style and ideas. It is well known that Franklin developed his literary style by copying from the *Spectator,* and Jonathan Edwards, the century's greatest American philosopher, had his philosophical awakening when he was exposed to the so-called Dummer collection, books donated to Yale library in 1714, which included, besides the new psychology of Locke, writings of Newton, Addison, Defoe, and many of the Anglican divines whose latitudinarian teachings so stimulated Edwards' own thinking. Even in matters of fashion the colonial Americans looked to their royal governors and their families for guidance. To make up for this lack of cultural resources the provincial Americans were forced to improvise and develop new ways of doing things. Book printers, lacking patrons to finance their enterprises, had to solicit subscriptions house-to-house, and came to rely more on newspapers and almanacs than on books to earn a living and to communicate ideas. Since America lacked an aristocratic class of patrons, she also lacked a distinctly intellectual class. Consequently, the Americans came to depend on their professional, business, and working people—their ministers, lawyers, merchants, and artisans—for their cultural productions.

Ideas are more easily imported than objects and institutions. Because of this, the Americans absorbed many eighteenth-century ideas while possessing few of the institutions, artifacts, and conventions that gave them special meaning. While this imposed obvious limitations on the American mind, it also presented the Americans with special opportunities. Institutions hamper ideas as well as sustain them, and their institutional shortcomings allowed the Americans, almost without thinking about it, to put many of their imported ideas to work without opposition. The most obvious example of this comes from the realm of political thought. As Louis Hartz has shown in his study *The Liberal Tradition in America,* the Whig tradition of political liberalism—the appeal for individual autonomy and for the rights of property over against traditional privilege and royal authority—found its "natural" environment in America, where the authority of the Crown and the Church was weak and feudal institutions were poorly grounded if not altogether lacking.[7] In a wider sense, America's lack of longstanding traditions and institutions meant that the political program of the Enlightenment would have smoother sailing in this country than abroad, and the Americans could accomplish things in areas like self-rule and religious tolerance that would seem like impossible dreams to most Europeans. Thus, if the provincial Americans worked under some severe limitations, they yet learned that in limitation there is sometimes unexpected strength.

Limitation, though it has advantages, remains limitation nonetheless. The American achievement in art, literature, science, and philosophy—while impressive under the circumstances—was clearly that of a "rude" and "unpolished" people. In ideas, the Americans were, as is frequently noted, importers rather than exporters throughout most of the eighteenth century. Only after the American Revolution did Americans make any substantial contribution to the Enlightenment, and this contribution—centering in the constitution of a Federal republic—was more on the practical than on the philosophical level. The practical nature of the American Enlightenment has been frequently noted and often praised. In their social thought, particularly, the Americans were not speculative, utopian, or grandly ideological, but down-to-earth and pragmatic, directing their wisdom to immediate problems of public policy. Such practicality went beyond social thought. When Samuel Miller pointed out that the Americans did their best in theology, politics, and textbook writing, he was referring to three eminently practical concerns of his time. (In eighteenth-century America, works of divinity were more popular and widely read than they are in our own day; hence, in meeting an immediate public demand, they may be considered more practical.) But was this practical emphasis an unmixed blessing? Unquestionably, American thought—and not just political thought—was closely related to practical needs and public concerns, but did this situation best serve the intellectual life of the country? Although the very phrasing of such a question suggests an answer, this is a very important and rather complicated matter, which we shall be examining from many angles.

III

Facing squarely the matter of the American Enlightenment, three questions have to be raised. First, what was the extent and how deep was the penetration of Enlightenment ideas in eighteenth-century America? Second, what was unique about the American Enlightenment, or more specifically, what was unique about the circumstances surrounding the American Enlightenment? Third, what is the time-period with which we are to concern ourselves in speaking of the American Enlightenment?

It is always hazardous to speak of the influence or penetration of ideas. When we use metaphors like "climate of opinion" or "spirit of the age," we run the risk of confusing the communication and influence of ideas with something else—like a weather front or pentecostal inspiration. Paris may have been the "center" of Enlightenment thought, but in the countryside only a few miles away the French peasant of the eighteenth century continued to live in a mental universe not fundamentally different from that of his great-great-grandfather. Still, the means available for the communication of ideas, thanks to the printing press, were rapidly expanding. And the reading public, led by an emerging middle class, was growing, particularly in Britain and her American Colonies, where literacy was more widespread than on the European continent. It would be a mistake, of course, to confuse literacy with higher thought. The almanacs and newspapers that people in the Colonies read, even though they sometimes contained quotations from Shaftesbury and Addison, Locke and Montesquieu, could hardly be considered important bearers of the Enlightenment. From what we know thus far about the cultural and intellectual life of the American Colonies, it seems safe to say that the Enlightenment was largely confined to the great seaboard cities and to a few notable plantations and estates, although at least one researcher has found evidence that Enlightenment writings got as far inland as St. Louis, a three-month journey up the Mississippi from New Orleans![8] In spite of occasional prodigies like Franklin, a few backwoods deists like Ethan Allen, and some interesting examples of popular enthusiasm for French ideas in the early 1790's, there is little substantial evidence of a popular Enlightenment in eighteenth-century America.

The influence of ideas, however, cannot adequately be measured simply by counting the heads directly exposed to them. Ideas have a qualitative as well as a quantitative impact, and may exert a subtle cultural influence that eludes our most careful counting techniques. This is where our second question comes in: What was unique about the circumstances surrounding the American Enlightenment? Put another way, What were the prevailing social conditions that would affect the way ideas were assimilated into America's intellectual life?

Using, for the sake of convenience, terms that admittedly present problems of interpretation, let us say that the American Enlightenment was unique in that it was a provincial, democratic, and nationalistic movement. The *provincial* character of the American scene we have already examined. We need only add here that our provincial circumstances served to filter Enlightenment thought, causing the Americans to become aware of some European developments only after long delays, and in some cases permitting them to receive only major ideas and themes from abroad, missing counterthemes and subtle variations because only the major works were considered worth the cost involved in shipping them across the ocean. Like a subway commuter reading a newspaper over another person's shoulder, the American got the gist of what was happening, but often missed the details and qualifications that went with it. A happy example of this is provided by Franklin's experiments in electricity. He was able to transform a curiosity into a science partly because he was largely unaware of the latest (wrong) European speculations in the new field.

The American Enlightenment was *democratic* in the broad sense that American society, being more mobile and less hierarchical and tradition-bound than European societies, permitted a wider dissemination of ideas and presented fewer institutional obstacles to Enlightenment thought. The monarchical, ecclesiastical, and aristocratic enemies of the Enlightenment were absent from the American social landscape. This meant, as we have noted, that ideas would be more easily translated into effective policies. But it also meant that ideas would never have to meet the challenge of determined and consistent intellectual opposition—a process that usually has the effect of sharpening distinctions and clarifying thought. America's democratic Enlightenment would be at once successful in realizing its ideals and something less than clear about the precise meaning or the long-range implications of those ideals.

Finally, the American Enlightenment was *nationalistic* insofar as its major impact on American thought came in the late eighteenth and early nineteenth centuries when the new nation was struggling toward a national identity, a sense of moral particularity. Drawing on the intellectual resources available to them, the Americans incorporated many of the basic assumptions of the Enlightenment—including its scientific humanism and its concern for the rights of man—into its own public ethic and official beliefs. The liberal social commitments of the age, in other words, became national goals; while the age's central convictions and values were officially included among the things the Americans liked to believe they believed in. By the first quarter of the nineteenth century the Enlightenment had been assimilated into the American social consciousness, though not, of course, without amendments and revisions. We are thus led to our third question, that concerning the matter of periodization.

What period of time are we considering when we treat the American Enlightenment? Henry F. May has recently reminded us that the American Enlightenment involves more than the events of the Revolutionary period and the political ideas of that time. In America as abroad the Enlightenment was both more and less than a political movement; and it was certainly more than the "infidel" and "skeptical" speculations associated with the extremes of French philosophy. May has divided the American Enlightenment into three periods.[9] The first, extending from the early eighteenth century until the time of the American Revolution, was marked by the quiet penetration of predominantly British ideas—including those of Newton and Locke. The second, extending through the 1780's and 1790's—a restless and critical period intellectually as well as politically—was characterized by fashionable Jacobinism, popular deism, and a vogue in French ideas. The final period—really a transition period in the first decade of the nineteenth century—saw the defeat of Enlightenment radicalism and the successful effort to contain the Enlightenment by seeing to it that its brand of rationalism worked for, not against, the fundamental religious and moral principles that were deemed essential to the well-being of the republic.

If we think of the Enlightenment in terms of the experimental philosophy and its application to other fields of inquiry, we may for the sake of convenience further break down this periodization by focusing on four especially important areas of concern, namely, religion, morality, political thought, and education. Although none of these concerns, obviously, is the exclusive preoccupation of any one time-period, it is not being entirely arbitrary to suggest that, in the first forty years of the eighteenth century, the religious concern was particularly prominent. During the middle part of the century there was a shift in interest from religion to more secular matters, accompanied by more adventurous philosophical speculation. This shift in emphasis was marked by a growing concern with standards of conduct in a rapidly changing and expanding society. The moral concern did not in all cases replace religion: Rather, pious and secular people alike exhibited growing interest in ethical questions and moral problems, an interest that is expressed in a new curiosity about the study of moral philosophy. During the Revolutionary period, though religious and moral concerns did not disappear, the nation's energies were drawn to matters of society and government, and politics moved into intellectual prominence. Finally, beginning in the 1790's, amidst growing concern over the fate of the young Republic in the face of the kind of philosophical "skepticism" and "infidelity" that had destroyed republican France, there was a fundamental shift in emphasis. Intellectual adventurousness fell into disrepute, and the effort was made to instill the principles of religion and morality into the public mind. The Americans turned to education, looking to their colleges, schools, and churches to promote public virtue by defending and promulgating sound philosophy and wholesome beliefs. In the process, the experimental philosophy was inducted into national service. The principles of the Enlightenment were shown to be in harmony with those of true religion, sound morality, and sane political thinking.

In exploring these four areas of emphasis, we shall concentrate on certain key figures who represent various aspects of American Enlightenment thought. Jonathan Edwards and Benjamin Franklin may be taken to represent the religious and the moral concerns respectively. Thomas Jefferson and John Adams show us somewhat different faces of the political thinking of the Revolutionary period, while John Witherspoon and William Ellery Channing suggest something of the range of the educational endeavor of the late eighteenth and early nineteenth centuries.

For a time, in the late eighteenth century, the Americans enjoyed a wonderful joining of public policy and philosophical debate, of power and intellect. Many Americans saw good reason to hope, moreover, that their nation would someday participate as an equal in the intellectual culture of the Western world. As it turned out, American intellectual history set off in quite a different direction. Reacting to the French Revolution and fearing the corrosive effects of Enlightenment thinking—fearing especially the secularism, naturalism, and positivism that were implicit in the age's humanism, scientism, and empiricism—the Americans pulled away from Europe, erected a moral barrier against radical ideas, stripped intellect of power, and pressed the experimental method of reasoning into the service of traditional values. If we think of the Enlightenment as giving shape to the modern mind, we may say that modernity successively intruded itself into various areas of American thought before it was finally tamed and rendered fit for the Republic. The Enlightenment became part of the fabric of American thought, but at a price. For, in becoming Americanized, the Enlightenment lost that critical spirit that makes it unique and innervating; it was transformed into something else. And in making the Enlightenment into an American institution, the Americans lost the use of a method of critical self-examination that might have added not only richness and texture to its intellectual life but also a redeeming note of moral discontent to its social and political life.

I

EXPERIMENTAL RELIGION

[1]

RELIGION AND THE EXPERIMENTAL METHOD OF REASONING

WHEN Franklin called his "the age of experiments," he identified the central theme of the Enlightenment. As the terms were used in the eighteenth century, "experiment" and "experimental" could refer to the process of testing hypotheses systematically (as in a laboratory "experiment") or, more generally, to matters pertaining to one's immediate experience— "experimental" knowledge of something being knowledge based on firsthand acquaintance rather than on hearsay or conjecture. In the first instance, the experimental method was that of Francis Bacon, the "father of experimental philosophy," as Voltaire described the great Elizabethan philosopher of science. In his *New Organon* (1620) Bacon had argued that simple, aimless observation does not constitute a scientific study of nature. Unstructured observation, he said, is only "groping in the dark." The scientist does not simply admire the birds and the bees for hours on end. His study of nature must proceed "in accordance with a fixed law, in regular order, and without interruption." The mind must ask very special, precise questions of nature, questions that can be answered through testing and whose answers will contribute to a more comprehensive framework of explanation that gives order to an entire range of phenomena. The "experimental method," in short, is the scientific method. And the scientist who uses it functions more like one of the dreaded Inquisitors, putting the question to a tortured heretic stretched upon the rack, than like a curious nature lover idly interested in knowing how things come to be. There is, in other words, the

3

element of systematic, relentless cross-examination in the experimental method of reasoning.

In the second instance, the term "experimental" identifies the approach of John Locke who wanted to raise the study of the mind to the status of a science. In the introduction to his *Essay Concerning Human Understanding* (1690), Locke expressed his determination "to search out the bounds between opinion and knowledge," between what we only assume and what we really know. To do this, Locke traced all knowledge—all possible human knowledge—to experience, the product of our five senses. Experience, then, the only source of knowledge, became the touchstone of philosophical empiricism and the starting point for a new, critical examination of all our ideas and beliefs. David Hume, Locke's famous eighteenth-century follower, spelled out some of the implications of the experimental approach to the study of mind. In making affirmations, Hume declared in 1739, "we cannot go beyond experience." Any hypothesis, even one that concerns human nature itself, that goes beyond experience and claims to disclose ultimate or transcendent qualities ought to be immediately dismissed "as presumptuous and chimerical."[1] Because of the work of Locke and Hume, and of others who followed in their footsteps, the legitimate range of philosophical speculation was to be severely restricted. Those "qualities," "potentialities," and "spirits" that had once animated existence were driven from the rational world, and the philosophical universe became disenchanted.

The experimental method of reasoning, then, is critical, precise, persistent, thorough, and rigorously analytical. It assumes nothing, and is even willing to admit that such things as natural law, cause and effect, and time and space are nothing more than mental fictions that serve mainly as logical conveniences. It does not try to justify itself, does not defend its own "first principles"—for it regards the quest for first principles as pointless. Beginning with facts rather than postulates, the experimental method of reasoning was able to accomplish two formidable tasks. First, in the natural world, it was able to describe the physical universe to everyone's satisfaction: Its experiments checked out, its figures proved accurate, its predictions came true. The well-known lines of Alexander Pope sum up his age's feelings on the subject as they apply to Newton:

> Nature and Nature's laws lay hid in Night.
> God said, Let Newton be! and all was Light.

Second, in the world of human faith and values, the experimental method functioned as an analytical scalpel, cutting away cherished beliefs as though they were no more than cysts on the body of philosophy. We may informally set forth five premises or assumptions that help define the frame of mind in which the experimental method of reasoning was applied to matters of faith and morals:

(1) There is a distinction between knowledge and belief, and although we may believe any number of things ranging from the sensible to the absurd, we actually *know* only those things that have been verified in our experience.

(2) Verifying something in our experience means more than just seeing it with our own eyes—as Thomas saw and felt Christ's wounds or St. Theresa saw holy visions. It means observing critically and, if necessary, rejecting what our senses tell us if what we see disagrees with our rational understanding of how things are. No new fact, in other words, may contradict the body of hard-won information we already have.

(3) Our knowledge must form a coherent whole. We must examine all our opinions and be ready to discard those that do not accord with the rest. Thus, if we believe that natural laws govern all natural phenomena, we have no right to make exceptions for an occasional miracle now and then.

(4) The preceding stipulations apply to every claim to knowledge, including our religious beliefs.

(5) When in doubt, the model to follow is that of the natural sciences, through which so much has so far been done in allowing us to understand the natural world for the first time.

For centuries Western man had felt that, despite all the mysteries of existence, he at least understood certain fundamental truths—about the existence of God, for instance, about right and wrong, about the purpose of life. Suddenly it was as though all the ultimate certainties were in danger of blinking away. Modern man, as H. G. Wells once put it, lit the candle of reason, expecting to find himself in a splendid cathedral. Instead, once the darkness of ignorance and superstition had dispersed, man found that he actually lived in a small closet, the only world he would ever really know.

Science alone did not cause men to doubt. The skepticism of the Enlightenment was part of a larger movement in Western thinking, away from the Christian world-view, in which the distinction between myth and history, legend and fact, poetry and truth would be drawn with increasing rigor and clarity. Science does not by itself account for this; for, though laking such science, the ancient Greeks experienced a similar crisis of belief in the days of Socrates. Perhaps, as the French positivist Auguste Comte believed, a civilization outgrows the beliefs of its youth, much as a person does, and eventually puts aside its old theologies as childish things. Perhaps as Western society grew more complex and sophisticated, as the European economy began to grow and the rate of social change began to accelerate, a common metaphysic became less and less possible. Perhaps such seemingly diverse things as the rebirth of classical humanism and the voyages of trade and the discovery of the fifteenth and sixteenth centuries made Europeans more conscious of themselves and of the intellectual options available to them—made doubt possible and, once possible, inescapable. For whatever reasons, European thought went through a fundamental change from, say, the emergence of Francis Bacon at the end of the sixteenth century to the French Revolution at the end of the eighteenth century. The philosophers were not far wrong when they claimed that the Western mind had for centuries been dominated by mythical thinking, pious superstition, and scholastic ratiocinations. Nor were they deluding themselves when they identified their own age as a time of awakening, a time when Western man's critical faculties began a process of reexamining all belief and rigorously testing all claims to truth. Formerly, the supernatural had been real for people—every bit as real as the fire in the hearth and the bread on the table; and the boundary between the natural and the supernatural had been vague, fluid, indistinct. The things of the world, living and inert, were seen as animated by spirits and forces that somehow controlled their cosmic destiny. Miracles, supernatural manifestations, and the most fantastic events had as casually prominent a place in the histories and chronicles as the most scrupulously documented, mundane occurrences. Now a small but rapidly growing segment of society not only demanded proof for what it believed, but emphatically dismissed as nonsense most of what people had commonly assumed to be truth. Witches and demons, angels and miracles, trolls and goblins, were swept away. It was becoming almost unnecessary to disprove the existence of such things. The burden of proof in fact was shifting. A miracle, David Hume blandly declared in 1748, "is a violation of the laws of nature." He took it as common sense "that no testimony is sufficient to establish a miracle, unless the testimony be of such a kind that its falsehood would be more miraculous than the fact which it endeavors to establish." He concluded that never—never in the history of the human race—had such clinching testimony ever been offered in support of a single recorded miracle. Nor, Hume was confident, would any such testimony *ever* be offered.

Although science alone did not cause men to doubt, it did provide doubt with a method. It offered a model for how rational thinking ought to proceed, what questions it should raise or refuse to entertain, and what evidence it should take seriously in arriving at an answer. And here is where the doubt became virtually inescapable. For though by no means all men were inclined to doubt the traditional beliefs—there were still many, like Pope, who would worship in the age of Voltaire—all thinking people, all those who laid claim to rationality and mental alertness in the eighteenth century, had to declare their allegiance to science and the experimental method of reasoning. Now, to declare oneself for the experimental method while determining to preserve one's faith is like inviting venomous snakes into one's home while determining never to be bitten. One may not want to doubt, but—living with the scientific philosophy—one cannot help questioning and criticizing, for that is the nature of science. So it was that even many who did not face doubt with the clear eyes and ready will of a David Hume found doubt a constant, if disagreeable, companion. It is little wonder, then, that the thinker who still wanted to keep the Christian universe at least partially intact labored mightily to bring science and the experimental method into the service of faith. In 1695, five years after publishing his *Essay Concerning Human Understanding*, Locke wrote his treatise *On the Reasonableness of Christianity, as Delivered in the Scriptures*. During the course of the eighteenth century there would be many who followed Locke's example, using the tools of the new philosophy to try to reestablish the old faith in a language acceptable to the times.

In England, in the late seventeenth and early eighteenth centuries, a number of writers addressed themselves to religion and attempted either to defend traditional Christian theology, to revise it, or to replace it with a more "rational" religion. These men wrote in a time and country in which the laws of censorship had lifted just enough to make speculative theological debate possible. Of these writers the ones who concern us most are those who found in the new experimental method of reasoning a liberating force, a means of releasing themselves from what they considered centuries of Christian superstition. They were called deists. Although they rejected many or most of the doctrinal peculiarities of orthodox Christianity, they were nevertheless sufficiently at home in the Christian cosmos that they were reluctant to abandon it altogether. They believed in a supreme being who created the universe to run according to natural and moral laws, and they believed—most of them did—that in some afterlife they would be rewarded or punished as their conduct in this life merited. Some accepted Scriptural revelation, others did not, but they shared one thing in common: They all maintained that claims to truth, in religion as in science, must be supported by (or at least must not run contrary to) the dictates of our critical rationality. Regarded as intellectual adventurers and even as closet atheists by some, the deists nonetheless helped smooth the way for many people at a time when the very mentality of a civilization was being altered, when, as it were, Western civilization was changing its mind. They tried to preserve, if not the richness and vivid emotion of the Christian cosmology, at least its orderliness and purposefulness. We may say that the English deists performed the overture that opened the curtain and announced the central themes of the Enlightenment.

Important though the deists are to our story, their names and writings seem remote and unfamiliar today. Simply to list some names and titles furnishes an idea of the concerns of the movement: John Toland, *Christianity Not Mysterious; Or, a Treatise Showing that There is Nothing in the Gospel Contrary to Reason nor above It; and That No Christian Doctrine Can Be Properly Called a Mystery* (1696); Samuel Clarke, *A Discourse Concerning the Being and Attributes of God, and Unchangeable Obligation of Natural Religion, and the Truth and Certainty of the Christian Revelation* (1705); Matthew Tindal, *Christianity as Old as Creation, or the Gospel of Republication of the Religion of Nature* (1730); and Thomas Woolston, *Six Discourses on the Miracles of Our Saviour, in View of the Present Controversy between Infidels and Apostates* (1727-29). These and many other similar works were read and debated, and had wide influence both in England and on the Continent. Naturally, they brought opposition, the best known being that of Joseph Butler (1692-1752), whose famous *Analogy of Religion* (1736) attempted to show that the same arguments used against orthodox Christianity could be effectively turned against deism itself. By the middle of the eighteenth century the "deistic controversy" had burned itself out, although deism or "freethinking," as it was often called, continued to attract adherents through the century.[2]

Among colonial thinkers, Benjamin Franklin was probably the most famous American deist. When, as a young man, he was living in England, in 1725, Franklin read William Wollaston's deistical treatise, *The Religion of Nature Delineated* (1722), and decided he could improve on Wollaston's logic. The result was Franklin's *Dissertation on Liberty and Necessity, Pleasure and Pain* (1725), in which he argued that if, as Wollaston and others contended, an all-powerful, all-wise, and all-good God has constructed the universe, it follows that there can be no such thing as evil and there can be no free will for men. How could philosophers claim omnipotence and wisdom for God, and at the same time contend that man is free to go his own way, to do his own thing? No sane clockmaker would (if he could) build a watch with a mind of its own; nor would an all-wise god design a world that could function independently of His plans for it. Man, said Franklin, "is a Part of this great Machine, the Universe," therefore, "his regular Acting is requisite to the regular moving

of the whole." Indeed, it is logically impossible for there to be
human freedom if God is omnipotent and omniscient; and it is
logically impossible for there to be evil if to divine omnipotence
we add benevolence. Triumphantly, Franklin concluded:

> If He is all-powerful, there can be nothing either exist-
> ing or acting in the Universe against or without his
> Consent; and what He consents to must be good,
> because He is good; therefore Evil doth not exist.

Franklin was later to regret this youthful foray into speculative
metaphysics; for, although he could find no flaws in his logic, he
nevertheless realized that this description did not accord with his
own reading of experience. Even though such speculation may
be true, he concluded, it is not very useful to one caught in the
midst of life and forced to make what every nerve insists are real
choices. Still, although Franklin greatly modified his deism as he
matured, this youthful insight tells us much about deism and
about Franklin.

As far as Franklin himself is concerned, the *Dissertation* shows
an eager young mind coming to grips with the Newtonian view of
the universe as a splendidly contrived machine that runs according to fixed laws. That Franklin, who had been raised in the
Calvinist tradition, could find no way of reconciling that machine
with free agency is understandable: Many thinkers besides
Franklin were to have trouble making a place for a moral world-
order within the Newtonian world-machine. But Franklin's
youthful willingness to jettison moral distinctions and human
freedom in the interest of logical consistency suggests the extent
to which his mind was liberated from the assumptions of former
ages. In the *Dissertation* we observe not only the brashness of
youth but also the intellectual flexibility of modernity: Franklin
could follow his logic wherever it led because he traveled light.
He was unencumbered by the theological baggage that so many
of his contemporaries, and countless others for centuries before,
were obliged to lug about with them. While perhaps no mind is
entirely free of metaphysical assumptions, Franklin's was remarkably free of metaphysical commitments and of the burden
of belief.

The *Dissertation* also tells us something about eighteenth-century deism. Although most deists would have dismissed Franklin's tract as an outrageous prank, since it puts aside the very morality that the deists so warmly defended, nevertheless Franklin's description of the world as a "great Machine" that tells us something about the existence and attributes of its creator was completely in line with deist thinking. Although some deists preferred to argue their way to God from man's moral nature, those who took their cue from Newton used the wondrous design in nature as their revelation of God's being and purpose. The position is well stated by Cleanthes, in David Hume's wicked *Dialogues Concerning Natural Religion* (posthumously published in 1779), a presumably deistical work that in fact demolishes all the deists' favorite arguments.[3] Told that we mere mortals can never with confidence speak of the attributes of God (since "our ideas reach no farther than our experience"), Cleanthes replies:

> Look round the world, contemplate the whole and every part of it: you will find it to be nothing but one great machine, subdivided into an infinite number of lesser machines, which again admit of subdivisions to a degree beyond what human senses and faculties can trace and explain. All these various machines, and even their most minute parts, are adjusted to each other with an accuracy which ravishes into admiration all men who have ever contemplated them. The curious adapting of means to ends, throughout all nature, resembles exactly, though it much exceeds, the productions of human contrivance. . . . By this argument *a posteriori*, and by this argument alone, do we prove at once the existence of a deity and his similarity to human mind and intelligence.

Nature, scientifically studied, was itself a work—some said the only authentic work—of sacred Scripture. God revealed Himself in His universe, and equipped man with reason that he might come to know Him through His handiwork. The experimental method of reasoning may free us of superstition but, as far as the deists were concerned, it would not injure—indeed, it would support and confirm—true religion, what Wollaston called "the religion of nature."

Franklin's *Dissertation* is representative, finally, in its cosmic optimism. Though his denial of evil was a triumph more of syllogism than of insight into the human condition, the assurance that God is in His heaven and all is right with the world was one of the reassurances the deists tried to offer a civilization that was abandoning its former theology and seeking new sources of hope and cosmic encouragement. Their Christian opponents, to be sure, doubted that the deists' optimism would be of much comfort in times of real crisis—as when one faces death or real human iniquity—but the deists bravely maintained that the fables on which Christians rested their hopes were no longer capable of sustaining an intelligent, critical person through any crisis, that only a rational belief—no matter how bland it may seem—is able to reassure and console an enlightened being. If today the deist solution seems pallid and unconvincing, we must nevertheless exercise our imagination sufficiently to try to recapture the mood of liberation and at times breathtaking confidence the deists experienced as they ventured forth from the gloom of ignorance into the light of reason and science. Their concern was philosophical, not pastoral. They were interested more in freeing the mind than in cuddling or comforting it. The terrors of freedom would become apparent soon enough. At the time, as was the case with young Franklin, it was the joy of deliverance, of release from superstition and credulity, that occupied them.

Franklin's early essay, of course, does not suggest the remarkable range of thinking usually covered under that difficult term "deism." The term has been applied, on the one hand, to the ideas of Christian writers who accepted the authority of Scripture as the revealed Word of God, but who championed the study of "natural theology," insisting that the existence and attributes of God can be rationally established by the scientific examination of the natural world. The position of the Christian deist, if we may so call him, is well represented by that latter-day Puritan, Cotton Mather, in his essay, *The Christian Philosopher* (1721). Mather set out to show "that *Philosophy* is no *Enemy*, but a mighty and wondrous *Incentive* to *Religion.*" God's works, seen in the light of the latest discovery of science, "should *excite* our *Acknowledgment* of His *Glories* appearing in them." Such a scientific or (in the language of the eighteenth century) "philosophical" religion, Mather hoped, would reach all people, cutting through sectarian controversy and appealing to all rational minds irrespective of station or calling:

> *Behold, a Religion,* which will be found *without Controversy;* a *Religion* which will challenge all possible Regards from the *High* as well as the *Low,* among the People; I will resume the Term, a *PHILOSOPHICAL RELIGION:* And yet how *Evangelical!*

On the other hand, "deism" is most often applied to positions that are assuredly not "Evangelical" and that exalt reason above revelation, placing supreme emphasis on formulating a thoroughly rational religion. Many such deists still considered themselves Christians—believing, for example, that even though the authority of reason is higher than that of the Bible, that nevertheless the Scriptures, properly interpreted, perfectly conform to reason. From here, however, the distance is not far to non-Christian deism, which at most regards Christianity as the best, but still only a fragmentary and corrupt, example of a more universal, natural religion whose principles derive solely from the rational (scientific) contemplation of the created order of things. Thomas Paine, whose provocative *Age of Reason* (1794, 1796) stirred such excitement in post-Revolutionary America, summed up this position nicely:

> That which is now called natural philosophy [*i.e.,* the physical sciences], embracing the whole circle of science of which astronomy occupies the chief place, is the study of the works of God, and of the power and wisdom of God in his works, and is the true theology.

Science is the true theology, and the created universe is the true

Scripture for the non-Christian deist. Among non-Christian deists there is, in fact, a wide range of opinions, moving from those, at one extreme, who are almost indistinguishable from Christians in their admiration for the Bible and their adoration of Jesus, through those who regard Christianity as an enemy of "true" religion, to those whose positions border on atheism.

Although many deists were resentful of orthodox Christianity and lost no opportunity to attack and ridicule its more exotic doctrines, deism had a positive as well as negative aspect. Negatively, it represented a reaction against theological dogma, mystery, and religious authority. Positively, it represented a quest for a rational faith—a faith that could flourish in a scientific age—and the confidence that the quest would prove successful. Through such a faith, a faith founded in nature and supported by reason, one could explain the working of the universe, for God was acknowledged as the creator and sustainer of the natural world. To this faith one could look for personal assurance that existence is purposeful and that human life has meaning that transcends man's earthly estate. On this faith one could establish both private and public virtue, for the Creator is a God of benevolence and justice who superintends not only the natural order but the moral order as well. Because the polemical debate over deism brought forth its negative and critical aspects, these positive elements have frequently been underrated. Usually, the deists are seen as transitional figures, men groping their way out of a mythical-theological world, who have not yet gained the intellectual confidence to reject the supernatural entirely. "If God did not exist," Voltaire wrote to Frederick William of Prussia in 1770, "it would be necessary to invent him." But, he continued,

> all nature cries aloud that He *does* exist: that there *is* a supreme intelligence, and immense power, an admirable order, and everything teaches us our own dependence on it.

The sorry lot of transition figures is that their concerns never seem quite real to later generations. Between the seventeenth and the twentieth centuries the question of the existence of a god was raised and vigorously debated in Western culture. The deistic controversy represents an important stage in that debate, a stage in which the traditional conception of God—that represented in the Judeo-Christian tradition—was coming under attack, but in which the god-idea itself still had a powerful hold on the imagination of the entire society, including its intellectual class. Many eighteenth-century intellectuals were morally unable to assent both to the new learning and to the traditional faith. On the other hand, certain elements of that faith—the existence of a creator on whom man is dependent, the Providential arrangement of things, the transcendent basis of morality—were so tightly interwoven in the fabric of thought that they could not be put aside as childish things. Without God how is one to make sense of experience? How is one to explain the existence of our world? These were not the misgivings of cowards but the concerns of reflective people who were, like all of us, prisoners of their age. The questions were raised with a mixture of anxiety and confidence that is hard to appreciate today, in an age that is less anxious about the question of God and less confident that a rational answer can be given to such a question. The answer given by the eighteenth-century deists reflects both the depth of their anxiety—"if God did not exist, it would be necessary to invent him"—and the extent of their confidence: "all nature cries aloud that He *does* exist."

It would be a mistake to imagine that the debate over deism marks the limits of experimental religion in the eighteenth century. There were many thinkers who counted themselves orthodox Christians who nonetheless spoke in behalf of experimental religion—insisting on the compatibility between traditional faith and the new method of reasoning. To be sure, many found it necessary to amend and modify that faith here and there in the interest of sound logic. And the Calvinists, who were always as much concerned with sound logic as with sound doctrine, were perhaps the group most severely challenged by the new thinking of the Enlightenment. The matter is well illustrated by the Calvinist doctrine of original sin. According to Scripture, when Adam and Eve disobeyed God by eating of the tree of knowledge in the Garden of Eden, they brought God's wrath not only on themselves but on all subsequent generations of mankind. We are all born into this world as sinners in dire need of divine grace and forgiveness. The Calvinists put great stress on this matter of sin and on man's inability to justify himself before God, and for years they managed to live with a paradox that, to them, summed up the predicament of unsaved man: Man is accountable for sin that he inherited; he is responsible for something over which he has no control. As the *New England Primer* put it back in the seventeenth century:

> In Adam's fall
> We sinned all.

This doctrine has been a source of much intellectual frustration, not to mention spiritual anguish, but in the eighteenth century it was challenged in a new way.

To the Enlightened mind, the doctrine of original sin seemed palpably absurd. It was no longer a profound paradox but pure nonsense, and psychologically harmful nonsense at that—for it makes us feel guilty about something over which we have no control. In one of many similar tracts on the subject, *The Scripture Doctrine of Original Sin Proposed to Free and Candid Examination* (1740), one John Taylor, an English Presbyterian who became increasingly anti-Calvinistic and eventually defected to liberal Unitarianism, flatly rejected the doctrine of original sin. One can become corrupt, he said, only by an act of one's own will. Guilt is incurred by personal action, not by heredity. "If we come into the World infected and depraved with sinful Dispositions," he maintained, "then Sin must be *natural* to us; and if *natural,* then necessary, and if *necessary,* then no Sin." One must be free if one is to sin; and one cannot be held accountable for what one cannot help doing. Our obligation to do something demands that we have the ability to do it: In modern jargon, "ought" implies "can."

The Calvinist doctrine of original sin was but one among many doctrines that became the subject of critical reexamination in the eighteenth century. This was not merely theological nit-picking—the kind of doctrinal quarrels theologians have engaged in for hundreds of years. In the case of John Taylor, he was expressing the new consciousness of his age. Mystery was to be banished. Language was to be made simple, natural, precise.

Paradox was to be arraigned as an agent of confusion. Science would not tolerate a paradox like matter without mass or momentum without velocity, and theology has no right to tolerate paradoxes like guilt without choice or responsibility without ability. It was no longer theologians debating the mystery of the Eucharist. It was an entire culture having second thoughts about all claims to mystery. If one wanted to remain a Christian and at the same time be taken seriously as a rational, Enlightened person, one had to follow Locke's example and defend the reasonableness of one's Christian faith. It was not an easy task in the age of experiments, but there were many who were willing to undertake the responsibility, nonetheless.

A large number of eighteenth-century people felt that they could accept their age's experimental method of reasoning without admitting to all its logical consequences. The fact is, most eighteenth-century thinkers had both a medieval and a modern mentality and wanted to remain at once Christian and Enlightened. It was an age not only of battles between freethinking deists and orthodox believers, but of that more intimate battle waged within the mind of any given person—a battle between two points of view, two mentalities, the Party of the Past and the Party of the Future clashing within one's very being. It is this clash of mentalities that gives the eighteenth century much of its drama and pathos, and that makes the eighteenth century in some ways so remote from us, despite its modernity. The world in which Franklin and Voltaire, Jefferson and Tom Paine, lived is indeed a lost world. The remoteness of the eighteenth century is perhaps most evident in its religious thought, and it is nowhere more manifest than in that elusive and troublesome American philosopher and theologian, Jonathan Edwards.

[2]

JONATHAN EDWARDS AND
THE REALITY OF THE UNSEEN

IT seems somehow preposterous to turn from deism to Jonathan Edwards, from the religion of the Enlightenment to the seemingly medieval faith of the last of the great Puritan theologians. One need only pause for a moment over Edwards' most famous single piece, his well-known sermon "Sinners in the Hands of an Angry God," to find oneself in a world that seems entirely remote from that of David Hume and Benjamin Franklin, his contemporaries. Edwards' "Sinners," preached at Enfield, Connecticut, in 1741, is a hellfire sermon—one, in fact, that comes close to raising that peculiar genre to an art form, if such a thing is imaginable.

In his sermon Edwards compared the sinner—virtually all of us, that is—to a particularly loathsome insect being dangled over a roaring fire by one who feels nothing but hatred and revulsion toward it. It is not just that someday God is going to call you to account, Edwards warned his self-satisfied hearers: The judgment is in; sentence has been passed; all appeals have been denied; and even now the headsman's blade is arcing down toward your exposed neck. Edwards used an array of picturesque metaphors to convey his message. He described heavy, leaden clouds about to break open, dams about to burst, the earth's fragile crust about to crack, an arrow—well aimed—about to fly from a taut bow. Everything is about to explode at once. Only God is holding it all back for an instant—for reasons known only to Himself. But He will not bother for long, maybe not even for one moment more. Why should He?

18

Now, Edwards spoke this way not because he hated people, but because he believed their only hope lay in their awareness of their awful danger. He called for repentance, but repentance could begin only in a heart that was frantic. So, to make the hearts of his congregation frantic, Edwards impressed upon them the fact of their own cosmic vulnerability. As Edwards pictured it, the very ground of reality is breaking up. The familiar world we have come to trust instinctively is ultimately untrustworthy. The enormous pressure of divine wrath is about to blot out existence. Soon—very soon—it will be too late to repent.

Can the man who preached this sermon possibly be considered a modern thinker? The question of Edwards' modernity has, in fact, been much debated by historians. On the one hand, it is undeniable that the supernatural realm had a vividness and immediacy for Edwards that it does not have for people, including people from Edwards' own century, who are usually considered modern. In Edwards' universe God acted personally both in the soul and in history. The major effort of Edwards' life, furthermore, was directed toward the preserving and restating of an ancient theological legacy. But, on the other hand, it is well known that Edwards knew and made use of the ideas of Newton, Locke, and other writers who were transforming the world of thought. He was a keen observer of natural phenomena, an informed student of human psychology, and an extremely sophisticated philosopher. As his famous sermon shows, he had a profound sense of man's cosmic jeopardy that makes him appealing to many in our own day. Finally, he was fully aware that he lived in an age of experiments and, in fact, referred frequently to his "experimental religion"—religion rooted in vital experience and not merely conforming to arid doctrine or ancient authority.

Of course, as Richard Hofstadter has remarked, there is a distinction between being modern and being merely up-to-date.[1] Perhaps the question of Edwards' modernity is an inappropriate one, after all. Only by doing great violence to the historical person can we fit him into the mold of a modern existentialist (as some have) or an eighteenth-century philosophe. But it is also misleading, as well as facile, to set him up only as a sad contrast to his countryman Benjamin Franklin. The two men were greatly different, obviously. But Edwards was not merely a Puritan (if there is such a thing as being "merely" a Puritan), a convenient relic from the seventeenth century. He is an eighteenth-century man, and although he is unique in many ways, he is a representative figure in some of his major concerns. In him we can observe the action of modern ideas on a premodern sensibility. He reminds us that the intellectual battles of the eighteenth century were fought, not only between the Enlightenment and its enemies, but also within the minds of thinking individuals who tried to accept new ideas without abandoning ancient beliefs.

Edwards was born in East Windsor, Connecticut, in 1703, the son of a Congregationalist minister who gave the precocious youth his early education. In 1716 Edwards entered Yale College, where he was exposed to the "New Learning"—the writings, not only of Newton and Locke, but of the liberal Anglican divines who were questioning many of the traditional doctrines in the name of reason and good sense. These works greatly agitated Edwards and stimulated his thinking, but did not cause him to lose his faith. Having experienced his personal conversion probably in 1721, Edwards was eventually ordained in 1727 at the Congregational church in Northampton, in western Massachusetts, as assistant pastor to his grandfather, the great Solomon Stoddard. He became sole pastor in 1729. Edwards remained in Northampton until 1751, when, following a period of increasing tension with his congregation over the qualifications for church membership (Edwards believed they were far too lax), he moved to Stockbridge, Massachusetts, where he served as the pastor of a frontier church and minister to the Indians. In Stockbridge, Edwards published some of his most important works and carried on a voluminous correspondence. In 1757 he accepted a call to become president of the College of New Jersey (now Princeton). On February 23, 1758, a week after arriving at Princeton, he was inoculated against smallpox. He died of that disease a month later.

Edwards' intellectual life may in part be understood as a struggle to maintain a balance between emotion and logic, on one level, and between piety and intellect, on another. He was a man with a deeply religious sensibility but with an alert and resolutely systematic mind. For Edwards, a faith that is not profoundly felt is really no faith at all. Yet the feelings of devotion and awe are not enough. The emotions, however crucial they are to man's spiritual life, must be examined and scrutinized intelligently so that one is not misled or deluded by them. Besides, faith involves a person's entire being: It is not just the rapture of intense devotion, any more than it is only the dry intellectual assent to a creed. Edwards firmly believed in things supernatural, in what William James has called the reality of the unseen. He was intellectually critical enough, however, not to rest content with his belief. He turned all his analytical skill to a relentless probing of the meaning of the supernatural within human experience. Edwards wanted to determine—insofar as it is humanly possible to do so—precisely how God's spirit acts in the human heart. He applied the tools of the new psychology to one of the oldest problems in Christian thought in the effort "experimentally" to establish the legitimacy of the experience of the Holy.

Three issues in particular occupied Edwards' mind: the mystery of conversion, the nature of authentic religion, and the riddle of human morality. The first of these Edwards dealt with in his own experience—subjecting himself to an almost clinical self-scrutiny. The second—the question about authentic religion—he handled as part of his brilliant defense of the Great Awakening of 1740. The third question was taken up in different ways in his best-known treatise, *Freedom of Will,* and his short, posthumously published work *The Nature of True Virtue.*

CONVERSION

Like a good Puritan, Edwards grew up under an ever-present threat and promise. His cosmos was at once dangerous and benign. As far as man's eternal destiny is concerned, existence was maddeningly ambiguous, fundamentally insecure. One lived life always off balance. The surface we stand on is icy, he said in his hair-raising Enfield sermon. We are liable to fall at any moment. Morally puny man, hideously corrupted by original sin, never knows where he stands in God's sight. This was at the heart of Puritan doctrine. Many in Edwards' times still assented to the doctrine, but a diminishing number really consented to it with their whole being—really suffered it. Edwards did suffer it.

In his *Personal Narrative,* probably written in 1739, Edwards tried to reconstruct his own personal religious history in order to comprehend the mystery of his conversion. The narrative expresses many of the themes that were to play a prominent part in his later thought. At the center was Edwards' vision of God's absolute and arbitrary sovereignty in choosing "whom he would to eternal life," an idea, Edwards tells us, against which he had been "full of objections" before his conversion. His conversion had effected "a wonderful alteration" in his mind, so that, henceforth, divine sovereignty was "a *delightful* conviction" for him. He put a characteristically Edwardsean twist on the Puritan doctrine. Not only is the fact of divine sovereignty to be faced squarely: It is to be embraced joyously.

To understand Edwards' change of heart, we must understand his idea of sin, an essential element in his thinking. With Adam's fall, sin had become the human condition—one of depravity and enmity against the Father. One of the things real conversion—as opposed to apparent conversion—accomplishes is to apprise one of the appalling depth of his sin. Edwards had experienced several conversions, but all save the last had proved illusory. Each time, he tells us graphically, he returned to his old ways, "like a dog to its vomit." Only after his true conversion—and Edwards had sufficient second sight to question even this one—did the depth of his wickedness appear so overwhelming as to seem "perfectly ineffable, and swallowing up all thought and imagination; like an infinite deluge, or mountain over my head. I know not how to express better what my sins appear to me to be, than by heaping infinite upon infinite, and multiplying infinite by infinite." Even this recognition seemed "exceeding small, and faint," compared with his actual guilt: "When I have had turns of weeping and crying for my sins I thought I knew at the time, that my repentance was nothing to my sin." From this feeling of ineffable sin and unspeakable corruption, Edwards reports, he was raised through God's grace to "a new sense of things," a new aliveness to what he was later to call "the divinity of divinity"—the beauty of things holy.

He described his conversion experience sensually. He had, he says, an "inward, sweet sense" and a "sweet burning" in his heart. "The appearance of every thing was altered; there seemed to be, as it were, a calm, sweet cast, or appearance of divine glory, in almost every thing." He realized that his pseudo-conversions as a boy had left him as blind as ever, with no more sense of divine things "than one born blind has of pleasant and beautiful colors." True conversion brought a new "sight" or "taste" of "the divine excellency of the things of God," a new perception of the "divine Beauty." Edwards' new sense of things stimulated his desires: "I felt a burning desire to be in every thing a complete Christian." Again:

> My heart panted after this, to lie low before God, as in the dust; that I might be nothing, and that God might be ALL, that I might become as a little child.

In his personal piety Edwards built on and added his own unique twists to Puritan doctrine. The sovereignty of God becomes something beautiful and ravishing—so ravishing as to assault and transform the heart of the penitent sinner. The beauty of God's holiness, like a kind of reverse Medusa, turns stone men into living human beings. This assault begins with a new sense, given by God and functioning in a way analogous to the five senses by allowing people to perceive a new quality, as the eye permits us to perceive a certain range of light rays. Possessed of this sense of things divine, we feel new desires—holy desires—urging us toward God. The blind man who gains his sight sees the beauty of a rose, delights in it, and reaches toward it. Similarly the converted sinner sees the beauty of divinity, feels love and joy, and reaches out, and, in reaching, finds fulfillment that no earthly experience can ever match. Edwards was to develop this theme in his later years, in his great works on the *Religious Affections,* the *Freedom of Will,* and the *True Virtue.*

RELIGION

"What is the nature of true religion?" This is the difficult question Edwards put to himself in the preface to his *Treatise Concerning Religious Affections* (1746). For the eighteenth century the question of the nature of true religion was a more urgent and important one than perhaps it is for the twentieth, for religion was then nearer the center of the intellectual culture. Studies in divinity were eagerly read, especially in New England. In fact, theology provided the basic clusters of metaphors through which most people could best come to terms with difficult moral and political matters. The distinction between claims to religion and true religion—always a matter of concern for orthodox Christians—received new emphasis in the eighteenth century because of the critical philosophy of the Enlightenment. Locke's crucial distinction between "opinion" and "knowledge," as we have seen, pervaded the sacred as well as the secular realm. In addressing himself to the question of true religion, therefore, Edwards was taking on a big assignment. In an age at once of religious concern and of skeptical questioning, Edwards would determine the area of authentic religious experience.

The question of religion had an even more immediate and direct relevance to the events of Edwards' time. The great religious revival that swept the American Colonies around 1740, although it brought new hope to many, including Edwards, prompted some to respond critically to what was then called its "enthusiasm"—its excessive religious emotionalism. The Great Awakening in America is most closely associated with George Whitefield (1714-70), a former English actor turned preacher, who arrived in Georgia in 1738, traveled through the Colonies, and drew huge crowds wherever he went, making thousands of converts. He charged the established clergy with being too comfortable in their sins, and dramatized not only the need for personal salvation but also the divisions in American society, as he and his followers attracted people from the established parishes. Edwards met Whitefield when the latter came through New England in the autumn of 1740, and is said to have wept during Whitefield's moving sermon. In Edwards' mind, Whitefield and others like him—whatever theatrical or emotional excesses they may at times have been guilty of—were important instruments of God's purpose. So, throughout his life, Edwards remained a staunch defender of the Great Awakening against the charges of those, like Charles Chauncy (1704-87) of Boston, who used the excesses of the Awakening to discredit it. Chauncy, a product of latter-day Puritan rationalism and a forerunner of American

Unitarianism, insisted on the centrality of reason in religion, arguing that "an *enlightened Mind,* and not *raised Affections*" ought to be the guide in religion as in all matters. Edwards' response to such criticism was, in effect, to make a rational excuse for irrationalism in religion. Using the new experimental philosophy to probe the true spiritual meaning of the religious revival, Edwards set himself the nearly impossible task of defending the Great Awakening against its informed and Enlightened detractors, and in terms they could understand.

The *Treatise Concerning Religious Affections* is an attempt to establish the primacy of emotion in religious experience. More: It is an attempt to distinguish between authentically "*religious* affections" and mere emotionalism, self-delusion, sentimentalism, or hysteria. It is easy enough to make the case for the emotions in religion, but it is difficult to say how the emotions are then to be circumscribed, once the boundary of decorous rationality has been crossed. Edwards began by arguing "that a great part of true religion lies in the affections." He defined these affections as "the more vigorous and sensible exercises of the inclination and will of the soul." Following the example of Locke, Edwards analyzed the mind into its two major functions: the intellectual, which involves perceiving and knowing (the "understanding"); and the active, which includes both volitions (acts of "will") and emotions (the "affections"). The will and the affections, Edwards insisted, "are not two faculties." The terms simply refer to one complex function, for when we act voluntarily (as in an act of free will) we do what we *want* to do, and our "wanting" is part of our emotional life. It is our emotions that spur us to activity. Without them we would be inert, like rag dolls. Appealing next to Scripture, to his own pastoral observations, and to the new psychology, Edwards argued that religious experience involves more than knowledge and belief—merely intellectual assent to some set of doctrines. True religion engages the feeling and acting, as well as the reasoning, person. He warned, however, that just as there is "no true religion" where the affections are absent, there is no authentic religion "where there is nothing else but affections." Furthermore, there are "false affections" that may easily deceive and mislead us. The problem, then, is to distinguish the truly "holy affections" of real religion.

The "distinguishing marks" by which we are able to recognize truly holy affections are the subject of the major portion of the *Treatise*. Edwards offered twelve signs by which truly religious emotions are distinguished. These include a love of divine things in and for themselves, apart from all peripheral or selfish considerations (we love God for Himself alone, not to guarantee our own salvation); a "new sense" of the beauty of divine things, an aesthetic appreciation of the Holy; a change in one's basic attitudes, and the cultivation of the Christian virtues of meekness, tenderness, and humility; a restless and urgent longing for holy things; and—the "chief of all signs of grace"—one's transformed conduct in the world.

For Edwards, the distinguishing marks of true religion include emotional, intellectual, aesthetic, and moral elements. True religion, in other words, provides one with an entirely new orientation toward life and a new aliveness to experience. The convert receives "a new spiritual sense" and, as a consequence of this, a "supernatural understanding of divine things" and a new, total responsiveness to "the beauty of the Godhead, and the divinity of Divinity (if I may so speak), the good of the infinite Fountain of Good." The divinity of Divinity, the good of the Good. Goodness and divinity have always been present, but fallen man lacks the eyes to see them. True religion provides these eyes: It gives man a "new sense," a new capacity for experience—in fact, a whole new dimension of experience, the experience of the Holy.

Edwards is not entirely clear about what this "new sense" really is. Is he speaking metaphorically, or is one truly given a supernatural sixth sense? Edwards is deliberately ambiguous on this point, and with good reason. This "new sense" is precisely where the supernatural impinges on the natural; it is, therefore, a mystery that the experimental method cannot successfully solve. In the best of Christian thought the spirit of God has always been a mystery and a miracle. But more than this: Are not *all* the senses fundamentally mysterious for the empiricist? Neither Locke nor Hume had been able to look outside of man's sense experience to study the connection between our senses and the external reality they presumably report on. When I look at the desk before me, for example, I speak of "seeing" the desk, but what enters my mind is only a collection of ideas of color and form that I have learned to associate with the notion of a desk. Can I leave my mind and examine my desk "directly"? Absolutely not. The mind is like a computer that is fed sense-data in the form of a computer-language we call ideas. Even as a computer cannot step beyond its own machinery and programming, so the mind cannot operate independently of the laws that govern mental life. We have our "ideas." They constitute our "world" for us, that is, our mental world. This is the only world we shall ever know. The so-called real world—out there, out beyond our ideas and our senses—is fundamentally mysterious. As Locke put it, we live in a "dark room" that we may never leave. Outside the closet we call our mind is (perhaps) a world of people and things, but all we will ever know about that world comes to us in hastily scribbled messages slipped under the door.

This fundamental mystery about the real world appealed to Edwards' imagination. As natural knowledge is ultimately mysterious, so is "saving truth." Sensation is always a stark intruder into the human psyche. Whence it comes, no one knows—not Edwards, not Charles Chauncy, not John Locke. This logical blind spot in Lockean empiricism seems to have delighted Edwards. It suggested that, behind our knowledge, behind our experience and ideas, behind our basic sensations is a fundamentally unknowable realm of Being. Man cannot break through his experience to being-itself. He is obliged to wait in a universe in which he is finally helpless and completely dependent on something or someone beyond himself. Like his Puritan ancestors, Edwards was always ready to remind himself what a poor, dependent, nothing-creature proud man really is. Did the highly regarded experimental method of reasoning change things? Not one bit. Lockean psychology served Edwards as a metaphor for the human condition.

As for the marks of "true" religion, they could be systematically enumerated, but they remained difficult to apply. What Edwards was really saying is that God works in mysterious ways, and the only sure mark of divine action in the soul is an entire life of soul-searching and dedication. He succeeded mainly in making it clear to anyone who would listen that the Christian life is no simple matter, and that what claims to be a religious experience can neither be lightly dismissed nor unthinkingly embraced. If nothing else, Edwards' *Treatise Concerning Religious Affections* reminded an age that prided itself on its experimental and critical spirit that a truly searching examination of a complex phenomenon does not yield a simple formula, and that the human heart is never easily explained.

MORALITY

Two of Edwards' most remarkable writings, his long treatise on the will and his brief essay on true virtue, concern themselves mainly with problems of ethics rather than of theology. This is not unusual in light of the fact that ethics—or moral philosophy, as it was often called—was a major preoccupation of eighteenth-century thinkers, both in Great Britain and in her colonies. Depending on one's mood and point of view, one may regard eighteenth-century ethics either as theology roused from its dogmatic slumbers or as piety anesthetized by secular rationality. That is, one may argue plausibly that the eighteenth-century concern with moral philosophy was a refreshing departure from the medieval habit of treating ethics as little more than a department of theology. Or one may suggest that, with the decline of religious authority in the modern world, matters of conduct had to be put on a new basis to guarantee that morality would survive theology. For whatever reasons, eighteenth-century thinkers undertook to study ethics as an independent subject, and came to regard ethical questions as unique. And questions of ethics came to occupy the mind of religious and nonreligious thinkers alike. Edwards was no exception.

What distinguishes Edwards from most moral philosophers of the eighteenth century is, of course, his profoundly religious orientation toward the subject and his determination to use the language of morality—even as he used the language of Lockean psychology—to reestablish the truths of faith. Edwards' apologetic purpose is evident in his famous treatise on *Freedom of Will* (1754), in which he addressed himself to the moral and logical objections raised against the traditional notion of the bondage of the will. For many years, in fact, strict Calvinists had been charged by their moderate critics, the Arminians, with relieving man of all responsibility for himself by insisting that man can do nothing either to ensure his salvation or even to resist it. God elects whom He will to salvation, irrespective of merit. Man can do nothing—well, virtually nothing—to alter his cosmic destiny, the orthodox Calvinists insisted. In the eighteenth century the Arminians—who wanted to give man at least the power of a beggar who raises a hand to receive alms—found new ammunition for their argument in the logical clarity demanded by Enlightenment philosophy. We cannot be responsible for what we cannot change. By the standards of ordinary language, obligation implies ability: One is accountable only for what one can control. The new logic of the Enlightenment seemed to strike at the heart of the Pauline paradox: "That good that I would I do not; that evil I would not, that I do." Edwards set out to defend the paradox in terms acceptable to his century. There can be no responsibility unless there be free will. Fair enough: But what is free will?

Edwards defined "will" as "that by which the mind chooses anything." It is, he says, "an act of choosing or choice." To act voluntarily is to make a choice, to opt for something. A person's choice is his preference, that is, what he wants or desires. Edwards followed Locke in closely relating will and desire, and in defining "free will" as freedom from physical restraint. Thus, an act of free will is an act in accord with one's desires; it is doing what one wants to do. In the final analysis, however, Edwards found it confusing and redundant to speak of "free" will. All choices made according to our desires are free. Hence:

> The plain and obvious meaning of the words *Freedom* and *Liberty*, in common speech, is the power, opportunity, or advantage that anyone has, to do as he pleases.

If we are sinful, then, it is because we want to be. Our desires are wicked, so our volitions or choices are wicked. The matter is as simple, and as logically tight, as the relation between cause and effect. Can we ever act contrary to our desires? Not voluntarily, Edwards maintained, for voluntary action is action in *accord* with our desires. We must follow simple, ordinary language after all, must we not? Can we ever change our desires? This, said Edwards, is a meaningless question, for it is logical nonsense to speak of someone's wanting what he does not want. The sinner turns away from God because he *wants* to. The only thing that can effect a change in his desires is the presence of a new possibility, a new object that is more desirable than anything the sinner has yet had before him. The new object, of course, is the beauty of holy things. How do we become aware of this beauty? Edwards' trap snapped closed: only through a supernatural sense that is the gift of God's Holy Spirit. If man is a victim in this scheme, he is the victim of his own desires; he is a willing victim. He lives in terrible enmity against God and cannot change his attitude because he does not *want* to change it.

At this point, one can well imagine Edwards' opponents tearing their hair in rage. Unquestionably, Edwards had given "desire" a very narrow meaning (narrower than Locke had), making desire functionally indistinguishable from volition. The alcoholic who takes that fatal glass of beer, the sinner who "cannot" repent, the sojourner who aimlessly takes the high road instead of the low road, the felon who chooses the gallows over the chopping block—all behave as they do because they want to, hence all are trapped in the logic of their volitions. Our purpose here is not to analyze Edwards' logic but to understand the thinking behind it. He was using the new philosophy to reaffirm a traditional doctrine against the charges of its Enlightened critics. Further, he was placing the moral agency of man within a constricted universe of cause and effect. Edwards' use of logic is almost metaphorical. It expresses the terrible limitations of human experience. Man's freedom makes him his own slave. Turning common sense upon itself, Edwards tried to show that the only cure for human nature is something totally other than man, something available only through "the interposition of divine grace." Even though the sinner cannot help sinning, yet he sins only because he wants to. Only the divine intrusion into human experience can alter the context of volition. Morally, as well as experientially, man remains confined within the "dark room" of his own mind.

Edwards addressed himself directly to moral theory in only

one major work, *The Nature of True Virtue* (1765). He defined "virtue" as "some kind of beauty or excellency." In taking this line, Edwards was following the lead of Anthony Ashley Cooper, the third Earl of Shaftesbury, who spoke of the "natural Beauty" of good actions.[2] This beauty, said Edwards, is beauty of "the disposition and will" or "the heart." (Somehow, every path of Edwards' logic leads eventually into the deep recesses of the human heart.) This beauty of the heart is benevolence—not the love and kindness we show our family and friends, but something far more mighty: "BENEVOLENCE TO BEING IN GENERAL."

All-embracing love of Being—a love that reaches out toward that mysterious realm beyond the senses! Benevolence to Being in general. The concept is at once puzzling and breathtaking. Can one love Being? Woodrow Wilson once said that he loved man but not men; and this was taken as a confession that Wilson was capable only of a very abstract and general concern for others, one that lacks specificity, intensity, or real meaning. Even love of God and of His Creation seems more concrete and real to us than "benevolence to Being in general." It is like a check for an infinite number of dollars made out to "cash" and left unsigned. The truth is, love of Being is inconceivable to any but the redeemed, the truly born-again Christian. It is a turning of the will in "consent" to the divine Beauty, a consecration of the self to universal blessedness, that is so total as to turn the heart inside out. The "dark room" of our selfhood at last bursts open and we stand face-to-face with the blinding divinity of existence. "True virtue," in other words, is not like any virtue we can imagine. It is nothing less than the sum of true religion: It is holiness.

Edwards wanted to put ethics back into a theological context. To his mind, an ethical system that is independent of religion is only systematic infidelity. One of the reasons moral philosophy is hampered, he believed, is that moralists are "so ready to leave the divine Being out of their view." Most people "allow that there is a God," Edwards acknowledged,

> Yet in their ordinary view of things, his being is not apt to come into account, and to have the influence and

effect of a real existence, as it is with other beings which they see, and are conversant with by their external senses.

This passage is a revealing one. Edwards' concern was not just with irreligion or with deism but with an increasingly secular habit of mind that made it easy to leave God out of account, as if by oversight. In a truly Christian culture, this would be inconceivable. Can there be a more urgent, living reality than God? Leibniz had been scandalized because the first edition of Newton's *Principia* contained no reference to the Deity. Now such theological nonchalance was becoming common practice. Deism, even militant atheism, can be fought and beaten. Casual indifference, though meaning no harm to faith, is a far more insidious enemy. For Edwards the life of faith had to be the vital center from which all human aspiration and endeavor flows. His psychology, his logic, his ethics—just as much as his preaching— all testify to this.

In his moral theory, Edwards took the latest speculations of his time and, like any good religious apologist, showed that they were incomplete or misdirected without the Christian faith. Shaftesbury's identification of virtue and benevolence, for example, permitted Edwards to introduce the idea of Christian love, showing what an expansive and profound thing benevolence really was. Again, Shaftesbury's relating of ethics and aesthetics provided Edwards with the opportunity to distinguish between natural and divine beauty and to raise ethics to a theological level. Finally, in his treatment of moral agency, Edwards was able to show that the doctrine of original sin, far from undercutting human responsibility, merely added a note of cosmic urgency to ethical discussion—the moral life being lived in constant expectation of the final judgment. Edwards succeeded in re-relating religion and morality in an evangelical frame of reference. In an age of rational criticism and advanced deistic speculation, Edwards pointed to man in all his moral brokenness and declared that there was yet hope for him—a hope that his age's finest philosophy could not begin to fathom.

Edwards' joining of morality and evangelical religion was to have unforeseen consequences for American thought because the Edwardsean synthesis could lead in two directions. On the one hand, it could lead toward perfectionism and the explicit identification of virtue (something expected of all people) and holiness (something possible only for the regenerate). Samuel Hopkins, Edwards' friend and student, made this identification explicit, and thus helped fashion the ideology for the evangelical radicalism of the early nineteenth century. On the other hand, Edwards' synthesis could lead in the direction of practical idealism. If religion and morality are too closely interrelated, then piety is likely to be treated as a moral obligation, and repentance becomes a duty. This direction of thought was taken by Nathaniel William Taylor, the great Yale theologian of the early nineteenth century, who advocated appealing to the sinner's moral sense—his conscience—in order to effect conversion, urging the sinner "to his duty—*to his duty—to his duty,* as a point-blank direction to business now on hand and now to be done." Once conversion becomes a moral duty, of course, it has to be considered a practical possibility (since duty implies ability), and it may end up as something less than the dazzling spiritual experience Edwards had in mind. The effort to translate the evangelical vision into the language of the public conscience was bound to alter the vision and transform the conscience.

Jonathan Edwards is a significant representative figure in our study of the American Enlightenment in two important respects. First, as we have seen, in his effort to reconcile pietism and the Enlightenment, Edwards suggests by his example that these two mental worlds cannot easily be set apart from each other. For many eighteenth-century people the new experimental philosophy, having accomplished wonders in the sciences, promised similarly to do many positive things in the study of philosophy and religion. This holds particularly true in England and even more so in her American Colonies, where the corrosive effect of the new experimental method on the traditional faith did not become glaringly obvious until later in the eighteenth century. Few really understood the meaning of this new mentality that was intruding itself into the realm of Western civilization's most precious beliefs and values.

Edwards is representative of the American Enlightenment in still another way. In America's provincial society, which was largely middle class and underpopulated, the intellectual life was necessarily very close to the public life. American society lacked the resources and leisure to sustain an independent intellectual class. Now Jonathan Edwards was probably as lonely an intellectual as colonial America was likely to produce—lonely, not just in the geographical sense, but in the psychological sense as well. Still, in his office as preacher and divine, he was serving a public function; and even his most theoretical treatises reveal the man as a thinker whose primary concern is the public influence of his ideas—not their popularity, but their practical effect in guiding and encouraging the devout life of the community. In treating weighty topics involving the religious affections, free will, and the nature of virtue, Edwards was, in fact, participating in a lively dialogue—a dialogue that was part of the New England culture of the early eighteenth century. What historians have sometimes called the tragedy of Edwards—the commitment of this brilliant mind to the cause of doctrinal theology—is largely a result (as he saw it) of his service to his community. What Edwards wrote on psychology and philosophy is not to be compared with Locke's *Essay Concerning Human Understanding* but with Locke's *Treatises of Government.* For he was not writing as a cloistered savant, whiling away some "idle and heavy hours," but as a responsible intellectual addressing himself to the immediate concerns of his society. It is altogether appropriate, in this regard, that we began our treatment of Edwards not with his great philosophical works but with his "Sinners in the Hands of an Angry God."

Edwards' system of thought was a remarkable personal achievement. But his position was tenable only because he lived when he did and where he did. The very conditions that were to allow Franklin to make significant contributions to electrical theory—a provincial culture and the primitive state of the new science—allowed Edwards to apply to Calvinist theology the not-yet-clearly-defined techniques of the new philosophy. Clearer definition of the experimental philosophy was to show that Edwards' synthesis was a brilliant but unrepeatable *tour de force.*

[3]

FROM PIETY TO MORALISM

HISTORIANS have rightly considered Evangelicalism and Enlightenment as representing what William G. McLoughlin calls "two contrasting ideologies" in American thought. The prominent themes associated with Evangelicalism, McLoughlin observes, include emotionalism, pietism, perfectionism, millennialism, supernaturalism, and a suggestion of populist radicalism, antinomianism, and fanaticism. Those associated with the Enlightenment include, besides experimental reasoning and scientism, moralism and a concern for measure and control. Although these ideologies are clearly "contrasting," McLoughlin maintains, they should not be considered diametrically opposed to each other. In fact, "as Americans have construed them," they share some important qualities, such as concern with a "higher law" and a belief in the moral order of the universe, the belief in a Supreme Being, the ideal of human equality, and an idea of Providence that came to be associated with America's national destiny. McLoughlin considers it evidence of the "pragmatic quality of American culture" that Americans judged Evangelicalism and Enlightenment by results rather than by philosophical argument, thus perceiving an ultimate harmony between them.[1]

McLoughlin's observation is worth pondering. Unquestionably, Evangelicalism and Enlightenment are central themes in American intellectual history in both the eighteenth and the nineteenth centuries, and students of American thought who stress one and overlook the other are frequently criticized for their oversight. It is true, furthermore, that many Evangelicals besides Edwards responded enthusiastically (in the modern sense of that word) to Enlightenment ideas; while a rationalist like

Franklin could appreciate the moral strengths of pietism. By the first third of the nineteenth century, finally, American thinkers had achieved a synthesis—though an unstable one—between some of the ruling assumptions of pietism and of rationalism. This synthesis was undoubtedly instrumental, moreover, in providing the new nation with a public philosophy that preserved traditional values and helped sustain the social order, while accepting intellectual innovation and encouraging social reform. The Americans were able to make ideas work for them, to serve the public interest, and this is surely an indication of their pragmatic temper. But is this all to the good? The advantages of this state of affairs are real and obvious, but did not American intellectual life suffer from the avoidance of extremes and the blunting of contradictions that made this compromise possible? Is moderation always an intellectual virtue?

Eighteenth-century America was part of the intellectual culture of Western Europe despite the ocean barrier that separated the two continents. Many of the intellectual conflicts that divided Europeans—including that between piety and rationalism—were felt by the Americans as well. By the 1790's, as we shall see, these conflicts came to a head, provoking a great deal of agitation, controversy, and anxiety in the new nation. Yet American thought had certain peculiar features even in the eighteenth century. For one thing, Americans were always a little behind the times. Often the latest intellectual vogue in Europe was already passing out of vogue by the time Americans were aware of it. Sometimes Americans remained entirely unaware of the controversy attending the introduction of a new idea abroad, and were able to accept that idea without much serious consideration of it. One thinks of Newtonian physics, which the Americans accepted readily as soon as it was known that Newton stood virtually unchallenged abroad. The intellectual battleground on which the Newtonians had won their victory and destroyed their enemies never had to be seen by the Colonials. The reception of ideas in America did not always work that smoothly, of course, but the circumstances were such that frequently the Americans would receive new ideas without having any real appreciation of the disputes attending their arrival or of the qualifications and amendments that had been added at their fringes. Intellectual passion and subtlety of mind, that is, were not encouraged. The Philadelphia printer and the Virginia planter, dependent on European middlemen for their books, received those that were considered "important"—that is, those that were most representative of prevailing taste. But it is often the "unimportant" books—the ones that petulantly attack a great idea or tediously belabor a small point—that give the thinking of an age its drama and texture. Provincial circumstances, then, encouraged in the Americans a habit of thinking the intellectual life to be something relatively smooth, simple, and straightforward.

Other circumstances contributed to the peculiarity of American thought. Those entrenched institutions, like the Church and the monarchy, that exercised such rigid control over the exchange of ideas on the continent of Europe were lacking in the British colonies of North America. Further, since the Americans were more closely linked to England than to any other nation, the generally more tolerant attitude prevailing there was, as one would expect, encouraged here. Finally, as we have seen, the intellectual life was much closer to the practical and public life in America. All of this contributed to a moderate, pragmatic, tolerant frame of mind. Americans would take ideas seriously (pragmatists always do that), but they would not take the intellectual life very seriously. For the intellectual life was part of the common life; and the life of the mind—or so it seemed—seldom involved matters of life and death.

It is against this background that the relation between Evangelicalism and Enlightenment is best understood. The central issues were defined during and following the "great and general awakening" that stirred the Colonies in 1739-40. Perhaps the major intellectual issue of the Awakening had to do with the claim that the events connected with it were inspired by the Spirit of God—were supernatural—and were not to be dismissed as the results—in Charles Chauncy's words—of "a bad temperament of the blood and spirits . . . a disease, a sort of madness." Were people dealing with a form of miracle or a species of psychosis? After the obvious cases of mental unbalance had been weeded out, was there evidence of divine agency? These questions led defenders and critics of the Awakening into debates over a diversity of subjects, including theological doctrine, the psychology of religion, and what may be called religious style. Religious style embraced matters of "proper" behavior, respect for authority (particularly the authority of the settled pastorate), and the proper balance between emotion and reason in religious life and thought. In the years after 1740, the friends of the Awakening—often called New Divinity men among New England Congregationalists—attempted a new formulation of Calvinist doctrines, emphasizing the sovereignty of God, the sinfulness and moral impotence of man, and the need for a regenerating experience—effected by the Holy Spirit—to give the convert a new life in Christ. The enemies of the Awakening were, in fact, a varied group that included the more traditionally orthodox, as well as representatives of various shades of religious liberalism. Those of most interest here are the ones who, speaking against religious "enthusiasm," upheld the belief that "Christianity is a rational Religion." To these rationalists—let us call them—the very fact that one affected by the revival claimed to have had a mysterious and supernatural experience, and to have received special knowledge as a result of this experience, served to discredit him. Such a person had, in effect, laid claim to a private revelation. Chauncy snorted his contempt for such a claim by observing that the person making it will not even admit of the possibility of rational counterevidence that might prove him wrong, so he is not "capable of being argued with; you had as good reason with the wind." True religion, Chauncy and the rationalists maintained, is characterized not by "high Affections" and private revelations but by good judgment and decorous behavior:

> *Reasonable* Beings are not to be guided by *Passion* or *Affection*, though the Object of it should be GOD, and the Things of another World: They need, even in this Case, to be under the Government of a *well instructed Judgment.*

The theology of these upholders of reasonable Christianity has been called "supernatural rationalism."[2] Although supernatural rationalism clearly distinguished itself after the Great Awakening, it nevertheless has roots going back into Puritan and

Anglican thought, and beyond that into medieval and ancient thought. It stems from the conviction that God, the Creator, has left His imprint on the natural world, and that therefore the study of nature and of her wondrous design will prove the existence and the benevolent attributes of the Deity. Supernatural rationalism does not stop with the study of nature and the effort thereby to prove God's existence. This is what was called "natural theology," and it was likely to yield no more than a belief in the impersonal and rather remote divinity usually associated with deism. Supernatural rationalism maintained that reason must be supplemented by revelation, the testimony of Scripture. God speaks through His handiwork, Nature, and He has spoken in the Old and New Testaments. In the first case, God's Word is known through Reason; in the second, it is known by faith supported by reason. (The divine inspiration for Scripture, it was believed, could be rationally demonstrated.) Ebenezer Gay, who served for seventy years as pastor of the First Church in Hingham, Massachusetts, put the matter succinctly in 1759, in a sermon on "Natural Religion." Religion, he maintained,

> is divided into natural and revealed: *Revealed* Religion, is that which God hath made known to Men by the immediate Inspiration of his Spirit, the Declarations of his Mouth, and the Instructions of his Prophets: *Natural*, that which bare Reason discovers and dictates.

Each is supplementary to the other, and each is a vital source of spiritual truth. Here was a reasonable Christianity that avoided the extremes of enthusiasm and arid deism. It combined a restrained and decorous pietism with a moderate and pious rationalism.

Overseas, as we have seen, a variety of forms of rational religion emerged, extending all the way from liberal Christian theism through deism and ethical paganism to outspoken infidelity and virulent anticlericalism. In America these extremes were less evident. To be sure, Franklin reports having met "one Dr. Brown," an innkeeper near Burlington, New Jersey, who was a self-proclaimed "infidel," but he offered a more accurate picture of things—and was not being ironical—when he observed, in 1782, that the "happy Mediocrity" of American society is evident also in American thought, and that the extremes of atheism and infidelity are rare or nonexistent in this country. By the 1790's there was evidence of a lively but short-lived popular deism in America. In general, however, even the arch-rationalists restrained themselves in publicly expressing their opinions; and the more respectable supernatural rationalism that was to develop into the cautious American brand of Unitarianism remained representative of American religious liberalism throughout most of the eighteenth century.

In the first half of the century, American religious liberalism was not intellectually adventurous or speculative. It was moderate, restrained, and highly moralistic. An excellent example is Jonathan Mayhew (1720-66), the famous Boston Congregationalist minister, whose well-known *Seven Sermons ... Preached at a Lecture in the West Meeting-House in Boston* (1748) set forth the central elements of his theology. The sermons read like a text in moral philosophy. Mayhew argued that mankind is endowed with mental faculties—including the reason and a "moral sense"—that allow us to judge between truth and falsehood, right and wrong. We have a built-in obligation, since God gave us these faculties for a purpose, to inquire into and question all things, including the basic principles of religion and morality. Although the dispassionate study of nature will make clear the existence and attributes of God—and will, furthermore, show the need for the additional light of Scripture—we must, above all, look within ourselves for the most vivid and impressive evidence of our spiritual and moral nature. God's moral law is inscribed in our hearts:

> There is such a *law written in our hearts*; such an internal consciousness of the moral excellence of virtue, and of the odiousness of its contrary, as really leaves us no room to doubt of our obligation to it.

In our religious life Mayhew believed in a sane balance between piety and rationality. Our love for God should be a "steady, sober, calm, and rational thing," but we

> ought not to run so far from *enthusiasm*, as to lose sight
> of real devotion; we ought not to be so fond of a *rational
> religion*, as to suppose that religion consists wholly in
> cold, dry speculation, without having any concern for
> the *affections*.

Mayhew's religion, then, is warm without becoming "enthusiastic," rational without being cold, and infused with moral concern. The last two sermons of the seven are devoted to a careful analysis of our moral duties—those of benevolence to man and love to God. "To exclude a God, and a righteous providence from the world," Mayhew insisted, "is . . . to deprive virtue of one of its greatest supports and guards."

The moral emphasis in Mayhew's *Sermons* deserves attention, for it suggests a significant common element that joins all parties in the theological debate in mid-eighteenth-century America. The rise of interest in moral philosophy in this country, reflecting a similar development in eighteenth-century England and Scotland, is an important episode in our intellectual history that has only recently stirred much interest among historians. The growing importance of moral philosophy is seen in the development of the American philosopher and educator Samuel Johon, whose interest in ethics grew over the years, to receive full expression in his massive *Elementa Philosophica* (1752).[3] Though not as great as Edwards, Johnson was an energetic scholar who taught himself the basics of higher mathematics in order to come to terms with Newtonian physics. His intellectual personality is not easily classified. He was a critic of the revivals who was converted from his Calvinist scholasticism to liberal Anglicanism, and who became increasingly Arminian—opposed to the limitations Calvinists imposed on man's free moral agency. His philosophy was a combination of Platonism and Berkeleyan idealism. Johnson's ethical system is something of a hodge-podge, for he revised it over the years, incorporating new ideas that his ever-expansive mind continually and hungrily absorbed. Like many thinkers, Johnson related "happiness" and "virtue," connecting private interest with the public good. He derived the moral obligation to practice virtue from man's external and internal understanding of the moral law. That is, externally it is evident that God has so constructed the universe that virtue is rewarded and vice is punished. It is, therefore, decidedly to our interest to live righteously. Internally, we are aware of a "moral sense," which is an "irradiation of the Deity in our minds," and which takes the form of a "disposition" to promote "the good of others." This moral sense is an "almost intuitive sense of right and wrong" within us. Following the lead of Shaftesbury and of the great Scottish philosopher Francis Hutcheson (1694-1746), Johnson was arguing, in effect, that morality is natural to man. The principle of benevolence is implanted in him. Johnson's mention of the moral sense, added only in the later editions of his work, reflects a new and significant emphasis in moral theory on experience and on the internal life. Moral duty is based not on God's arbitrary commands, nor upon man's calculation of enlightened self-interest, but on human nature and consciousness. This new emphasis on the moral sense (sometimes called "conscience") was to influence American philosophical, religious, and social thought for the next century or so.

In the mid-eighteenth century moral philosophy was, as Norman Fiering observes, the "semi-secular way station" between an age dominated by theology and a new age increasingly dominated by science.[4] It provided a common language through which people could communicate their views on ultimate matters without necessarily committing themselves on the issues that divided doctrinal theology and the experimental philosophy. It was, in other words, part of that pragmatic adjustment between pietism and rationalism that we spoke of at the outset.

For the rationalists the adjustment was fairly easy. For those who represented the new pietism of the Great Awakening, the matter was less simple, but the results were no less striking. Edwards, in his treatment of "true virtue," had shown what evangelical moralism really involves. One may, in fact, question whether Edwards was really describing morality at all. There is something contradictory in the very term, "Christian ethics," if by "Christian" one means the tradition of piety going back to Augustine and to Paul before him. In the Pauline frame of reference the emphasis is on faith over works, and the Christian is made entirely dependent on God's grace. All Christian "virtue" is simply the fruit of God's spirit at work within the heart of the regenerate, and all the virtues of the unregenerate count for nothing, being, as Augustine put it, merely "splendid vices." Certainly, in such a context, terms like "duty" and "responsibility" take on peculiar meaning that has little to do with the moral life as most people think of it.

In fact, the history of New England theology since the time of Edwards is one of continuing tension; it is the story, to use Joseph Haroutunian's phrase, of "piety versus moralism."[5] Calvinism was attacked by its enemies often on strictly ethical grounds. In effect, the Calvinists were asked: When you preach that God preordained everything that is to happen, and that one's good character and righteous conduct are of no help in winning salvation, are you not providing an excuse for *immorality*? If the sinner can do nothing to avoid damnation, then why should he mend his ways? Calvinism, especially the Edwardsean restatement of it, even suffered at the hands of its friends—a result of their very effort to defend it. Haroutunian has shown in his study of the "passing of the New England theology" how Edwards' followers came to place increasing emphasis on man—his freedom, responsibilities, duties, and abilities—while losing the awesome sense of God's total sovereignty that had inspired Edwards when he wrote, "Absolute sovereignty is what I love to ascribe to God." Calvinism was further subverted when its supporters tried to use philosophy—particularly the so-called Scottish philosophy of common sense—in its behalf. In the late eighteenth century, Scottish philosophy, which enjoyed wide influence in America, actually provided a good defense of the transcendence of God and the spiritual nature of man: It was a good weapon against materialism, idealism, and skepticism. But it was also strongly humanistic in emphasis, optimistic in its anthropology, and rationalistic in its approach. The long-range effect of turning to Scottish philosophy was to make traditional Calvinism look cold and lifeless as a theological system.[6]

Of course, we must not make the picture seem too simple. While it is true that Calvinism increasingly was put on the defensive and pietism after the Awakening became more prim and moralistic, Calvinism nevertheless remained a formidable system for years to come ane pietism was destined to become a potent force in American life. The truth is, neither the rigorous, Calvinistic pietism of Edwards nor the decorous rationality of Chauncy and Mayhew was to win the field. America was to be dominated neither by the overpowering vision of Edwards, nor by the so-called "consistent Calvinism" of his followers, nor by the "rational religion" of the Boston liberals, but by a blend of pietism and common-sense moralism that manifested itself, at times, as an urgent demand for moral and social (as well as spiritual) regeneration, and, at other times, as a lofty appeal for sterling character, honesty in government, and high-mindedness in foreign relations. The American ethos, when it finally took form in the nineteenth century, was a peculiar combination of Evangelicalism, Populist radicalism, and middle-class gentility.

The experimental philosophy of the eighteenth century was ultimately destructive of traditional theism in Western civilization, for it was the cutting edge of a critical mentality that would sever all unverifiable affirmations about the supernatural from legitimate claims to rational belief. The critical mentality would relentlessly distinguish between "opinion" and "knowledge," myth and fact. In this respect, rationalism and pietism were mutually antagonistic. Until around the seventeenth century, atheism had never been a viable intellectual choice in Western culture. By the mid-twentieth century, theism, in the traditional sense of a belief in a Supreme Being, was no longer a live intellectual option.[7] Belief in God would survive, but only as an act of faith, or through a series of drastic redefinitions of "God." In the meantime, habit, custom, tradition, and the Church had kept faith alive in Europe. But what about America? Thomas Paine once hopefully predicted that, because they lacked most of the traditional restraints on freethinking, the Americans would easily shrug off the weight of dogma and superstition and develop a rational religion to complement their liberated institutions. This was not to be, because the experimental philosophy and the critical mentality it fostered did not enjoy a free hand in America. They were, from the point of view of a rationalist, to be restrained by an attachment to sentiments and emotions—a sentimental trust in the heart over the understanding—that was to distinguish

American thought from the time of Edwards to that of William James.[8]

The matter goes deeper than sentimentalism, however. American philosophy has always been a public matter. As such, it has been in the service of a common faith, a philosophy for the average citizen, a democratic ideology. This has meant that American philosophy has never been free to push to the edges of its assumptions or to be consistently and unrelentingly critical. Just as pietism was constantly put into the service of conventional morality, so rationalism was forced to temporize in order to avoid a direct assault on public principles. The American Enlightenment—to the disappointment of many of its greatest spokesmen—was destined for the happy mediocrity of being made safe for democracy.

II

EXPERIMENTAL MORALITY

[4]

THE CIVILIZED AMERICANS

WHEN the "first drudgery of settling new colonies" is over, Franklin declared in 1743, and the people are no longer preoccupied with the task of merely securing the necessities of life, it becomes possible at last "to cultivate the finer arts and improve the common stock of knowledge." Such was the state of affairs in British North America in the mid-eighteenth century: The Americans could now develop their cultural and intellectual life, and join in the general advancement of learning. The land was so vast, however, and the colonies were so far to the edge of civilization, that communication and the transmission of ideas posed a serious problem. A discovery might die uncommunicated with the person who made it. Because of this, Franklin proposed the formation of a society "of *virtuosi* or ingenious men" to maintain constant correspondence—particularly in the area of science and invention—among its members throughout the colonies. Although Franklin helped to organize such a society in the 1740's, it took more than twenty years for the American Philosophical Society to begin its activities in earnest. Nevertheless, Franklin's assessment of the colonial situation and his scheme to create an organization to facilitate the transmission of ideas offer, like so many of Franklin's schemes, a valuable clue to the intellectual life of eighteenth-century America. There was increasing opportunity to think, but if thought is to have cultural relevance, ideas must be disseminated. Where the necessary vehicles for this dissemination are lacking, they must be built. The intellectual life can flourish only in a congenial institutional environment.

Colonial America was what Louis Hartz calls a "fragment culture," self-consciously a part of something larger than itself,

49

namely, European civilization. Such a culture, "hurled outward unto new soil," suffers the psychological discomfort of being isolated from the whole, and must eventually develop an identity of its own, a sense of its own cultural integrity. The process is a slow and painful one. In the case of British North America, it was not until after the mid-eighteenth century, when tensions with the mother country began to mount, that the colonists even began referring to themselves as "Americans" with regularity.[1] A fragment culture measures its achievements in terms defined by the wider culture from which it derives. In the eighteenth century those provincial achievements most likely to win recognition abroad included the advancement of science and of literary culture, or "letters," as the latter was called.

Scientific accomplishment has been called the "intellectual passport" into the intellectual society of the eighteenth century.[2] While most colonists would admit that in the area of art and poetry America's contribution lagged far behind Europe's (it takes time, Jefferson reminded his country's detractors, for a civilization to mature sufficiently to produce a Shakespeare or a Milton), many nevertheless insisted that America had much to be proud of in its energetic pursuit of science. Here America could contribute, if nothing else, her own endlessly fascinating natural environment; and, as it turned out, colonial Americans became busy collectors of natural miscellany. Through contacts with men like Peter Collinson, the London merchant and international correspondent, colonial men of science could bring their discoveries and observations to the attention of the "world."

Today, we would label most of those who showed interest in science in colonial America "amateurs." If we do, we are obliged to remember that the amateur was a more important figure in eighteenth-century science—especially in Britain—than he is in our highly specialized age. The natural sciences were in such a rudimentary state that the part-time collector or experimenter might still make significant contributions; and any educated gentleman might consider it his intellectual duty to have a basic familiarity with all of the sciences. James Logan, the Philadelphia Quaker merchant and statesman in the first part of the century, was a gentleman-scholar in the tradition of the English *virtuosi*— Elizabethan gentlemen of wide interest in the arts and sciences.[3]

His library, perhaps the finest in the colonies at the time, included the first three editions of Newton's *Principia Mathematica*.

By the mid-eighteenth century, American interest in science clearly extended beyond the concerns of the well-rounded Renaissance gentleman. Colonial Americans showed themselves to be capable collectors of botanical specimens, alert observers of natural phenomena, able experimenters in the field of public health, and even accurate recorders of astronomical events. Newton himself once complimented the Americans on their careful observations of comets. The highpoint for colonial science was probably the study of the transit of Venus in 1769, when American observers contributed much to the accurate measurement of the solar parallax, thereby permitting a more precise estimate of the distance between earth and the sun. The occasion earned the Americans applause throughout Europe, and gained them recognition as being more than mere collectors.[4] It is true that Americans contributed little to scientific theory, if we except Franklin's truly significant experiments with electricity. Still, America produced men who were capable scientists: David Rittenhouse, a clockmaker and amateur physicist whom Jefferson once extravagantly hailed as a "genius . . . second to no astronomer living," and who in fact did offer a workable theory of magnetism; John Winthrop III, who established the first experimental laboratory in physics at Harvard College; John Bartram, the versatile naturalist, whose scientific travel narratives stirred much interest abroad; and Benjamin Thompson, who did pioneering work in thermodynamics.

In the realm of scientific organization, the Americans further worked to develop their intellectual culture. Franklin was not the only one to propose the formation of an American scientific society. In 1765 Ezra Stiles, who was shortly to become president of Yale, drafted the constitution for a proposed American Academy of Science, an organization designed to collect all manner of scientific curiosities and to "maintain a correspondence all over the world." Stiles' precise scheme never materialized, but in 1780 the American Academy for the Advancement of Science was established in Boston and received the support of many prominent Americans of the time, including John Adams, its second president. The Americans' effort to establish scientific societies reflects their recognition of the need for communication and organization in their intellectual life. It also reflects their awareness of the prevailing passion in Europe for the organization of learning. Early in the seventeenth century, Francis Bacon, in his *New Atlantis* (1624), had dramatically proposed that science is a cooperative endeavor in which men work together for the benefit of humanity. According to Bacon's notion of the experimental method, the collecting of data is no desultory occupation but a demanding job that requires a degree of concentration and persistence that even the most dedicated individual cannot be expected to put forth. Bacon's ideas seem to have appealed to the gregarious seventeenth century. Perhaps the first scientific academy dedicated to the experimental method was the *Accademia del Cimento*, founded in Florence, Italy, in 1657 by Leopold de' Medici. In England and France the rise of scientific societies exhibited a wider base of support and greater spontaneity. Informal groups meeting in London and Paris to discuss new ideas and discoveries eventually formed the Royal Society (1662) and the *Académie Royale des Sciences* (1666), respectively. During the course of the eighteenth century nearly every Western nation developed its own scientific academy. The rise of the academy contributed to the gradual transformation of European science from an intellectual amusement of the amateur into a professional enterprise in which the dilettante was replaced by the specialist. The scientific correspondence (the medium Franklin used in reporting his electrical experiments) and the diverting scientific essay were eventually replaced by the highly technical paper, published in the society's "transactions," and intended only for the expert in the "field." The rise of the scientific society was perhaps the first in a series of developments that would take science out of the hands of the gentleman amateur and place it in the hands of a new scientific class, a new kind of intellectual elite. In America, where organization came only late in the eighteenth century and the specialist had not yet begun to emerge, science was still very much the avocation of the gentleman or the hobby of the professional, business, or even "leather-apron" man. The greatest name in science at the time, Benjamin Franklin, was himself a leather-apron virtuoso who recorded his electrical experiments in homely letters that somehow resemble his recipes for hickory tea and gallstone medication rather than anything we think of as a scientific treatise.[5] Franklin the scientist resembles Europe's philosophes—Voltaire, Diderot, d'Alembert—more than her greatest men of science—Laplace, Lavoisier, Buffon. To put it another way, American science remained part of the general culture and was not yet on the way to becoming a culture of its own. Science was still an integral part of the Republic of Letters.

In the wider area of letters the American record is more ambiguous than in the realm of scientific discovery. Samuel Miller called the story of eighteenth-century American literature a "history of poverty," a judgment that has to stand when we compare America's literary output with that of Europe at the time. Fully to appreciate the literary situation in colonial America, however, we must broaden our understanding of literature to embrace, besides the great works of poetry and fiction, "the best expression of the best thought reduced to writing," as James Fitzmaurice-Kelly once defined it. It is in this sense that David Hume could acknowledge Franklin as the "first great man of letters" for whom Europe is beholden to America. Literature and letters in this broader view have been called a "Third Realm," distinct from those of Church and state, a cosmopolitan realm where men of learning may meet, irrespective of political or religious differences.[6] In the eighteenth century, this Third Realm, the Republic of Letters, came into its own. The philosophe (the term "publicist" has been suggested as a good synonym) could converse with others like himself across national and creedal boundaries, could consider himself, by virtue of his status as an intellectual, a citizen of the world. The philosophe, considered as an international figure, wanted to break out of the narrow confines of the local and the provincial, to free himself from the habits of custom and from cultural stereotypes (what he called "prejudice"), to be a part of a cosmopolitan civilization, to identify himself with what was universal and essential to "human nature." This attitude often resulted in oversimplification, particularly in ethical and theological matters, for when one pursues universals, one is tempted to overlook those exciting and indispensable particulars that give human experience its richness and complexity. But it also produced good results, in art criticism, for example, and served as a stimulus for such social sciences as economics, sociology, and anthropology—all of which were born in the eighteenth century. The universalist ideal helped sustain a truly cosmopolitan frame of mind in which no particular expression of culture, in Paris or London, say, could legitimately be offered as the standard of all culture. To be sure, because even the most enlightened minds are still ensnared by "prejudice," this ideal was never fully realized. The salient point is that, in the Republic of Letters, there was little excuse for dismissing the output of a cultural province as being necessarily inferior and therefore unworthy of serious consideration. On the contrary, in its very newness and primitiveness, a colonial culture like that in British North America might offer what eighteenth-century intellectuals were looking for—a new angle of vision, a new point of view from which to reexamine some of their own cultural assumptions.

At this point it would be natural to point out that, in the minds of some Europeans and Americans, America offered above all else a valuable counterstatement to Western standards of civilization. America represented closeness to nature, spontaneity, and innocence in contrast to the "artificiality," overrefinement, and corruption of Europe. Franklin, certainly, captured Paris as much with his animal-skin hat as with his wit and politesse, and among Parisians it would have been the cause of some consternation as well as much amusement to learn that John Adams' first positive reaction to France was that it seemed to contain nothing to "disgust" him. By the end of the century Americans were accentuating the positive when they stressed their simplicity and wholesomeness, making a strength of their weaknesses, as it were. What else could a new nation show for itself?[7] All this, however, must not cause us to ignore the fact that the Americans desperately wanted to be civilized, in the sense of being sophisticated, learned, appreciative of great things, and part of a splendid cultural tradition. The simple, good-natured provincial—*Le Bonhomme Richard*—had his virtues, but they were those of a bumpkin. Franklin was willing to be such a person only on a part-time basis; Jefferson, despite some of his rhetoric, was reluctant to be such a person at all. The authority of Western culture was immense in the eighteenth century. Despite its romantic fascination with the primitive and the pastoral, Europe had not yet suffered a real failure of nerve. If America were to participate fully in Western culture, she had to do so on its terms and not merely on her own.

Any contribution that America could make to Western culture under the circumstances would be modest, but that was not important. In the mid-eighteenth century, the Americans were happy to be part of civilization and did not insist on being particularly unique, much less superior. The ideal of the Republic of Letters was helpful. If the American could read and think, and if he could write, his participation in the world of letters would be welcome. He would suffer humiliations, would be patronized as rude and unrefined, but he could always parry the charge of provinciality by turning the tables on his critics: He could claim that they, not he, displayed narrowness and prejudice, for he was participating (however tentatively) in a culture that transcends any national or local embodiment of it, no matter how grand that embodiment may be. This tone pervades Jefferson's *Notes on Virginia*. Given the cosmopolitan cultural ethic of the eighteenth century, the Americans could afford to take pride in their achievements while being appropriately modest about their contributions. The true cosmopolitan holds no cultural effort in contempt. The Americans, moreover, were the advancing front of European civilization; they were the bearers of the arts westward.

Precisely what the American achievement was—particularly in the areas of morals and politics—will concern us shortly. Here we are concerned more with the material conditions that made any achievement possible. These conditions include institutions like the nine American colleges that, for all their limitations, introduced young men to the liberal arts and, by the time of the Revolution, managed to transcend the sectarian purpose many of them had originally been established to serve.[8] They also include voluntary associations—both formal and informal—that range all the way from nascent scientific societies and (at that time) philosophical organizations like the Freemasons to intercolonial networks of acquaintance and correspondence. Regarding this last item, it should be noted that in those days before the telephone, the electronic media, and the hasty memo, letter writing was a passion among highly literate people and was regarded as an art. Of greater importance to American civilization than either colleges or voluntary associations, however, were those "seedbeds for the emerging culture of the New World," the colonial cities.[9] In the eighteenth century, Boston, Newport, New York, Philadelphia, and Charleston were becoming thriving centers of culture, as well as commerce. The greatest of these was Philadelphia.[10]

America in 1750 was a rural society with an urban population of merely four percent. Philadelphia at that time had a population of still under twenty thousand and somewhat fewer than three thousand houses; but it was growing rapidly as a busy trading center supplied by the fertile farmlands and resources of the Delaware and lower Susquehanna river valleys. In an average man's lifespan, Peter Kalm observed in 1749, Philadelphia had grown from a newly established Quaker community into the most cultured and cosmopolitan city in North America, and one of the largest cities in the British Empire. Carl and Jessica Bridenbaugh, in their detailed study of Franklin's Philadelphia, *Rebels and Gentlemen*, have well described the richness of Philadelphia's cultural life. Although colonial Philadelphia is usually associated with the name of Franklin (a habit encouraged by Franklin himself, who, in his *Autobiography*, identified Philadelphia's rise with his own), the Bridenbaughs name hundreds of eighteenth-century Philadelphians who contributed to that city's cultural flowering. It was only through the combined effort of many individuals that Philadelphia was able to advance as it did in areas of education, the fine arts, literature, medicine, and science. By the time of the Revolution, moreover, Philadelphia's culture was not only cosmopolitan, but broadly based as well—the possession of her "middling sort," her artisans, craftsmen, and businessmen, as well as of her upper class.

In the mid-eighteenth century Philadelphia was large enough to offer the amenities of an urban culture but still small enough for people to know one another personally. In studying the city in this period, one is impressed by the number of personal quarrels and animosities one witnesses among her famous and not-so-famous residents. This is not just because people were more contentious (they certainly were more litigious) in the eighteenth century, but because people were in such close contact with one another and knew one another so well. The anonymity and impersonality we associate with city life today are not evident in Philadelphia in 1750. It is hard to imagine a modern Franklin parading his diligence and thrift with much effect in present-day Philadelphia. The city's intimacy facilitated the spread of ideas in a time of poor communications. It also encouraged, and was, in turn, reinforced by, the rise of a variety of voluntary organizations, which not only contributed to the city's cultural life but also promoted many essential civic projects—in the area of public health and safety, for example—that are today considered governmental responsibilities.

As a printing and communications center, Philadelphia reached far beyond her own city limits. In 1782 Franklin wrote to the English Unitarian clergyman and philosopher Richard Price, contrasting the dissemination of ideas in the eighteenth century and in the ancient world. In ancient Greece and Rome, he said, when the bulk of the people were illiterate, it was the orator who communicated ideas, but only to those citizens within the sound of his voice. Now, thanks to the printing press, we can speak to entire nations, and books and pamphlets have wide influence. During the middle decades of the eighteenth century some fifty booksellers opened shop in the city, distributing their merchandise throughout the colonies. Printers produced thousands of items, ranging from almanacs and newspapers to sermons, self-improvement manuals, political tracts, and occasional philosophical and scientific treatises. Meanwhile, Philadelphia's economic growth and social mobility stimulated increasing interest in reading and education as keys to social advancement and badges of social distinction.

The Enlightenment was an urban and interurban phenomenon, and it is difficult to know how deeply it penetrated the countryside. In France, the available evidence suggests that the prevailing mentality in the provinces was medieval throughout most of the eighteenth century.[11] In England, where society was more mobile and literacy more widespread, the picture is somewhat different. Partly because of the rise of the circulation library and of the popular magazine—those *Tatlers* and *Spectators* of Joseph Addison—there was much interest in new ideas among

England's merchants and artisans, more interest, probably, than among her aristocracy. This interest, moreover, was not confined to London but is evident in provincial cities like Manchester and Birmingham as well. America was an even more mobile society than England and looked to the mother country for its intellectual inspiration. Periodicals like the *Spectator* and *Gentleman's Magazine,* or reprinted articles from such magazines, were eagerly consumed by a growing reading public. Franklin founded America's first subscription library in 1731, and by the end of the colonial period such libraries were to be found throughout the colonies. The American cities were centers of thought, but it is reasonable to suppose that their influence on the countryside was somewhat greater than was the case abroad. In the first place, America's rural population was predominantly middle class and largely literate. In the second place, because America was a newly established society with seemingly endless land resources and no traditions, with much hope and no history, there was little of that acquiescence to custom and authority that Jefferson, for one, observed in Europe. In America, expectation and accomplishment replaced resignation and submission. The Americans are animated, observed J. Hector St. John de Crèvecoeur,

> with the spirit of an industry which is unfettered and unrestrained, because each person works for himself . . . We have no princes, for whom we toil, starve, and bleed: we are the most perfect society now existing in the world.[12]

Allowing for exaggeration in the above description, it remains true that the Americans enjoyed a control over their destiny unknown among the populace overseas. American society could be expected to produce minds that were active and open to intellectual stimulation. Perhaps, for the American farmer, this stimulation came in the form of his annual almanac, to be studied carefully and placed in a position of respect second only to that of the Bible. Indisputably, there is a great difference between Montesquieu's *Persian Letters* and *Poor Richard's Almanack* as great as that between being literary and merely being literate. Admittedly, too, the American farmer had limited horizons and was provincial, even parochial, in his thinking. But when all the limitations are acknowledged, and the American plowman is stripped of all Jeffersonian pretensions regarding his intellectual accomplishments, a significant mental element remains. That element is identified by words like "alertness," "curiosity," "consciousness," and "awareness." What all this comes down to is that, if the American farmer was not cosmopolitan or as well read as Jefferson liked to think, he was in all likelihood mentally more alive than his European counterpart. The American farmer was hardly a philosophe, but he stood closer than did the French peasant or even the English countryman to that ideal of the awake and liberated individual the philosophes had in mind. He was more aware of his circumstances and more willing to fight politically in behalf of his own interests. The extemporaneous speeches and harangues delivered by common, frequently illiterate people during the Revolutionary period demonstrate this popular awareness and show that ordinary men could hold forth eloquently on matters like civil liberties and political rights. The American farmer, furthermore, had a new sense of space and time. Living in a relatively mobile and very young society, he was neither rooted in his place nor imprisoned by changeless centuries. We may infer that it was easier for the American farmer than for his counterparts overseas to envision new possibilities and determine to change things for the better. The product of a provincial culture, his mind might yet break through the political and perhaps even the intellectual constraints of provinciality.[13]

Concerning the state of civilization and the diffusion of ideas in America in the mid-eighteenth century, the following generalizations seem in order. By the 1750's the Americans could feel themselves to be part of an Atlantic civilization. The growth of American cities in particular helped stimulate the life of the mind, but so did the growing economy and increasing prosperity. If the Americans as yet contributed little to the advancement of learning, they could still take some comfort in the fact, or at least in their belief, that the colonial population on the whole was more literate and mentally alert than the population in European countries. If the Republic of Letters had fewer contributors on this side of the Atlantic, it nonetheless had a somewhat wider base. Influenced by the middle-class moral perspective of the

English Enlightenment and by the strains and tensions involved in being a fragment culture, eager to widen their cultural horizon and to become fully "civilized," the Americans received new ideas eagerly and without significant controversy in these years. In science and in letters the Americans worked energetically to keep abreast of new developments and to offer, wherever possible, something of their own. When an American received recognition abroad, as Benjamin Franklin did, it was the occasion for what can only be called *national* pride.

[5]

BENJAMIN FRANKLIN AND THE ART OF VIRTUE

IN the eighteenth century, the intellectual—the man of letters—could feel that he was understood and appreciated by his society. He had not yet become the alienated figure that frequently comes to mind when we think of intellectuals in the modern world. Far from being the cultural foe of the businessman, for example, the intellectual-as-philosophe held the rising merchant class in high regard; and Diderot and the other collaborators on the *Encyclopedia* were unblushing in their admiration for manufacturing and industrial technology, the "mechanical arts." From the other side, although the intellectual risked persecution for his more adventurous opinions, particularly when they were considered subversive of the standing order, he could also win acclaim as a champion of liberty and human dignity, as Voltaire eventually did at the end of his life. If the eighteenth century was a time of "honeymoon" between the intellectual and the wider public, as Crane Brinton contends,[1] then no man better serves as a symbol for the age than does Benjamin Franklin.

One is always a bit embarrassed about introducing Franklin. The man seems to need no introduction at all, so well is he known. The fact is, Franklin *does* need to be introduced, for in many respects he is as remote from us as is his contemporary Jonathan Edwards, who was born only three years before Franklin and little more than one hundred miles from Franklin's birthplace, Boston. To be sure, the two men had contrasting destinies and different mentalities. Edwards, until the very end of his life, seems to move farther into the hinterland: East Windsor to Northampton to Stockbridge. Franklin moved from one metropolitan center to another: Boston to Philadelphia, with extended visits to London and Paris. Edwards was a preacher and theologian. Franklin was a go-getter, printer, businessman, booster, philosopher, scientist, politician, wit, *bon vivant*—America's homegrown philosophe. Edwards was a Puritan among Puritans, whose vision of God was intense, vital, overwhelming. Although Franklin was born into a devout, Presbyterian home, all that survived of his Puritanism was that strenuous moralism and sober diligence that Max Weber identified with the Protestant Ethic. Still, for all his appearance of familiarity and of brisk modernity, Franklin remains essentially mysterious to us. He is one of the least-known of our best-known Americans.

The outlines of Franklin's early life are familiar to most Americans, thanks in part to the popularity of his famous *Autobiography* (written in two installments, 1771, 1788). It is with the *Autobiography*, however, that the trouble starts. The work is so readable and seemingly so candid that we fail to realize that it presents not the real Franklin but a carefully constructed *persona*—a fictive being, a sort of "New-World Tom Jones," as Robert Spiller calls him, who combines an essentially good heart with Yankee shrewdness and a resolute will to overcome both weaknesses of character and the hazards of fortune in his rise from rags to riches.[2] We think of the young Franklin trudging up Market Street with those three puffy rolls of his, or of the genial older man, balding and bespectacled, in breeches and three-cornered hat, sending his famous kite up into the thunderclouds. We think of Poor Richard's homely sayings. We find it difficult to take Franklin seriously; or, if we do, to have much appreciation for him. He is either the vaguely comical self-parody of the autobiography or a penny-pinching Polonius preaching the gospel of success. It is often observed that Franklin did himself a disservice in his *Autobiography*, that the character he presented there has lived to obscure the memory of the man who created it. The fact is, Franklin was a determinedly private person who never fully reveals himself in any of his writings. It is always Franklin the public figure with whom we are presented and with whom we must deal.

Franklin was an astonishingly versatile man who possessed

incredible energy. Carl Van Doren called him a "syndicate of men" and a "harmonious multitude." A list of his scientific interests alone would fill a page, provided one did not bother to explain or elaborate on anything. At age eighty, on the eve of his return to Philadelphia after serving for six years as America's Minister Plenipotentiary to France, Franklin wrote a touching farewell to his friend the British diplomat David Hartley. Recalling their mutual labors to restore peace after the American Revolution, Franklin announced that he was "going home *to go to bed!*" "Wish me a good night's rest," he asked, "as I do you a pleasant evening." As it turned out, Franklin himself had nearly five years of "evening" left when he penned those words. On his sea voyage home, the old man found the energy during his "Leisure at Sea" to write three substantial treatises: one on ship construction and maintenance, one on the causes and cure of smoky chimneys, and one setting forth a new idea for a stove. If ever the middle-class virtues of industry, perseverance, practicality, and ingenuity can meet the measure of the heroic, they do so in Benjamin Franklin.

Although Franklin would rank as a foremost eighteenth-century American by any standard, it is precisely with his middle-class moralism, his interest in the "Art of Virtue," that we shall concern ourselves. Franklin's moral philosophy—if it is proper so to call it—leads us in many directions. It involves more than rules and prudential maxims. It forces us to consider Franklin's theory of the individual and his moral growth, of society, and of God. Franklin, of course, established his international reputation as a man of science. But if he was truly America's "first great man of letters," it was as a moralist that he earned this renown, and it is especially as a moralist that Franklin reveals himself, in Bernard Faÿ's phrase, as the "apostle of modern times."

THE INDIVIDUAL

At the beginning of his *Autobiography* Franklin observes that his ancestors lived in the same English village, Ecton in Northamptonshire, for "at least three hundred years." His father, Josiah, moved in the 1680's to Boston, where Benjamin was born in 1706. Seventeen years later the young Franklin made his fateful journey to Philadelphia.

To understand Franklin's moral perspective as it pertains to the individual, we must see it in this historical setting. Franklin's life exhibits a mobility that would have been unthinkable to his ancestors, who for centuries had remained rooted to the land. It was not merely that Americans were more mobile than Europeans, although they were. Western society was changing rapidly by the eighteenth century from a tradition-directed, hierarchically arranged community to what is called an associative society in which the individual and the family unit are perceived apart from society as a whole, and in which fundamental social relationships are deliberately and rationally established to satisfy specific interests or to realize certain goals. Young Franklin grew up in what may be called either a post-medieval or a premodern society—a society in which the old restraints and guidelines were vanishing or losing their authority, but in which new principles of social order were only dimly apparent. In the 1920's it was fashionable to dismiss Franklin's ethics as the expression of middle-class Babbittry. What was too frequently forgotten is that the middle class—always an elusive social division—scarcely had an identity in Franklin's century, and the boosterism and status anxieties of Sinclair Lewis' character were still remote from this earlier world of privilege, deference, and aristocratic standards of "virtue." Franklin's recent ancestors had lived in a society in which, as Peter Laslett has shown, virtually all the wealth, power, and prestige were in the hands of about twenty percent of the population.[3]

The playful good humor and easy cheerfulness of Franklin's *Autobiography* presents us with a misleading picture of his rise in life. Franklin's society was a dangerous place for a young tradesman just starting his career. A person could easily fall into debt and end up in prison or in indentured slavery. Beware of debts, Father Abraham admonished his listeners: Your creditor has the power to put you in "Gaol for life, or to sell you for a Servant, if you should not be able to pay him!" This was a fearsome warning. Young Franklin had to make his way in a society that was hostile and uncertain, in which guidelines were absent and deceit was common. Seen in this light, his moralism and catchpenny maxims take on new significance, and his *Autobiography* may be seen as a practical manual on how to outwit society and on its own terms.[4]

Each age, each society, asks its own central question. For the seventeenth-century Puritan, it was: "What must I do to attain salvation?" For the twentieth century, perhaps it is: "Is life worth living?" or, as Albert Camus put it, "Why should I not commit suicide?" For the eighteenth and nineteenth centuries it was the question of the conduct of life: "How should I live?" The question is one both of ends and means: It involves both the ultimate goals toward which one should direct one's efforts and the most effective means of reaching these goals. Life's goals had once been taken for granted, had been set for an individual by his society. Actually, the idea of individual goals—personal ambitions and ends that one sets for oneself—was foreign to the medieval mind. Now, as society changed and the individual came to distinguish himself as a private center of consciousness with legitimate interests and aspirations of his own, the problem of goals became a pressing one. The crucial problem was that of voluntary choice. One's life became the sum total of the countless choices one made. Choice shaped character and character determined destiny. It was important, therefore, that the faculty of choice—the will—receive proper training and instruction.

Franklin's recognition of the need for moral instruction is evident in his decision to create the famous Junto, a group dedicated to the mental, moral, and material improvement of its members. The list of two dozen questions that Franklin drew up in 1732 as a kind of catechism to be reviewed at each meeting clearly shows that one object of the club was to raise the consciousness of its members along these lines:

Have you met with any thing in the author you last read, remarkable, or suitable to be communicated to the Junto?

Have you lately heard how any present rich man . . . got his estate?

What unhappy effects of intemperance [or of imprudence, passion, *etc.*] have you lately observed or heard?

Have you lately observed any encroachment on the just liberties of the people?

Such a ritual may seem quaint and naïve in our day when moral autonomy is taken for granted. In Franklin's day Western man was morally like one learning a new skill. Habits that seem natural to us had to be painfully acquired. New concerns—involving one's character, one's fortune and fate, one's civil liberties—were being identified. One's earthly destiny was no longer determined by one's birth; unquestioning obedience to the Church was no longer expected; and morality was no longer governed exclusively by custom and tradition. Now one cultivated good character as one learned a craft or established a business reputation. Virtue, no longer just the adornment of nobility or the badge of piety, had become an "art" to be mastered by Everyman.

The word "art" was used variously in the eighteenth century. It referred not only to the application of one's talent and skill to the creation of beautiful things, like music, painting, and poetry—the "fine arts"—but also to the pursuit of any industrial calling, as in the "mechanical arts." Above all, "art" referred to the collection and systematic arrangement of those rules and measures by which some object is achieved; the object in question may be skill with a saber, expertise in navigation, a condition of contentment, or virtuous character. One might choose to make any aspect of life into an "art." When Franklin speaks of the "Art of Virtue," he is referring to rules for the cultivation of good character. In 1760 Franklin wrote to Lord Kames (Henry Home) explaining his intention to write "a little work for the benefit of youth, to be called *The Art of Virtue.*" Many people lead bad lives, he observed, who would prefer leading good ones, "but they know not *how* to make the change." Further, most people have some virtues, but no one has all the virtues. The problem, then, is to "acquire those that are wanting, and secure what we acquire." This is the appropriate "subject of *an art.* It is as properly an art as painting. navigation, or architecture." Franklin never completed his book.

Nevertheless, he developed and practiced an art of virtue, the outlines of which he presents in the middle of his *Autobiography*.

Even the most casual student of Benjamin Franklin is aware of the famous list of thirteen virtues, and of the elaborate method he devised for concentrating on a virtue each week, keeping track of all his transgressions in an ivory-paged memorandum book. These virtues—temperance, silence, order, resolution, frugality, industry, sincerity, justice, moderation, cleanliness, tranquillity, chastity, and (last of all) humility—constitute a kind of secular version of the basic Christian virtues. Absent from this catalog are such heroic virtues as courage and devotion, as are the gracious virtues of benevolence, charity, and forgiveness. In fact, Franklin's approach to the "art" of virtue is so methodical, businesslike, and matter-of-fact that his critics have accused him of presenting a picayune morality that neither challenges the human spirit nor recognizes its true greatness. Franklin "fenced a little tract that he called the soul of man," D. H. Lawrence charged, "and proceeded to get it into cultivation."[5] Although this charge has some truth to it, it remains misleading and unfair, nonetheless.

First of all, Franklin was not trying to present a complete ethical system. He was aware of the wider dimensions of the moral life, but was not trying to cover the length and breadth of the subject. One of the virtues that Franklin most assiduously cultivated, as a matter of fact, that of toleration, does not even appear on his list. He assumed that he was addressing people who were well disposed toward humanity—who were, like himself, seeking to improve their character. Seen in this light, it becomes clear that his list of virtues was never intended to be definitive. That he added "humility" to the list only as an afterthought reveals more than his arrogance: It reveals a flexible, open-minded attitude toward the entire subject, a problem-solving frame of mind. Franklin approached morality as he approached so many other things, with the mentality of an engineer. He was not primarily concerned with "why" a job is to be done but with "how" it can most efficiently and economically be undertaken. For a man like Franklin there is no sense in arguing about why one should be good: The person who raises such a question is either a fool, a knave, or an academician, and in each case argument would be futile. Rather, morality is to be treated as a problem that can be solved by proper planning and technique. This includes a careful job analysis—breaking the abstraction "virtue" into a number of identifiable traits; it also calls for the development of some kind of program by which we modify our behavior by consciously focusing our attention on certain areas of conduct, thereby acquiring a "habitude" of certain virtues, as Franklin called it. "I concluded," he writes,

> that the mere speculative conviction that it was our interest to be completely virtuous was not sufficient to prevent our slipping, and that the contrary habits must be broken and good ones acquired and established before we can have any dependence on a steady, uniform rectitude of conduct.

Franklin was not concerned here with ultimate goals but with what John Dewey calls instrumental ends. He was saying, in effect: "Define 'virtue' as you will; here is a practical way to go about the business of self-improvement, however you measure it." The eighteenth-century physiologist Pierre Cabanis, one of many French intellectuals who admired Franklin, was particularly impressed with Franklin's method of teaching the art of virtue, "in the same way as one would teach playing an instrument or fencing." Lawrence was indeed correct in calling Franklin "the first downright American": Franklin applied Yankee know-how to the age-old problem of human conduct.

Franklin is criticized not only for his superficial moralism and for the banality of his virtue but also for his concern with appearances. He candidly says of humility: "I cannot boast of much success in acquiring the *reality* of this virtue, but I had a good deal with regard to the the *appearance* of it." And everyone knows how careful he was to present the appearance of industriousness and frugality. Although he was a man of strong opinions on almost every subject, moreover, he took pains to present his ideas modestly—offering to others the façade of the "humble inquirer" and avoiding outright contradiction of another's opinion. To shallowness is added disingenuity and hypocrisy, say Franklin's critics. This is not the art of virtue but the artifice of public relations. Franklin is not trying to arrive at "moral perfection," as he claims, but only to win friends and influence people.

To such a charge one may say, first, that our century values frankness and spontaneity more highly than did the eighteenth century. In Franklin's day, order, self-control, discipline, were more highly prized, and even the clothing and furniture of the time reflect a life-style that we today would consider constraining. Twentieth-century people take for granted what the eighteenth century was only coming to appreciate, the sanctity and importance of the private sensibility. Although hypocrisy, duplicity, and guile were condemned in that earlier time ("Use no hurtful deceit," Franklin wrote under his seventh virtue, sincerity), the self was not perceived as something so sacred as never to be compromised. In the deferential and still hierarchical society of the eighteenth century one's public behavior was prescribed and was not considered a reflection of one's personal feelings. The latter, indeed, counted for little. Franklin lived in a society that was changing from an aristocratic to a democratic order, using these terms broadly. More than this, it was a society in which the private man was becoming aware of himself. In this changing, more mobile, and self-conscious society, patterns of behavior that had once seemed "natural" now had to be learned and cultivated as an "art." A person of the "middling sort," who was neither noble nor plebeian, had to pick his way with care when he moved about in public. Franklin, in offering guidelines to help such a person, revealed himself not only as the first American glad-hander but also as one of the last of the commoners: a man groping his way into a new social order, a new age. Since it was through the world of business that Franklin—and the bourgeoisie generally—rose in society moreover, it is understandable that he would see a similarity between social relations in the new society and economic activities. Thus, if, as Gladys Meyer maintains, Franklin treated acquaintanceships as "business transactions"—as mutually profitable exchanges[6]—he was merely translating the traditional terms of social intercourse into the language of the new society. As loyalty, deference, obedience, had been the appropriate qualities for commoners under the old regime, so compromise, reciprocity, persuasiveness, and tact seemed appropriate for the rising entrepreneur under the new order of things. If the "business civilization" that eventually emerged exhibits undeniable limitations as a civilization, we are not necessarily justified in putting these limitations at Franklin's door. The fault is not Franklin's if those who followed him could not fit his shoes.

Franklin's concern with appearances can be explained, further, in terms of his engineering approach to morality. This approach clearly has limitations which Franklin seems to have recognized. It would be truly dishonest to maintain that one can make oneself humble or can "will" sincerity. (The motto "Be sincere" inspires mirth.) Franklin's Calvinist counterpart, Jonathan Edwards, wrestled mightily with his heart, always seeking "some new *contrivance*, and invention," to make himself feel his own sinfulness and to love God above all else. But he knew the arrogance of humility; and he knew that divine grace alone turns the heart from a state of enmity against God to one of loving obedience. For a secular Puritan like Franklin, one who could not count on God's gracious intrusion into the inner heart, all that could realistically be expected is a change of behavior. The hypocrite in a secular society is not the one who acts according to his best interest but the one who lies to himself, who persuades himself that he can respond with total ingenuousness and innocence in the myriad transactions in which he daily engages. In modern society each of us is, in fact, many people: Integrity in this context is keeping our many selves in some kind of moral harmony with one another. Franklin's psychological genius lay in perceiving this. His moral tough-mindedness is manifest in his determination to incorporate this insight into his "art" of virtue.

In the final analysis, Franklin's calculated tactfulness has to be understood with reference to the times. From he pages of his *Pennsylvania Gazette*, as well as in the *Autobiography* and other publications, Franklin gave his readers helpful advice on how to be an agreeable companion by avoiding the "Spirit of *Wrangling* and *Disputing*," and cultivating an air of courteousness, affability, and modesty. An "indiscrete Zeal for spreading an Opinion," Silence Dogood once advised, "hurts the Cause of the Zealot." The available evidence suggests that Franklin was temperamentally averse to personal conflict and went out of his way to avoid it.[7] If this be true, his personality nevertheless reflects his changing society and the new burden social mobility placed on interpersonal relations. Success in life depended on influence and goodwill; and one can win this only with one's charm and manipulative skill. The Enlightenment, moreover, marks an important step in Western thought "from force to persuasion," to use Whitehead's phrase, from belief based on authority and superstition to conviction based on private judgment and personal inclination.[8] The eighteenth century saw the rise of what we today call public opinion. Increasingly, no man's opinion was accepted solely because of his station, and more and more men with no station were expressing opinions. Like everything else, persuasion became an "art." Nor was it simply a matter of "reason" replacing "force," for even the authority of reason could be questioned. Had not Locke and his followers condemned the logic of the "schools"—that monkish scholasticism that bewildered common sense with airtight demonstrations of pure nonsense? Persuasion was a more delicate matter than merely bettering your opponent with logic. In 1808 Jefferson quoted Franklin in advising his grandson, Thomas Jefferson Randolph, "never to contradict anybody." The "age of reason" was an age of political passion and rising popular feeling. There were times when more could be gained by cajolery and tact than by argument, however rational. It is interesting that the very word "tact," defined as a "delicate sense of what is fitting and proper in dealing with others," was first recorded in the late eighteenth century. The corresponding French word, "*tact*," was introduced by Voltaire.

In approaching Franklin's moral philosophy, we are met with something that is at once more than just penny wisdom—tips on how to win success—and different from what had traditionally been encompassed by ethics. Ethics was no longer the concern exclusively of the philosopher or of the cultured gentleman. As society grew more free, as it became possible for a lowly printer's apprentice to rise to a position of power and influence in life, and as traditional coercive institutions gradually lost their control over people's thought and conduct, a new universal ethics became necessary. Moral philosophy had to be made into a marketable public commodity. Franklin did his best to package and advertise such a product. Like his literary model, Joseph Addison, Franklin tried to reach the public through the popular press. He showed that virtue, besides being its own reward, insures one's material success in life as well. More than this, virtue, considered as an art, was revealed as part of an enjoyable and fulfilling life-style. This is Poor Richard's real message. Virtue is not an ornament of nobility but an ennobling of the common life. The way to promote virtue, Franklin found, is not to hold forth a high ideal, nor to preach endless sermons, but to begin with life as it is, seek out what is potentially good and fine in it, and cultivate these qualities—coax them forth. Admittedly, Poor Richard concentrated on what he called the "humbler virtues," like industry and frugality. His intention was not to deny grander ones like justice and benevolence, but to approach people on a moral level with which they were familiar. Franklin helped establish an ethical tradition in America that was to have its culmination in pragmatism. The virtuous life must begin with the concerns and aspirations of people as they actually are; it cannot be imposed from above, nor can it be presented as a remote moral galaxy with the charge "Go thither!" The problem—perhaps the weakness—in this tradition concerns the matter of transcendence. Will man be able to rise above his immediate concerns? Will he aspire beyond the level of his present aspirations?

SOCIETY

A noteworthy, if not unique, feature of Franklin's ethical philosophy is the way it relates the individual and society or, more in line with Franklinesque thinking, the private and the public man. In his study of Franklin as a man of letters, Bruce Granger rightly observes that Franklin addressed himself more to the public than to the individual consciousness. His tone was not one of inward reflection and brooding but of social commentary. This was in the neoclassical tradition of the eighteenth century, but with the difference, says Granger, that it was more clearly directed to the needs and strivings of the rising middle class.[9] Still, there is throughout Franklin's works, but particularly in his autobiography, a recognition of the uniqueness of the individual life and of the legitimacy of private hopes and ambitions. There is no contradiction here. Franklin perceived the individual as man-in-society rather than man-in-solitude. He viewed society not as something existing in itself, apart from the individuals composing it, but as the sum of a multitude of individual variables. Thus, although he might speak of the public good, to his mind the public good and private interests were never far apart. With disarming candor, Poor Richard could present his thirteenth annual almanac in 1745 "for the Benefit of the Publick, and my own Profit." Franklin could identify Philadelphia's rise to greatness with his own, because a society's success is the sum total of the successes of the individuals composing it. Conversely, an individual is successful, by Franklin's reckoning, only insofar as he contributes to society's, as well as his own, well-being.

Along with the harmony between individual success and social progress, Franklin also perceived a harmony between moral and material advancement. In this way he skirted the English controversy between those, like Thomas Hobbes, who reduced morality to calculated selfishness and those, like the third Earl of Shaftesbury, who traced virtue to altruistic impulses in human nature. Virtue and happiness coincide or, in the words of Poor Richard, "Virtue and Happiness are Mother and Daughter." We must not state this too baldly. Franklin did not simply regard virtue as a means to an end: "be good and you will be rewarded." Poor Richard describes the relation between virtue and happiness as a familial one in which, presumably, there is mutual affection and responsibility. True, the "humbler virtues," like thrift and industry, constitute the way to wealth. But, in advancing the individual, they also promote the social good, as we have seen. Furthermore, the cultivation of virtuous character in all its dimensions is, for Franklin, a kind of happiness in itself. One may compare it to the development of an athletic skill. In undertaking an athletic regimen, one improves one's strength and health, but the exercise itself becomes increasingly enjoyable as one's skill and endurance increase. A person may take up a sport like tennis in order to keep fit, only to find that he ends up pursuing it out of sheer love for the game. As physical man needs and enjoys physical exercise, so social man needs and enjoys the possession of various social graces, one of which is good character. Everyone has a "natural desire of being valu'd and esteem'd by the rest of his Species," proclaims Franklin's Busy-Body. Why do so few realize that, more than learning, wit, wealth, or good looks, virtue is the primary social grace? If we were

> as industrious to become Good as to make ourselves Great, we should become really Great by being Good, and the Number of valuable Men would be much increased.

The element of self-interest here is undeniable. Franklin never considered the desire for esteem and good reputation a base or unworthy motive. But if goodness is the key to greatness, this does not mean that goodness is not to be valued in itself—any less than learning, wit, or wealth. If virtue is a tool, it is indeed a splendid tool that the skilled craftsman enjoys using and values as an indispensable part of his craft. That craft is not "success" or "popularity" but a full, rich life. Franklin once referred to "the Beauty and Usefulness of Virtue." He saw virtue not just as a means to an end but as an intrinsic part of the greatest of "arts," the art of living.

Society, as well as the individual, is part of the moral order of things by which virtue and happiness are so intimately joined. Franklin's social ethic has been excellently presented by Paul W. Conner who, in his analysis of *Poor Richard's Politicks*, treats Franklin's overriding concern for a harmonious social order that provides the chance for each of its citizens to rise in the world by his own efforts.[10] Franklin's concern with order is understandable. He lived in a time of great change when even the most adventurous mind might yearn for a measure of stability. His demand for opportunity reflects his own struggle upward, the frustration he felt as an ambitious young businessman pitted against upper-class privilege, and his appreciation of the immense material promise of the New World. Franklin saw America as the land of opportunity. It was a land destined not only to become wealthy, but also to encourage a wide distribution of that wealth among its energetic and industrious population. But a society's prosperity depends on its virtue, which includes the quality of its government, the justness of its laws, the serviceability of its institutions, and the character of its citizens. In his many projects to organize and improve, as well as in his office as a didactic publicist, Franklin labored throughout his life to influence each of these aspects of his nation's character. In the final analysis, both the virtue and the prosperity of society are, to his way of thinking, the products of individual initiative, willpower, and cooperation.

In his almost geometric correlation of virtue and happiness, at one level, and of the individual and society, at another, Franklin deserves to be acknowledged as the person who formulated what Gladys Meyer calls the American liberal ideology. He provided the first coherent statement of what later generations thought of as the promise of American life. His formula may be diagrammed:

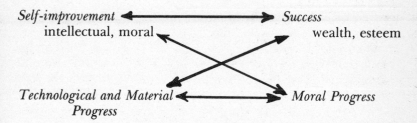

THE INDIVIDUAL

Self-improvement ←————————→ *Success*
  intellectual, moral   wealth, esteem

Technological and Material ←————————→ *Moral Progress*
     Progress

SOCIETY

The individual, in devoting himself to his own intellectual and moral improvement, insures his success in life. His moral and intellectual growth, moreover, is what ultimately determines his society's moral progress, which, in turn, insures its material progress. A society's material progress is measured by the success and productivity of the citizens composing it. Finally—and this is crucial but often overlooked—both the individual's and society's material progress are to be regarded as enabling conditions for future moral progress. The wealthy and powerful nation has more moral responsibilities to its citizens and to the rest of the world than the underdeveloped country. The man of means has increased responsibilities as a citizen and neighbor. (Having himself become wealthy, Franklin retired from business in his early forties to devote his life to public service and further self-improvement.) This is the substance of Franklin's moral philosophy. It was to become part of the American ethic.

GOD

Franklin's ethical world view, with its marvelous harmony between self-interest and public service, presupposes the existence of a moral cosmos, a universe that is not only an intricate mechanical system but a moral order as well. Here is where the religious element enters Franklin's scheme. Besides being an expert architect and builder of the natural world, Franklin's God is also a moral governor and sustainer of virtue. He sees to it that virtue and happiness do indeed coincide—that virtue is rewarded and vice is punished. He also sustains the virtuous man in his course—providing him with both courage and comfort. God's first office, as moral governor, is widely recognized by students of Franklin. His second function—that of sustainer and comforter—has been somewhat less widely acknowledged.

Obviously, Franklin lacked Edwards' piety. Edwards used every imaginable psychic "contrivance" to keep himself always on moral tiptoe—ever reminding himself of his cosmic jeopardy, of his soul's precarious state, in order to live with all his might in God's service. Among his famous "Resolutions" he recorded his determination "To think much, on all occasions, of my own dying" and to "live so, as I shall wish I had done when I come to die." Edwards saw life in the context of a perilous, urgent, and infinitely desirable Eternity. In striking contrast to this, Franklin reports saying farewell to a friend who, it turned out, was soon to die:

He and I had made a serious agreement that the one who happened first to die should, if possible, make a friendly visit to the other and acquaint him how he found things in that separate state. But he never fulfilled his promise.

Such casualness is to be found only in one who no longer lives in the presence of a blinding divinity and whose concern about the hereafter and feeling for things eternal is temperate.

Franklin's earliest reading included his father's small library of works in polemical theology. He later regretted having bothered with them. Throughout his life Franklin had no interest in and saw no use for the intricacies of theology. Although he was generous in supporting numerous sects and maintained a very cordial relationship with George Whitefield, the great evangelist, he was always impatient with "sectarian" doctrines, distrustful of "enthusiasm," and committed to what he considered those beliefs that would "satisfy the professors of every religion, but shock none." These included belief in a god who created and who governs the world, belief in immortality and a future state of rewards and punishments, and belief that the most acceptable service to God is doing good to one's fellowmen. His mature theology was a moderate deism with a strong moral emphasis.[11] Whatever inclinations he had to worship God and demonstrate a spirit of reverence and praise were apparently satisfied by his private devotions and the kind of ceremonies performed by the Freemasons, of which he was a staunch member. He seldom attended church and seems to have gotten little out of it when he did. It is to be emphasized, above all, that Franklin's religion was always neatly confined to a department of his experience, as were all his interests and concerns. For him, what Edwards called "divine things" were never a matter of ultimate concern.

To say all of this is not to deny that religion was important for Franklin. Its primary importance for him, however, was moral. In our day, acknowledging this may seem like admitting Franklin's religious insincerity and superficiality. Franklin simply reduced religion to ethics, it is sometimes charged. The ethical religion that was so appealing in the eighteenth century appears shallow to the twentieth century, a kind of halfway paganism that lacks both religious conviction and the courage to abandon the faith entirely. Such an interpretation misrepresents the thinking of Franklin's age. Eighteenth-century liberals did not "simply" reduce religion to ethics, for there was nothing simple about the operation. Ethics was an extremely important subject in an age of new philosophical awareness, an increasingly liberated private conscience, and declining institutional authority. In Britain, moral philosophy seemed to attract particular interest. It is hardly surprising that in colonial America a secular intellectual like Franklin would transfer his cosmic loyalties from religion—which seemed to him either coldly doctrinal or vulgarly "enthusiastic"—to morality, the area in which the truly worthwhile and vital questions of the day were being raised. Twentieth-century people have trouble seeing the significance of this, not because they are more religious than eighteenth-century people, but because they are less moralistic. Because the ethical issues of Franklin's day are no longer alive to us, we are unwittingly grudging in our sympathies.

Franklin was being clever and pert when he published his *Dissertation on Liberty and Necessity, Pleasure and Pain* in 1725, denying both moral agency and the validity of moral distinctions on the basis of God's presumed omnipotence and benevolence. But he was in earnest when he drew up his "Articles of Belief and Acts of Religion" in 1728, and when he wrote to his father ten years later arguing that opinions and beliefs "should be judged by their Influence and Effects"—that in a "vital" religion virtue is always more important than orthodoxy. In 1735, when a local Presbyterian minister, the Reverend Samuel Hemphill of Philadelphia, was charged with preaching unsound doctrine, Franklin came to his defense in the *Pennsylvania Gazette*. Faith is not an end in itself, he argued. It is

> recommended as a Means of producing Morality: Our Saviour was a Teacher of Morality or Virtue.

Human nature is so prone to error and misconception, he continued, that it

> little becomes poor fallible Man to be positive and dogmatical in his Opinions. No Point of Faith is so plain, as that *Morality* is our Duty, for all Sides agree in that. A

virtuous Heretick shall be saved before a wicked Christian: for there is no such Thing as voluntary Error.

For Franklin, then, religious faith—one's beliefs about God and the universe—is ancillary to conduct. It is, nevertheless, still important. And it is here that our historical imagination most often fails us.

In the broadest sense, faith is important as a backstay of public virtue. It is a stable and orderly society's most precious possession. Where men are free and opportunity is abundant, where behavior is no longer dictated by custom and authority, virtue is a matter of individual choice. One makes one's moral choices on the basis of one's understanding of the nature of the universe and of man's place in it, that is, on the basis of one's religious beliefs. One of the advantages of studying history, Franklin suggested in his *Proposals Relating to the Education of the Youth of Philadelphia* (1749), is that it shows "the Necessity of a *Publick Religion*" to the well-being of society. In Franklin's estimation, the various Christian sects are all beneficial to the social order insofar as they contribute to this generalized belief. Doctrinal peculiarities are, to his mind, harmless idiosyncrasies that should be tolerated by the state but are of no special interest or concern to the thinking person. Just as one appreciates people for their essential humanity and joyfully accepts the variations of attitude and personality that add so much flavor to life, so one seeks, in the varieties of belief, that common faith that constitutes a society's metaphysic, its ideological cement. Franklin, of course, shared the widely held assumption of his century that the intricate design and order of the universe is adequate testimony that it was created by a Being who is not only intelligent and all-powerful but benevolent as well. To believe in such a Being, as any rational creature would, is to identify oneself as a responsible moral agent.

Important as the social function of faith is, there is another, more personal, aspect of faith that is equally central to Franklin's outlook. God not only sees to it that men behave themselves, He provides the individual with cosmic encouragement and reassurance. To put it another way, God not only discourages the wicked man from indulging his worst impulses, He also lends warm support to the good man in his pursuit of virtue.

Peter Gay, in his many writings on the European Enlightenment, has shown that the philosophes' criticism of traditional Christianity was not undertaken flippantly or with superficial optimism. Gay has reminded us of the anguish of secularism—the doubts and misgivings, the feelings of cosmic loneliness, that assailed those who had the courage to challenge a system of belief that had sustained and comforted Western man for centuries. There were some atheists like Baron d'Holbach, to be sure, who proclaimed the universe empty of divinity. For most eighteenth-century thinkers, even those who attacked and satirized Christian doctrines, the atheistic stance was an impossible one. The notion of an uncreated world system was still logically unthinkable to most. More, the idea of man's eternal solitude—marooned on a tiny fragment in an endless and empty universe—was psychologically intolerable.[12] In times of personal crisis, particularly, one needed the reassurance of traditional faith. In 1757, in a letter to his niece on the death of her father, John Franklin, Franklin wrote that this earthly life is merely

> an embryo State, a Preparation for living. A Man is not completely born until he be dead. Why then should we grieve, that a new Child is born among the Immortals, a new Member added to their happy Society?

Creeds and dogmas may be jettisoned, but the promise of the life everlasting is not easily renounced.

In living as in dying men still needed cosmic support. A close reading of the daily prayer that Franklin presents in his *Autobiography* reveals that close, and important, relation that obtains between faith and morals in his view of life:

> O powerful, bountiful Father, merciful Guide! Increase in me that Wisdom which discovers my truest Interests; strengthen my Resolutions to perform what that Wisdom dictates. Accept my kind Offices to thy other Children, as the only Return in my Power for thy continual Favours to me.

Franklin's God is a god of mercy, graciousness, and goodness, in gratitude for whose blessings one dedicates one's life to the service of others. From God Franklin asks wisdom, resolution, and acceptance. Wisdom reveals that, in the moral order of things, interest and happiness coincide. The moral life begins with this knowledge. It follows from this that virtue consists in the unflinching resolution to act according to one's moral understanding of things; and, in pursuing the life of virtue, one gains strength of will through the assurance that there is in the universe some power that supports us in our efforts to do good, because it is itself good. In a later century, William James was to define religious belief as the conviction that the better things in life are the more eternal. Human striving does not take place in a morally indifferent universe. Our moral sentiments and our best efforts count for something because they take place in a divine milieu. Hence, Franklin asks for acceptance, for cosmic recognition of his desire to live benevolently and justly among his fellow creatures.

Franklin's informal moral philosophy and his moralistic religion may not appeal to us today. For one thing, the intellectual life has become increasingly separated from the life of faith under the impact of scientific philosophy. For another thing, we are on the whole more casual about the kind of ultimate questions that concerned Franklin and other eighteenth-century thinkers. Finally, we are considerably less didactic and less concerned about matters of "publick and private Virtue" than were people of Franklin's day. For this reason Franklin's moralizing often seems either stuffy or insincere to us. By placing Franklin back in his own century, however, we are able to appreciate the part he played in American thought, not only as a creative genius but as a representative man. In this latter role, Franklin represents the conciliatory and moralistic frame of mind that introduced the experimental philosophy to the New World in the middle years of the eighteenth century. If Enlightenment ideas were more quietly absorbed in this country than they were on the European continent, it is partly because of the way they were communicated. Ideas were not treated as weapons to destroy oppressive institutions, but as the necessary tools to civilize a provincial society, to establish "the fundamental Principles of all sound Religion, and to promote the end of publick and private Virtue."

[6]

THE ETHICS OF BELIEF AND
THE CONDUCT OF THE MIND

"IT will be proper to observe," Franklin wrote in the *Pennsylvania Gazette* in 1730,

> that the great Truths of Religion, of Morality, and of Politicks, such as are the Cement of Society, come within a narrow Compass and may be apprehended by a plain Capacity, that shall diligently enquire into their Nature, with a Teachable Disposition, and Willingness to be informed.

The various efforts of "speculative Men" to introduce "Refinements" into these areas of knowledge, and to construct grand "Systems," are to be deplored, Franklin continued; systematic and speculative philosophy can cause only confusion when applied to these important human concerns. The basic truths are accessible to all who desire to learn; the speculations of the philosophers contribute nothing but bewilderment. It would be inaccurate to say that these words sum up the Enlightenment attitude toward philosophy, but it is fair to say that they reflect at least a recurring mood of the eighteenth century. For too long, it was thought, Western man had been misled and confounded by philosophers and theologians who were apologists for superstition and authority, who used reason not to enlighten the mind but to mystify the understanding.

Many of the developments we have discussed in the preceding two chapters have a decided bearing upon this philosophic temper. Science and the movement to facilitate the exchange of scientific ideas, rising literacy and the ideal of the Republic of Letters, increased social mobility, the erosion of traditional authorities—all these helped set the stage for a philosophic program that stressed clarity, simplicity, the wide dissemination of ideas, and relevance to the common life. It is "one of the great advantages of our century," said Voltaire in his article on the Man of Letters in the *Encyclopedia*, that learned men display a new breadth of knowledge that covers everything from mathematics to poetry, and that they are as "adapted to society as to study." The intellectual no longer wastes his time on ancient fables and abstruse speculations: He now turns a "searching and purified reason" to all matters of contemporary concern, and is thus contributing much to the "instructing and refining of the nation." The criticism offered by learned men, Voltaire believed, has "destroyed all the prejudices with which society was affected," and has

> relegated to the domain of puerility a thousand sectarian controversies that formerly were dangerous. . . . People are sometimes astonished that what previously convulsed the world no longer troubles it today. We are indebted to the authentic *men of letters* for this state of affairs.

It may be, as Whitehead charged, that "*les philosophes* were not philosophers," that they too eagerly applied a number of abstractions drawn from science to complex areas of experience, and that their vision consequently lacked depth.[1] The fact is, their mission was social as well as philosophical, and their frame of mind was moralistic as well as experimental. They wanted not only to clarify thinking but also to show the possibility of a new consciousness, a new wholeness of experience, in which the critical mind would concern itself with the common life, and the concerns of daily life would inform and stimulate the intellectual life. David Hume, who was both a philosophe *and* a philosopher, summed up the matter in the first chapter of his *Enquiry Concerning Human Understanding* (1748). Man needs to refine his thinking, he said; but man "is a sociable, no less than a reasonable being." He is also "an active being," involved in the business of living. It would seem, then,

> that nature has pointed out a mixed kind of life as most suitable to the human race. . . . Indulge your passion for science, says she, but let your science be human, and such as may have a direct reference to action and society. . . . Be a philosopher; but, amidst all your philosophy, be still a man.

Be still a man. Whatever philosophical difficulties this motto may lead to, we cannot overrate the debt of gratitude we owe—as Whitehead acknowledged—to the men who lived by it. It is with respect to "the great Truths of Religion, of Morality, and of Politicks," furthermore, that their contribution proved most enduring.

As far as the "great Truths of Religion" are concerned, we have already discussed the faith of the Enlightenment, particularly the deistic frame of mind; and we have seen that—superficial though it may seem to our own age—the deistic point of view was instrumental in helping many thinking people cope theologically with the cosmic uncertainties of a post-Christian world. Deism, moreover, was not only a halfway station in the flight from Christianity, a stopover on the way to unbelief. It was also a positive religious response to the times, an attempt to construct a truly rational, scientifically plausible faith that both met the critical standards of modern philosophy and offered truths that would appeal to all men, and were not intended only for a chosen few. These two positive characteristics of rational religion are often overlooked and deserve our attention. We may, for want of better titles, call them the spirit of criticism and the passion for simplicity and universality.

By "criticism," of course, is meant the questioning frame of mind that is determined to distinguish between opinion and actual knowledge, and uses the method of experimental reasoning to make the distinction. Science had used this method with astonishing results in the study of nature. Now, applying it to matters of faith, it would at last become possible to separate superstition from fact. Eighteenth-century thinkers were earnest about the ethics of belief: Man as a rational being was responsible for the things to which he gave intellectual assent; he had no "right" to believe whatever he chose. In a sermon on "The Right and Duty of Private Judgment" (1748), Jonathan Mayhew summed up the basic tenets of the ethics of belief. Except for a discrete number of "first principles," which do not extend to doctrines of religion, "all propositions are the proper subject of inquiry and examination," he asserted. It is our duty to inquire into the truth of all things, and to accept nothing on the basis of mere authority:

> Thus, for example, we ought not to believe that there is, or that there is not a God; that the Christian religion is from God, or an imposture . . . till we have impartially examined the matter, and see evidence on one side or the other.

Our duty critically to examine all our beliefs arises from our very constitution as rational beings:

> Our obligation, therefore, to inquire after truth, and to judge what is right, may be found within us, in our own frame and constitution. This obligation is as universal as reason itself; for every one that is endowed with this faculty, is, by the very nature of it, obliged to exercise it in the pursuit of knowledge.

Forty years after Mayhew delivered his sermon, Jefferson was advising young Peter Carr to fix reason "firmly in her seat, and call to her tribunal every fact, every opinion," no matter how august its source: "Read the Bible, then, as you would read Livy or Tacitus."

The spirit of criticism, thus, was more than contrariness or an adolescent impulse to topple the idols of an older generation. It arose among people who took the rational life very seriously, and who felt that free and unlimited inquiry was not only a right but a solemn duty. In the performance of their intellectual duty, however, their mood was predominantly hopeful and optimistic. This optimism stemmed from the conviction that the universe is orderly, purposeful, and morally governed. Relntless intellectual probing would finally reveal the truth; and this truth would ultimately confirm mankind's fondest hopes and satisfy its deepest yearnings. For beneath all the superstition and error that had accumulated through centuries of fear and ignorance lay a body of universal truths to which all rational beings must assent. Thus the spirit of criticism goes hand-in-hand with the passion for simplicity and naturalness, the desire to reduce all faiths to a few basic beliefs and principles that are common to humanity. Is this not analogous to what the Newtonian philosophy did in the physical world? Surely the Creator had not made the principles of religion and morality more complicated than those of physics and astronomy.

The ideal of a common religion of humanity, a religion based on the study of man and nature, a religion that somehow expresses the kernel of truth in all religions, must have been an inspiring one. After a century of persecution and religious warfare, and centuries before that of ignorance and superstition, here at last was the way to unity and concord among all people. After the American Revolution, the so-called militant deists— men like Paine and Elihu Palmer—considered deism the appropriate faith for a republic of free men. But even earlier, in the thinking of more discreet deists, like Franklin, we recognize the quiet conviction that a more "primitive" Christianity—a "pure" and essentially deistic Christianity, stripped of all its eccentricities and superfluities—is the true faith for the common, plain-speaking man who reads, thinks for himself, and is no longer content to be led (or misled) by synods or writers of dry divinity. The passion for simplicity, stirred by a new confidence in common sense belief, inspired the search for a common faith.

For the deist and the professors of rational religion generally, the great truths of religion seemed intimately connected with the question of morality. Although many things remain unknown to us, Voltaire said in a letter to the Prince of Prussia in 1770, we know that the "Lord of nature has given us the power of thinking and of distinguishing virtue." Like the truths of religion, those of morality may be "apprehended by a plain Capacity," as Franklin observed. If the deistic controversy of the early eighteenth century looks cold and sterile to us, the century's debate over morality exhibits additional vitality by contrast. Indeed, it has been plausibly argued that the primary concern of the deist was ethical. As the "enlightened reason" triumphs over superstition, fanaticism, and despotism, Elihu Palmer declared in 1801, and knowledge becomes more universal, "moral virtue" must inevitably triumph and bring "the ultimate extirpation of vice." A universal religion, unblemished by sectarian partiality and hence no longer the occasion for constant bickering, is the surest friend of virtue. A militant deist like Palmer might seek to replace the Christian sects with a universal deistical religion; while a moderate like Franklin cheerfully contributed his "mite" to any sect that preached what he considered "the fundamental Principles of all sound religion." In either case, the advancement of morals was the great test of faith.

Eighteenth-century Americans took their clues mainly from Britain in their ethical thinking.[2] Three developments in British ethics deserve particular attention. First, there was a determined move to make ethics independent of theology. Ethics emerged in this period as a secular and independent field of investigation, and questions like the one concerning the basis of moral obligation ("Why *ought* I . . . ?") were examined afresh. God's arbitrary will was no longer sufficient either as the basis for right and wrong or as the reason for pursuing the one and shunning the other. The noteworthy result of all this is that, as ethics established its intellectual autonomy, various theoretical problems arose that made ethics a fertile area of inquiry. In the English-speaking world, at least, ethics became a lively topic of discussion among thoughtful people.

Second, as ethics established its independence of religion, so, for a time at least, morality lost much of that burden of guilt and shame that the sinner must inevitably feel when he becomes aware of the impossible demands of God's Law and the meager resources of his own corrupt nature. Morality could be treated as an aspect of the art of living—part of a well-bred person's total life-style—and not merely as a system of rules that rigidly control conduct or that measure the depths of one's depravity. Franklin's

name for a proposed sect of young men dedicated to the cultivation of good character—the Society of the Free and Easy—
suggests this new mood of cheerful (but not easy) virtue. The
English essayist Joseph Addison, in his efforts (following the
Restoration period) to make virtue once again fashionable, and to
join moralism and wit, reinforced this tendency toward a secular,
temperate, stylish moralism.[3] So too did the Georgian fascination
with the classical tradition and particularly the later Stoic
philosophy, with its emphasis on self-mastery, obedience to the
moral order of things, and the coincidence of virtue and
happiness. This was a gentlemanly, even an aristocratic ideal, but
Addison had adapted it to the tastes of England's upper-middle
class. In America, Franklin adapted it to the sentiments and
aspirations of the rising bourgeoisie. So closely did Franklin's
own views reflect the English ideal of the secular gentleman that,
when he reprinted two of Shaftesbury's dialogues in the
Pennsylvania Gazette in the 1730's (without attribution, as was
customary), Franklin scholars for many years attributed the
pieces to the Philadelphian. Shaftesbury's argument, only he *truly*
loves himself who "rightly and judiciously loves himself" and who
regulates his "passions" according to the principles of his own
better nature, was so similar to Franklin's own judicious ethic,
that the distinguished English moralist seems to speak for the
rising American artisan. For both, the virtuous life is an expression of what is best in human nature, and since its careful cultivation is, in fact, self-realization in its noblest form, the practice of
virtue is the surest way to that feeling of accomplishment and
contentment we call happiness. The good life and the life of
goodness are one.

Third, in both America and Britain—particularly Scotland, the
eighteenth century brought a new examination of human nature
and its relation to the moral life. This was largely due to the
influence of Locke, who had undertaken his own study of the
human understanding because he thought such a study offered
the most promising approach to questions of morals and religion.
Locke, then, served as an inspiration in applying new techniques
to an old problem—using the experimental method of reasoning
to explore the human mind, the better to understand the moral

and spiritual life. But Locke had raised many disturbing questions. If, for example, all our knowledge—including our ethical knowledge—derives from our five senses, what validity do our judgments of right and wrong have? Many feared that Lockean empiricism led in the direction of a purely hedonistic ethics, where the good is equated with the pleasurable; and Locke's own tentative suggestions in this area did little to allay their fears. In the effort to avoid ethical hedonism or worse, philosophers like Francis Hutcheson began to look into the workings of our moral consciousness, searching for the true source of our ideas of good and evil, virtue and vice. They offered an imposing variety of answers. Hutcheson, although he himself qualified his theory through the years, traced our ideas of good and evil to a "sense" that is analogous to, but different from, our normal five senses. Our "moral sense," as he called it, rooted in our emotions, prompts us to react positively and approvingly when we witness certain kinds of conduct (an act of beneficence or of gratitude, for example) and negatively when we witness other kinds of conduct (cruelty, injustice). This is the psychological origin of our moral ideas. As man matures and reflects on his feelings, he develops very elaborate and subtle ethical theories; but the moral life springs from the warm, affective life, the life of feeling and emotion. It is reducible, that is to say, to certain fundamental principles in human nature. Thus, any description of human nature that is complete will include the recognition that man is by nature a moral being. Our love of virtue is, as it were, instinctive. What better sanction for morality can be asked?

Francis Hutcheson's was only one of many efforts to trace morality to a principle in human nature. The great Scottish moralist deserves special mention, however, because he was particularly influential in American thought in the eighteenth century. Later British writers, like the English divine Joseph Butler and the Scottish academicians Thomas Reid and Dugald Stewart, were to modify Hutcheson's theory, placing more emphasis on the rational element in our moral judgments. For all these writers, however, man possesses a moral nature. He has a faculty of mind—the "moral sense" or "conscience"—that enables him to make distinctions of which no other animal is capable: moral distinctions. This ability brings with it all the duties and responsibilities of the moral life.

Although the moral sense is part of man's natural endowment, this faculty, like the understanding, has to be properly nurtured and instructed. In the Lockean world there are no innate ideas, moral or otherwise. Human nature, moreover, is plastic and educable. Locke himself, in his *Thoughts Concerning Education* (1693), had placed heavy emphasis on moral education, the training of good character. Education, he said, should provide the young gentleman with four things: virtue, wisdom, breeding, and learning. The first three qualities Locke defined strictly in terms of Christian character, business acuity, civility, and bearing—all practical, temperamental, and moral qualities. Learning came last of all. Locke regarded learning as secondary to character training and the cultivation of worldly graces. Locke was not original in his formulation of the ends of education. Many of his ideas may be traced to the Commonwealth period and, in some cases, to the Elizabethan Renaissance. But Locke's prestige as (what we today would call) a psychologist gave his educational writings great influence in Britain and America. His emphasis on the utilitarian and moral aspects of the educative enterprise, furthermore, was appealing to a mobile society that stressed the relation between morality and social order, learning and advancement in life; and that recognized the importance of education in promoting all these causes.

When we think of education today, we usually think of the school and the academic subjects taught there. In fact, education includes much more than academic subjects, and goes on constantly, with or without schools and colleges. Locke, for instance, thought of education as a household enterprise undertaken with the help of a tutor, and intended to produce not a cleric or a scholar but a secular gentleman of affairs. In a posthumously published work, *Of the Conduct of the Understanding* (1706), Locke conceived of that advanced stage when the mature person undertakes his own education. The *Conduct* was written as a kind of instruction manual to provide guidelines in that undertaking. The fact is, schooling was much less available in the eighteenth century than it has since become. Many aspiring men, like

Franklin, were obliged to become their own teachers. Even those who had the advantage of formal education through the college level were subjected to rigorous discipline and instruction from their parents in their early years, and were taught to regard life itself as a system of moral and intellectual discipline. The inference to be drawn from all of this is that, in the eighteenth century, education extended far beyond schooling, that it was a constant and conscious part of life, and that it had a decidedly moral emphasis. Older men were prone to write long letters of advice and counsel to younger men and women, lavishing on them sound advice on the conduct of life. Such expository epistles to the young by a Franklin or a Jefferson may strike us as insufferably pompous and pontificating in our less didactic age. To get closer to the spirit of the eighteenth century, we should perhaps think of character building as an esoteric and demanding sport—like rock climbing—where one's interest may become totally absorbed in perfecting one's skill, and one is always eager to learn from a person who has distinguished himself as a master of its techniques. Such was the athletic mood in which many approached the art of living. This mood stems in part from the Renaissance ideal of life as a graceful expression of self-mastery and, at least in Britain and America, from the Puritan demand for self-control and discipline. But it contains a new element that reflects the spirit of the eighteenth century: a new sense of mastery over the circumstances of life—what Peter Gay means when he speaks of the "struggle to impose man's rational will on the environment."[4] The art of living involved a lifelong regime of mental, moral, and physical discipline in the determined effort to triumph over the brutality and callous fortuitousness of existence. The goal was not only survival but success—that is, arriving at that unspecifiable state that the people of the eighteenth century called happiness. Such was the aim of education. The state of happiness, of course, is never fully reached, so education is a never-ending process. The joy—the happiness, perhaps—is in the game as well as the goal. Happiness does not lie in repose, Jefferson wrote to William Short in 1819: We must be prepared "to meet and surmount difficulties." Only in the active, disciplined, involved life may we expect to enjoy that tranquility of mind we seek. In this respect education was at once a means to an end and an end in itself. It was preparation for life; it also *was* life.

In the process of society's continuing education, the press and the man of letters had crucial roles to play. The man of letters was an important character in the Enlightenment drama. One of the features that distinguishes the eighteenth century was the extension of the printed word and the rise—particularly in England and America—of a reading public. The much-celebrated "Republic of Letters" may, in fact, have been tiny, particularly on the European continent, but its social and cultural influence was immense. And the leading citizen of the Republic of Letters, the publicist, the man of letters, enjoyed growing influence throughout the century. His thinking, if not always profound, exhibited impressive range; and his concerns were not only theoretical but practical and determinedly down-to-earth. His overall influence in Western cultural history was great. It was the man of letters who introduced the experimental method of reasoning into other areas of the intellectual culture. It was he who championed the critical spirit and used it to probe society's beliefs and practices. And it was he whose writings—intelligent, witty, irreverent, angry—began a process of cultural consciousness raising that is without precedent in Western history. The man of letters provided the vocabulary and grammar through which the modern consciousness emerged. At the same time, he set forth the guidelines for the self-improvement of Everyman. He served his age not only as a critic but as an educator and moral pedagogue, whether he wrote didactic essays, moral maxims, sentimental novels, or political pamphlets. He helped cultivate the moral sensibility and stir the public conscience of his century.

Thanks in large part to the efforts of the man of letters to awaken his readers to their own humanity and to the needs of those about them, we observe in the eighteenth century a new consciousness of human suffering and a growing resolution to reduce it. As Whitehead remarked, the eighteenth century, with its common sense, "its grasp of the obvious facts of human suffering, and of the obvious demands of human nature, acted on the world like a bath of moral cleansing."[5] Science and technology, of course, encouraged this new moral sensibility by promising to increase the sources of human comfort and to make them available to more and more people. But it was the man of letters who taught the reading public the great moral lesson of material progress: that with man's growing *capability* for changing things for the better there comes too a concomitant *obligation* to improve the circumstances of everyone and to provide for the general welfare of all. When this moral insight was finally translated into social policy, the pursuit of happiness became the publicly sanctioned right of all citizens. The Enlightenment politicized the good life.

Thus we arrive at the third great set of truths that Franklin placed within the grasp of ordinary intelligence, that of "Politicks." In an age when science expanded human understanding and power, when improved communications greatly spread information, and when the middle classes were becoming conscious of their own interests and potential influence, it was natural that politics should become a subject of new interest and inquiry. Ideas about government, sovereignty, and institutional authority—ideas that had, for centuries, guided Western thought—came in for critical reexamination. In the British colonies of North America, during the last half of the century, this critical reexamination of traditional political beliefs was undertaken with a sense of resolution and urgency that inspired the whole world. "Happy that nation," Poor Richard shrewdly observed, "fortunate that age, whose history is not diverting." If we were to apply this rubric strictly, then we would have to conclude that Poor Richard's creator ended his life in a world that enjoyed neither happiness nor good fortune. For, in America, the great truths of politics were not simply to be studied and debated: They would be subjected to a dangerous but epoch-making experiment—an experiment that began in the violence of revolution and resulted in the creation of a new nation.

III

EXPERIMENTAL POLITICS

[7]

SCIENCE, RHETORIC, AND REVOLUTION

WHEN we think of the American Enlightenment, we think mainly of the Revolution and the events surrounding it. We think of political theory, of the Declaration of Independence and such things as self-evident truths, natural rights, and government with the consent of the governed. Yet the relation between the Enlightenment and the American Revolution is a complicated one, so complicated as to prompt some to downgrade and even deny entirely the impact of Enlightened thinking on Revolutionary America.

Even to begin to make sense of the problem, we must distinguish two important elements in Enlightenment thinking, particularly in its social thought. They should by now be familiar. The first has to do with the experimental philosophy and concerns the philosophical effort to base our knowledge on experience, critically analyzed. It is the effort to arrive at a new scene of thought that dispels mystery and allows man, for the first time, to understand his social world as it really is—the way he was beginning to understand nature—and not through the lenses of authority and superstition. Society was to be studied scientifically. The second significant element, best characterized as the rhetorical element, expresses the moral concern of the Enlightenment. It represents the effort not only to understand society but to control it, thereby making man society's master rather than its prisoner. To accomplish this, it is necessary both to understand how society works and to alert people to the new possibilities before them—to inform and stir society, to make it conscious of itself. The social thought of the Enlightenment, then, reflects both a method of knowing and a way of appealing to the moral sensibility, a determination to learn and a resolution

97

to awaken. This combination of the experimental and the rhetorical gives Enlightenment thinking its special quality, and suggests the relation between ideas and political events in the eighteenth century.

The experimental approach to social studies is evident in Montesquieu's pioneering study of social institutions, *The Spirit of the Laws* (1748). In the Preface Montesquieu affirmed: "I have laid down the first principles, and have found that the particular cases follow naturally from them." He added: "I have not drawn my principles from my prejudices, but from the nature of things." He used "prejudices" to mean "not that which renders men ignorant of some particular things, but whatever renders them ignorant of themselves."

These assumptions distinguish the eighteenth-century science of society. Western thinkers had sought out "first principles" and had appealed to "the nature of things" for centuries, to be sure. What is noteworthy is Montesquieu's way of linking these ideas and his sociological use of them. In his study of the "infinite diversity of laws and manners" Montesquieu drew on the experience of many nations, ancient as well as contemporary, non-Western as well as European. His understanding of the "nature of things," therefore, was informed by a twenty-year comparative study of social life: It was grounded in experience. Proceeding inductively, Montesquieu derived his "first principles" from the myriad data he had gathered, on the basis of which he could make generalizations about such things as the kinds of government that exist and the spirit that animates each, or about the influence of climate and geography on a nation's social life. At all times, Montesquieu tried to preserve a critical attitude, seeing things as they are and not through a medium of fictions and preconceptions. "When I have been obliged to look back into antiquity," he says, "I have endeavored to assume the spirit of the ancients, lest I should consider those things as alike which are really different, and lest I should miss the difference between those which appear to be alike." He gives assurances that he writes "not to censure anything established in any country," but rather to see to it "that the minds of the people be enlightened," to help "make mankind recover from their prejudices" and gain true self-knowledge. Montesquieu was but one of many eighteenth-century thinkers who helped apply the experimental method of reasoning to the investigation of society and politics.

Inductive reasoning, comparative studies, the quest for universals, the effort to free the mind from "prejudices"—these are the intellectual and moral qualities that link Montesquieu with thinkers as diverse as David Hume, Lord Kames, Rousseau, Voltaire, John Adams, and James Madison. These methods and assumptions did not put them above criticism. Later historians, for example, were to deal as harshly with Montesquieu for his supposedly naïve environmentalism as they were with Hume for his famous remark:

> Mankind are so much the same, in all times and places, that history informs us of nothing new or strange in this particular. Its chief use is only to discover the constant and universal principles in human nature.

It has been charged that, in trying to overthrow ancient prejudices, the philosophes constructed fictions of their own and imposed simplistic models of explanations on very complex areas of human experience. The charge cannot be casually dismissed. The philosophes were often guilty of simplistic explanations, although neither Hume nor Montesquieu in this instance offered so one-dimensional a view of history and society as some critics maintain. Whatever their shortcomings, in any case, their contribution was immense. The eighteenth-century thinkers did nothing less than fashion the *science* of society as we know it. The disciplines not only of history but of sociology, anthropology, economics, and political science owe their inceptions to these men, who made the determined effort to explain social phenomena, and to do so without reliance on myth and fable or with reference to God's will. What scientists were doing in the physical realm would now be accomplished in the social realm and by similar methods.[1]

This means, following the advice of Francis Bacon, not only that data must be exhaustively gathered but also, as we have seen, that these data must be manipulated, rearranged, and set in a new perspective. To take an obvious example, if one supposes that "mankind are so much the same, in all times and places," one is then bound to give new attention to those historical, cultural, and environmental circumstances that make one society different from another. One can no longer avoid explaining differences among peoples by saying simply that people are by nature different. Used this way, Hume's statement serves as a kind of mental lever, forcing us to consider our facts from a new angle, prompting us to see man in a wider context. More: If we suppose human nature is a constant, we are in a position to learn from history and from the study of other societies. The decline of political virtue would have as deleterious effect on a modern republic as it did on ancient republics, and we might do well to be on our guard against a recurrence of the circumstances that preceded such a decline among, say, the ancient Romans. The science of society, then, has a practical application to present policies. Just as the Baconian method gave rise both to science and technology in the physical world, so it produced both fresh insight and new moral possibilities in the social world.

In their social thought the philosophes were often simplistic in setting up models and in treating history as a moral lesson. If this was their vice, however, it arose as an excess of their virtue. They suffered the limitations of the pioneer exploring and settling a new land. For all their shortcomings, the social thinkers of the eighteenth century realized that society could be made the object both of human understanding and of human control.

This leads us directly to the rhetorical element in Enlightenment thought. The rhetorical element is evident in the concepts we most readily associate with the social thought of the Enlightenment, those of natural law, natural rights, and the social contract. All three of these formidable ideas have roots going back into medieval and ancient thought, so in a sense they cannot be considered exclusively themes of the eighteenth century.[2] The idea of natural law, furthermore, a metaphysical principle that predicates a rational, transcendent law above all human law, was already passing out of fashion among European thinkers by the time of the American Revolution precisely because of its speculative, metaphysical, nonempirical character. These ideas are nevertheless important to the revolutionary rhetoric of the late eighteenth century. Whatever problems they may present to the social theorist who hopes to develop a strictly empirical "science" of society, moreover, the ideas of natural law, natural rights, and the social contract express important moral truths that relate to the Enlightenment concern for social justice, and this makes them central to our understanding of the age's social ethic.

Natural law, natural rights, and the social contract were variously interpreted by seventeenth- and eighteenth-century thinkers from Hobbes to Rousseau. For our purposes, a few central features may be highlighted, drawn mainly from John Locke's famous *Second Treatise on Government* (1690). Man as a human being, prior to the formation of any political society (that is, in the "state of nature"), has certain rights with respect to others. These include the rights of life, liberty, and property, and they are guaranteed by the law of nature, which is the law of reason. As Locke put it:

> The state of nature has a law of nature to govern it which obliges every one; and reason, which is that law, teaches all mankind who will but consult it that, being all equal and independent, no one ought to harm another in his life, health, liberty, or possessions.

Because, in exercising his rights, each individual ran the constant risk of clashing with each other individual similarly engaged, man found it expedient to organize into political society, thereby sacrificing certain liberties (social man is no longer free to do whatever he pleases) but gaining new security. Society exists to serve and protect the individual in the proper exercise of his rights. Its authority over the individual, in other words, is limited, and its government may rightly be overthrown should it violate these basic rights.

These ideas have been severely criticized in the eighteenth century and since. Not only has the law of nature been dismissed as a fiction and the whole notion of "natural" rights existing apart from society been questioned, but the idea of the social contract—sometimes interpreted literalistically as an actual event in history or prehistory—has been vigorously attacked, particularly in the nineteenth century, for failing to account either historically or logically for the origins of the body politic. Even the historical influence of these ideas on the political events of the late eighteenth century has been questioned. It has been convincingly argued, for example, that of the two greatest proponents of the social contract theory, Locke and Rousseau, the latter's version had almost no influence in Revolutionary America and the former's was used more for rhetorical than for analytical or interpretive purposes.[3] The Declaration of Independence, which incorporates so much of this thinking in its Preamble, seems to have attracted little attention in Europe at first, and it set forth ideas that were at the time already losing respectability abroad. What, then, makes these theories significant in a discussion of the American Enlightenment?

As we have seen, it is exactly in the area of moral rhetoric that the ideas of natural law, natural rights, and the social contract are most important. The ideas may be treated as elaborate metaphors that describe the individual's moral status in society. The social-contract theory, for instance, suggests an element of voluntarism in any social order: Society exists to serve man, not vice versa. The idea of natural law directs us beyond society and its positive laws. It suggests that when there is a real dispute between the individual and society the matter may be shifted from politics to ethics: We are called to put aside our "prejudices" and customs, and to examine the individual's claims from the most universal perspective available. Finally, if one removes natural rights entirely from the theological-metaphysical realm, its metaphorical meaning becomes clear. Man as an individual has to be appreciated for himself, apart from his society. He has a dignity and a moral identity that transcend his social milieu. Society, that is, may be judged according to its willingness to satisfy (or to frustrate) human needs and aspirations. The theory of natural rights, furthermore, permits one to speak of human dignity and worth specifically and enumeratively—translating benign sentiments into a concrete program, as when one draws up a list of basic "rights" to fight for. Following this line of interpretation, we avoid such questions as "Do rights exist outside of society?" Instead, the matter may be put thus: "Although governments may trample human freedom, as long as one is conscious of his or her own worth and dignity no government can ever nullify that person's humanity." It may be that the theory of the free individual apart from society is a fiction—that the very definition of humanness is a product of social life. Still, this quality of humanness, howsoever it arose, is not to be crushed by society's *institutions*. Human dignity always has a moral veto over an oppressive institution or an unjust government.

In eighteenth-century America such thinking as this served to sanction political actions of protest, of resistance, and, finally, of rebellion. When, following the war with France and the Treaty of Paris in 1763, Britain turned to her North American colonies for financial help in paying her postwar debts and meeting her military expenses, enacting various revenue measures and enforcing trade laws that had for years gone unenforced, she was met with determined colonial opposition. The Americans, suffering themselves from a postwar business recession, condemned outside "interference" in their internal colonial affairs and protested against taxation without meaningful representation in the English Parliament. They reacted with mounting resistance to measures like the Currency Act (1764), the Stamp Act (1765), the Townshend Acts (1767), and—later—to retaliatory measures like the Coercive Acts (1774). Defiant declarations by colonial legislatures seemed to be ratified in the streets of the American cities as angry mobs demonstrated, rioted, and sometimes clashed with British troops. By the mid-1770's resistance had become rebellion, and the Americans prepared to declare themselves an independent nation. In the course of this struggle the Americans drew on the rhetoric of their age to define and defend their position. The language of natural rights, natural law, and the social contract did not simply justify the American rebellion to other nations: It broadened the moral perspective on political actions so that the actors themselves could come to terms with events that seemed to shatter all existing structures of explanation. If these ideas suggested metaphysical as opposed to empirical thinking, if they seemed to violate the scientific spirit of the times, they were nonetheless useful, perhaps indispensable, to people living through a period of social upheaval. More is needed at such times than the spirit of criticism. People seek inspiration to act and reassurance that their action—undertaken in defiance of law and custom—is yet grounded in some firm principle. The ideas of natural law and natural rights were particularly helpful to people trying to cope morally and psychologically with political revolution. Thus, to understand the social thinking of the American Enlightenment, we must consider seriously its rhetorical as well as its philosophical aspects. Faced with a revolutionary crisis, the Americans drew not only on science but on what Jefferson called "the harmonizing sentiments of the day" for moral guidance. They demanded truths that were not only probable and approximate (and the surest empirical truths are nothing more) but sacred and undeniable, even self-evident. The American Revolution and the events following it provide a case study not so much of the influence of ideas on events as of the way events affect the reception and appropriation of ideas.

The American Revolution is one of those cataclysmic events that, at first glance, seems to bring intellectual history into sharp focus but which, the longer one looks, actually tends to blur everything. Interpretations that had once seemed obvious—that the Enlightenment was a significant "cause" of the American war for independence, for example—have not merely been qualified but completely turned around. It has been maintained, thus, that the American Enlightenment would more accurately be described as an effect rather than a cause of the Revolution; that the political turmoil of the period 1765 to 1783 forced the Americans to reexamine their old ideas and consider new ones, finally developing a new mentality altogether.[4] Though it seems an obvious inference, considering documents like the Declaration of Independence, that Enlightenment ideas played a significant role in shaping the revolutionary mind, on closer inspection we find it was not the ideas of Voltaire, d'Alembert, Diderot, and Rousseau that were most influential in the American colonies. The American revolutionary ideology owed its major debt to a number of British thinkers of the seventeenth and eighteenth centuries, men like Algernon Sidney, Benjamin Hoadly, Robert Molesworth, Thomas Gordan, John Trenchard, and others, who were known as "real" or "honest" Whigs, and whose radical political thinking stirred more interest in England's colonies than in England itself. Natural rights, the contractural basis of society, government with consent of the governed—all mingled with a profound respect for the British constitution—

were part of radical Whiggery and became part of American thinking tough this channel.[5] We may, speaking loosely, consider the real Whigs as representatives of the Enlightenment (and some of the later radicals, like Joseph Priestley and Richard Price, undoubtedly were), but this would ultimately do violence to the concept. The real Whigs were opponents of arbitrary government and champions of freedom, both political and religious; but in the final analysis they looked not outward and forward but backward, to the political ideas of the Commonwealth period and to the opportunities offered by the Glorious Revolution of 1688. They were not philosophes with a truly internationalist perspective. Ultimately, they were concerned not with society but with English society, not with the rights of man but the rights of Englishmen, not with the promise of the future but with the corruptions of the present. Inasmuch as these writers shaped the thinking of Revolutionary Americans, then we have to agree with those who minimize the influence of the Enlightenment on the American Revolution.

The picture becomes blurrier still. When we consider the transmission of revolutionary ideas among the colonists themselves, we find evidence to suggest that it was not primarily radical Whiggery, much less Enlightenment thinking, that shaped *popular* attitudes on the subject, but religion, particularly the Calvinist doctrines concerning God's demands on His people in working His purposes on earth. Perry Miller and others have shown how the American clergy set the events of the time in the context of divine Providence, making resistance to British "tyranny" not only a right but a solemn religious obligation resting on a people sworn to preserve their Christian liberties in order totally to serve their Creator.[6] The authority of magistrates, said the Reverend Samuel West in an address before the Massachusetts House of Representatives in 1776, derives from God and is given that God's purposes may be served. When these magistrates frustrate God's purpose and act in disobedience to His Law, as the British have done, they lose their legitimate authority,

> and it is so far from being a crime to resist them, that in many cases it may be highly criminal in the sight of Heaven to refuse resisting and opposing them to the

utmost of our power; or, in other words, that the same
reasons that require us to obey the ordinance of God,
do equally oblige us, when we have power and
opportunity, to oppose and resist the ordinances of
Satan.

It is possible to overemphasize the role of religion in the
American Revolution, indeed, one historian has referred to the
American colonies in the mid-eighteenth century as "perhaps the
most unchurched regions in all Christendom."[7] The available
evidence suggests that the overwhelming majority of the colonists were not even church members, church membership being
estimated at somewhere between only two and ten percent of the
population. Still, such statistics can be misleading: For church
membership, in an age in which it was not casually granted and in
which the devotional life was often informal and noninstitution-
al, reflects neither church affiliation and attendance nor the
extent of religious concern. In fact, Protestant Christianity was
deeply a part of American culture in the eighteenth century, and
Richard Hofstadter is certainly right to observe that many
Americans who participated in the Revolution did so "as Christians for whom it was intellectually necessary that the Revolution
appear as an incident in some providential scheme."[8] The
revolutionary leaders might argue from secular principles of the
common law, radical Whiggery, and Enlightened social theory,
but as Perry Miller reminds us, a "successful revolution . . . requires not only leadership but receptivity." Protestant Christianity provided this for many ordinary folk by furnishing the
appropriate metaphors and myths through which they could
make moral sense of the rush of political events.

To bring all this together, we may offer the following summary
concerning the intellectual "causes" of the American Revolution.
We may suggest, first, that ideas alone are seldom the only or
even the major cause of great historical events, and it is always
risky—though sometimes quite useful—to try to specify the
degree to which ideas are behind significant events. Some
historians, observing how unoppressive the British administra-
tion of colonial affairs really was, even in the years immediately

preceding the outbreak of fighting, have laid much stress on colonial thinking and perceptions. They have argued, along with Moses Coit Tyler, the great literary historian of the nineteenth century, that the Revolution "was pre-eminently a revolution caused by ideas, and pivoted by ideas." The colonists, according to Tyler, "made their stand, not against tyranny inflicted, but only against tyranny anticipated."[9] If we follow this line, however, we must ask ourselves whether we are speaking of ideas-as-theories or ideas-as-perceptions. Are we discussing political philosophy or social psychology? The obvious answer, of course, is that we are discussing both. The colonists interpreted such political events as the Stamp Act of 1765 as part of a wider "conspiracy" to undermine traditional English rights and liberties in the New World. In interpreting such events, further, colonists drew on both secular and religious ideas that were available to them—the theories of the real Whigs, the social rhetoric of the Enlightenment, the lessons of the Old and New Testaments, even the doctrines of the covenant theology—and came to see the corruption of public virtue that was presumably so shockingly a part of English political life at the time as a kind of disease that was spreading to the colonies. Growing "elegance," "idleness," "luxury," and "effeminacy," alarming signs of the times, were lumped together with religious indifference, unjust laws, and alleged violations of the prerogatives of colonial legislatures. The colonists came to see isolated events as part of a greater whole, a conspiracy to impose a corrupt tyranny on colonial America, a threat to constitutional government, an assault on political virtue, and—for some—an attack on true Christianity. As relations between the mother country and her colonies deteriorated between 1765 and 1776, the conceptual frame of reference within which these events were interpreted and by which counterstrategies were formulated and defended became at once clearer and more comprehensive. What had begun as a defense of the rights of overseas Englishmen ended as an appeal to natural law and divine Providence. The right to resist became the duty to rebel. Throughout this entire course of events, however, we find little evidence that specifically Enlightenment thinking played an especially noteworthy part.

The social and political aspect of the American Enlightenment is much more evident later, after America finally declared her independence. It is then that both the analytical and the rhetorical features of the Age of Reason become prominent, and in a way peculiar to the American experience.

[8]

THOMAS JEFFERSON AND THE
RHETORIC OF REPUBLICANISM

ON January 1, 1766, shortly before the Stamp Act was repealed, John Adams wrote in his diary:

> The eyes of all America are fixed on the British Parliament. In short, Britain and America are staring at each other; and they will probably stare more and more for some time.

Many years later, Adams recalled that the American Revolution began long before the fighting began at Lexington, and that it took place, not on the battlefield, but "in the Minds of the People." What took place in the minds of the American people between 1760 and 1775 was the development not so much of a philosophy as of a new consciousness. Historians have described how the Americans, as they stared at the British Parliament and reacted to its developing colonial policy (if indeed there *was* a policy), became increasingly sensitive about their rights, gave both clearer and increasingly audacious definition to these rights, and in the process experienced a dawning sense of national identity. By 1776 they were no longer staring at Parliament. The Declaration of Independence directed its charges not at Parliament but at the King, the very symbol of British nationality. The Americans were Englishmen no longer.

What did independence mean? What did it mean to be an American? The questions are important and difficult ones. The Americans were the first colonial people in the modern world to declare their independence of the mother country. They were doing something new in history, and they were fully aware of the fact. Moreover, the American Revolution opened an era of revolution in the Western world; and while the American Revolution was primarily a political and not a social upheaval, it was to play a significant part both in democratizing American society and in promulgating the ideals of freedom, equality, and human dignity. Finally, coming at the end of an age of Enlightenment, it was viewed by many in America and abroad as a practical demonstration of many of the ideas that had become fashionable in the preceding century. The American "experiment" was to serve as the practical test of current theories concerning man and society. All this added up to a weighty assignment for the new republic. For the generation just coming to political maturity in 1776, the years immediately ahead imposed the considerable burden both of defining America's Americanness and of locating the Revolution amid the startling events, social and intellectual, of the eighteenth century. Adams spoke with a prophetic exuberance when he wrote to his wife, Abigail, following the Congressional vote for independence in 1776,

> Yesterday, the greatest question was decided, which was ever debated in America, and a greater, perhaps, never was nor will be decided among men.

In considering the wider meaning of the American Revolution it is easy to think in broad generalizations, and to lose sight of the more immediate and personal elements that go into making a historical era. We forget that questions about the American identity, the social and historical meaning of independence, and the cultural implications of independence were raised by living people who suffered their history at firsthand. The people are there—Washington, Jefferson, Adams, Hamilton, Madison, Franklin, not to mention the lesser figures like Patrick Henry, Richard Henry Lee, Samuel Adams—but they loom before us like so many legends or marble busts, collectively named The Founding Fathers, as if to make them more remote and imposing than ever. Just as Edwards is distant from us in his seeming antiquity, and Franklin eludes us with his very familiarity, the first American nationals are remote from us because they are seen not as men but as national monuments. Interestingly, too, just as Edwards clung to that antiquity that separates him from us and Franklin cultivated that evasive familiarity of his, so the first American nationals grandly construed their actions and consciously thought of themselves in monumental terms. To understand their historic meaning, it is not really necessary to strip away the legend, but to come to terms with it. Thomas Jefferson provides us with an excellent chance to do this. He is the American philosophe, *par excellence.* His ideas are closely associated with the social and intellectual meaning of the American Revolution. And, next to Washington, no man of his age more clearly seems to represent monumental Americanism.

Jefferson, born in 1743, was only thirty-three when he wrote the Declaration of Independence. His mother was the daughter of a fine old Virginia family, and his father was a prosperous Virginia planter. As a member of Virginia's upper class, Jefferson is as representative (and as unique and unrepresentative, in some ways) of that part of the Chesapeake Society as Franklin is of bourgeoisie Philadelphia or Edwards is of Puritan New England. He enjoyed all the privileges, including the wealth, the personal associations, the political influence, the refinements, and the education, available to the Virginia aristocracy. After graduating from William and Mary College in 1762, Jefferson studied law and practiced for a short time before entering politics in 1769 as a member of the Virginia House of Burgesses. In 1775 he went to Philadelphia as one of Virginia's delegates to the Second Continental Congress. Already acknowledged as a skillful writer, Jefferson, in 1776, was appointed to a five-man committee charged with the responsibility of writing the formal document that would declare America independent of Britain. With some revisions by Franklin and John Adams (who also served on the committee) and by the Congress, the composition of the Declaration is largely Jefferson's. Everyone knows that Jefferson's document did more than declare American independence. It declared that governments are established to secure certain "inalienable rights," including "life, liberty, and the pursuit of happiness," with which all people are endowed. It declared, further, that governments derive their "just powers from the consent of the governed," and that, when a government acts in a way destructive of these fundamental rights, it "is the right of the people to alter or to abolish it, and to institute a new government." There was nothing original here. Jefferson did not intend the document to be philosophically innovative. As he later said, he mainly wanted to give "an expression of the American mind," setting forth the "harmonizing sentiments" of the day. What *was* original was the vehicle through which these sentiments were expressed—an official document announcing a policy of historic importance. Many of these ideas may indeed have already been passing out of vogue among European thinkers. The important point is that these ideas were not being discovered or analyzed; they were being used for a political purpose. The theories that European intellectuals had debated were now being put to the test of practical service in the public realm.

Jefferson himself was hardly an *avant-garde* social thinker in 1776. Although the intellectual record is somewhat meager up until that time, the evidence that is available, such as his *Commonplace Book*—his personal record of the reflections of great social thinkers—suggests that his was a rather conservative and legal mind, much influenced by Lord Kames and the basically conservative Montesquieu. In fact, it was only after Jefferson went to France, between 1784 and 1789, that his thinking took on that egalitarian and politically adventurous quality that we associate with Jeffersonian liberalism. While he was there, his correspondence exhibits little of the ideological exhortation that one today usually expects of revolutionaries abroad and in which the French revolutionary, Citizen Edmond Genêt, indulged when he came to America in 1793. Clearly, Jefferson was not a revolutionary ideologue.

Jefferson's thought is not easily abstracted from his life in its fuller dimensions. His ideas, never systematically set forth, have to be studied as they appear, almost incidentally to various practical and immediate concerns, in public documents and private correspondence. Jefferson was always both more and less than a social philosopher. He was less in that his thought was neither original nor systematically, nor even consistently, set forth. He was more in the sense that, in the tradition of the Renaissance humanist, he energetically applied himself to an astonishing variety of activities (in the context of his whole life, Jefferson's eight-year career as President of the United States seems incidental), and truly was, as Adrienne Koch has remarked, "superbly and notoriously versatile."[1] Besides being a politician and political theorist, Jefferson was an architect and builder of note, an inventor, a writer (if not the originator) of scientific geography, an educational theorist and planner, a hard-working plantation owner, and a student of the natural sciences, anthropology, philology, the classics, law and legal philosophy, history, and *belles lettres*. His reading schedule, even in his last years, can only be called heroic by today's standards. One of his biographers reports that once, when he was Secretary of State, Jefferson was asked for an appointment so he could be shown an experiment in the distilling of salt water into fresh. He would be available at any time, he replied, "from five in the morning to twelve at night, all being equal to me."[2]

Jefferson was a philosopher and a Virginia planter. To overlook either of these sides of the man is to miss his intellectual significance. In calling him a philosophe, we are simply acknowledging that he was a member of that international circle of articulate, thinking people who shared a common commitment to the experimental method of reasoning and the critical examination of all questions. Like them, Jefferson was aware of his modernity and of the intellectual gap that separated his age from those preceding it. He subscribed, like other philosophes, to the ethics of belief, and considered it a moral duty to cultivate what he called "the habit of testing everything by reason." Above all, Jefferson was intellectually cosmopolitan for all his national and local loyalty. In his intellectual life he was first and foremost a citizen of the eighteenth century and only secondarily an American or Virginian. He shared the philosophes' common admiration for the Greek and Latin classics and was most content when he could devote himself to the world of books. He wrote from retirement at Monticello to John Adams in 1812: "I have given up newspapers in exchange for Tacitus and Thucydides, for Newton and Euclid; and I find myself much the happier." Ideas, he said, are "like fire, expansible over all space, without lessening their density at any point." He praised internationalist scientific and literary societies that continued their communications even during wartime and formed "the republic of letters . . . a great fraternity spreading over the whole earth." The man who considered London superior to Paris but inferior to Philadelphia nevertheless regarded the Republic of Letters as inclusive of all.

Besides being a cosmopolitan philosophe, Jefferson was a Virginia gentleman with all the privileges and responsibilities such a position brings. Although we must use the term cautiously when discussing the American scene, Jefferson was an aristocrat, a well-born son of the Virginia oligarchy, which, through most of the eighteenth century, led Virginia politics and owned her richest land. The Virginia planter class established within itself a system of kinship and loyalty and developed a sure sense of its own honor and worth, cultivating an elegant life-style commensurate with this self-image. To be sure, Americans lacked the traditional badges of aristocracy, like titles, hereditary social rank, and long-standing traditions. Furthermore, the American aristocracy, as Richard Hofstadter observes,[3] constituted itself out of the business class; and most Virginia planters, far from being leisured nobles, were busily engaged on a day-to-day basis in the task of managing a plantation. Still, class lines had steadily hardened since the beginning of the eighteenth century, and it had become increasingly more difficult for one to enter upper-class Virginia society. By the time of the Revolution the best families of Virginia had developed that subtle, unaffected self-esteem, that quiet acceptance of rank—evident no less in the architecture and decoration than in the private diaries and correspondence—that distinguishes the aristocratic temper. Thomas Nelson Page, himself a Virginian, once expressed it thus:

> To be a Virginia gentleman was the first duty; it embraced being a Christian and all the other virtues.[4]

It is not really odd that liberal political ideas circulated among this upper class. In colonial Virginia, there was a fairly broad voting base among property owners, who nonetheless usually elected the larger landowners, the members of the gentry class, to the important political offices. Understandably, Virginia's upper class came to feel that it could trust the judgment of "the people," and someone like Jefferson might naturally be expected to endorse republican principles enthusiastically: His fellow citizens consistently displayed the good sense to choose the "best men" to govern them. If the Virginia gentleman was receptive to liberal ideas, then, it was not merely because political liberalism was enjoying a certain vogue at the time among Enlightened types, but also because of immediate, firsthand experience—which, incidentally, also provided the Virginia aristocrat with a practical lesson on how a republic ought to work.[5]

The republican gentlemen of Virginia have been much admired for their political "realism" and "pragmatism." No fuzzy theorists nor vain ideologists were these canny statesmen, for they had received their training in the school of practical political experience. In admiring the Virginians for their practicality and political experience, however, we must remember that the school of experience has limitations as well as strengths. It is sometimes difficult for the student to break free of his own experience in trying to master a subject with which he has had direct acquaintance, and sometimes one must "unlearn" things one has taken for granted for years. This was true of Virginia's liberal aristocrats, whose tendency it was to project the Virginia experience onto the national scene, interpreting the nation's problems and possibilities in terms of their local concerns and prospects. It was difficult for Jefferson to understand John Adams' reservations about the people or his fear of the mob: In rural Virginia the mob did not exist, and the people were, in fact, the trustworthy and still deferential freeholders. More seriously, it was too easy for Jefferson and others like him to read the future of the United States as a bigger version of Virginia politics. As Henry Adams put it: "The republic which Jefferson believed himself to be founding or securing in 1801 was an enlarged Virginia."

Jefferson's dual identity as cosmopolitan philosophe and Virginia planter helps us to understand many things about his place in the American Enlightenment, particularly regarding his social theories, and about his horizon of values generally. For example, in building his home at Monticello, Jefferson, a skilled architect (at least by the time he had finished building, then rebuilding it), erected a monument of classical symbolism that "states a creed," as Alan Gowans puts it, exressing "the classical conviction that men could control their destinies and mould their worlds to their will."[6] It symbolized the hopeful future of the new nation and, in its classical lines, linked the United States with that ancient embodiment of republican principles the Roman republic. Yet Monticello is set high on a hill looking west toward what was, in Jefferson's day, thousands of miles of unexplored wilderness. Environmental circumstances and wilderness conditions made it necessay for Jefferson, who was his own builder as well as architect, to study local timber, establish his own nail factory (using slave labor), train slaves as carpenters, masons, and cabinetmakers, and develop a mortar and a clay (using buttermilk in the latter formula) suitable to the damp climate of the region. Monticello expresses the contradictions of Jefferson's Virginia-style cosmopolitanism. Committed to classical aesthetics, Jefferson could sacrifice interior comfort and convenience to exterior expression: He gave up his originally spacious second-floor library, when he redesigned his home, in order to build a dome and portico that served no function but more nearly conformed to the architectural notions Jefferson had picked up while visiting Europe in 1784-89. On the other hand, Jefferson could sacrifice the aesthetic unity of Monticello's classical interior to his passion for mechanical gadgetry and New World artifacts. His incredible cannonball calendar for telling the days of the week adds nothing to the beauty and ambiance of the front hall. And the animal heads, Indian maps, and other curios on the walls make the hall resemble a pioneer museum more than the entrance to one of the country's great homes.

The architectural example of Monticello—with its curious mixture of Old World forms and New World experience—is only one clue to the wider meaning of Jefferson's dual identity as cosmopolitan philosophe and Virginia planter. One finds another in his carefully planned life-style and the ethical principles by which he sought to govern it. Here one observes a quite harmonious blending of new theories about man and prevailing standards of gentlemanly conduct. Jefferson was a moderate deist who— in the permissive intellectual climate of eighteenth-century

Virginia—could yet consider himself a good Anglican. In fact, Jefferson was not primarily interested in theological doctrine either positively or negatively. His secular temperament was such that he could politely put theology aside and adhere to his own moralized version of the Christian message.

Jefferson was no less concerned than was Franklin with the art of virtue. As might be expected, Jefferson was much less concerned with the relation between one's moral and social advancement, although the link between virtue and happiness was no less strong in Jefferson's mind than in Franklin's. Like Franklin, Jefferson blended ethics and aesthetics with a kind of athletic strenuosity and the rational planning of an engineer. Even as Jefferson tried to express moral themes in his architecture, so he approached ethics with an architect's concern for precision and aesthetics. Finally, in ethics no less than in architecture, Jefferson's taste ran to the monumental.

What strikes us first about Jefferson's moral outlook is his concern with will training and with the technology of virtue. Although later in his life he was to express disapproval of excessive novel reading, he warmly recommended fiction along with history to his in-law Robert Skipwith in 1771, as a means of refining one's moral perception. To experience a feeling of charity or of sympathy is "an exercise of our moral dispositions," he advised. "And dispositions of the mind, like limbs of the body acquire strength by exercise." By reading history and fiction (the moral lessons of history alone "would be too infrequent if confined to real life"), we engage in this exercise. Fifteen years later he admonished his nephew Peter Carr:

> Exercise all your virtuous dispositions, and exercise them whenever an opportunity arises; being assured that they will gain strength by exercise, as the limb of the body does, and that exercise will make them habitual.

What was said earlier should perhaps be repeated. This kind of moral didacticism should not be dismissed as the pompous garrulities of the older generation addressing itself to youth. The cultivation of virtue was crucial to the art of living, and as such was treated seriously by all. Coming from an older man who had lived through much, Jefferson's moral advice was undoubtedly appreciated. He was the master of a skill—a professional, as it were—whose tips to a youthful novice were to be interpreted as kindly offered expertise.

Jefferson never articulated a systematic moral theory, but in his correspondence, particularly, we get a good idea of what he believed. Along with many eighteenth-century people, he believed that human nature is by nature moral. Man is endowed with a "moral sense" (which allows him to distinguish good from evil), a free will, and a reasoning mind. He is intended by his Creator to pursue the good and to try to live the virtuous life. Now, all this may sound trite today. The very word "virtuous" has a quaint and prim sound to the modern ear that makes it difficult for us to take the idea of the virtuous life altogether seriously. It is useful to remember that "virtue," which often denotes female chastity in modern usage, once meant manly courage—the Latin word *virtūs* means manliness and strength. This is not to suggest that when Jefferson spoke of virtue he really meant virility. Rather, in the eighteenth century, the practice of virtue was more than a preoccupation with modesty or an obsession with social taboos. Jefferson's virtue includes various things that we today would identify as poise, compassion for others, a sense of justice and fair play, and an appreciation of one's own worth as a person. It includes as well the resolution to live life fully and yet in a disciplined way—according to some code that one has adopted as one's own. Such virtue is surely a long way from the kind of vulnerable and naïve chastity that the Marquis de Sade mocked and the Victorians tried eternally to preserve. It is, instead, at the very essence of human dignity as this might be understood by an eighteenth-century gentleman. Jefferson's virtue is that of the self-assured aristocrat.

In 1819, in his well-known letter to William Short, Jefferson identified himself as a follower both of Epicurus and Jesus. The former, he said, has given us "laws for governing ourself," the latter has provided "a supplement of the duties and charities we owe others." Both of these men, if we consider their ideas in their pure form and not as misrepresented and muddled by their enemies or their enthusiastic followers, offer moral codes that are both humane and sensible. Jefferson warned especially against misinterpreting Epicureanism as being a life of complacency and sensual gratification. Fortitude was one of Epicurus' four cardinal virtues, along with Prudence, Temperance, and Justice. It teaches us, Jefferson said, "to meet and surmount difficulties; not to fly from them, like cowards; and to fly, too, in vain, for they will meet and arrest us at every turn of our road." The pleasures offered by the Epicurean philosophy are those of the strenuous life and the well-balanced mind: It is a life of activity, discipline, and of "facing up" not "dropping out." Jefferson offered his own syllabus of the doctrines of Epicurus, which included the following formula:

> Happiness is the aim of life.
> Virtue the foundation of happiness.
> Utility the test of virtue.

For Jefferson, as for Franklin, the coincidence of virtue and happiness is firm, and the End or Goal of life is to be found in the process of living it fully. Jefferson left "happiness" undefined and open-ended. The man who made the "pursuit of happiness" part of the American heritage never told us what happiness is.

Jefferson's moral ideas, including their loose ends, are important because they help us form a more accurate idea of his broader social philosophy. To be sure, Jefferson offered no formal, coherent social philosophy (John Adams clearly was more of a social philosopher than Jefferson; but America produced no Condorcet, Rousseau, or Bentham). His social theories, set forth in a seemingly random collection of observations, criticisms, and slogans, are scattered throughout his public and private papers. They were usually occasioned by some immediate concern or interest, and reflect both his wide reading and his practical experience.

Although Jefferson was an eclectic thinker, sometimes given to statements that sound extreme, he was not the dreamy idealist he is pictured as being, nor is he simply a shrewd hypocrite who merely used democratic rhetoric to further his political ends. In many ways, he was representative of his age, and he is well described by Winthrop Jordan as being important for his "breadth of interest and his lack of originality."[7] In his intellectual personality he blends the two traits that we described as being central to the social outlook of the Enlightenment: a commitment to the experimental method and a propensity to use the rhetoric of political moralism. As an American, however, Jefferson was a uniquely placed philosophe. Both the experimental and the rhetorical aspects of his social thought were affected by his American identity. As a social thinker applying the new reasoning to politics, Jefferson not only appealed to history and comparative studies, but to his own firsthand experience in republican politics. America was itself a kind of political experimental station where Enlightenment ideas could be tested, and like many of his contemporaries he liked to refer to the American political "experiment." His American experience allowed Jefferson to see the limitations and "heresies" in Montesquieu's interpretation of society and history. As a social moralist and rhetorician, on the other hand, Jefferson not only invoked high ideals, like those of natural rights, but he had the opportunity of reading them into the public record, of making them official, so to speak, part of an emerging national creed. He could regard the new republic as "a standing monument and example for the aim and imitation of the people of other countries." Both the empirical and the moral-rhetorical elements of Enlightened social thought are present in Jefferson: America was at once an "experiment" and a "monument."

We observe this blending of approaches in Jefferson's conception of natural rights. Jefferson's defense of the rights of man was anthropological and empirical, not legal or metaphysical. His political rhetoric was grounded in his science of human nature. In 1816 he wrote to Adams that, in his view (in contrast with Hobbes'), justice is an "instinct, and innate," and the "moral sense is as much a part of our constitution as that of feeling, seeing, or hearing; as a wise creator must have seen to be necessary in an animal destined to live in society." Mankind, in other words, is equipped with a feeling of obligation and of duty to others. Jefferson traced human morality not to man's calculating faculty, the understanding, but to his heart, the realm of his deepest feelings. From this stress on man's innate and essential moral instinct comes Jefferson's conception of justice and human rights.

By taking this position, Jefferson brought moral man and natural man together. He did not simply join them in one body, but showed that the one was, in fact, indistinguishable from the other. Man was a moral being by nature. Man's moral character was a natural fact of roughly the same logical order as his mammalian identity. This provided Jefferson with a "higher" court of authority on which to rest his defense of the right of revolution. He could defend the overthrow of government by appealing beyond social institutions to the wider natural order that sustained all things. The moral appeal of the rebel was solidly grounded in nature. This is the insight behind Jefferson's assertion that a little rebellion now and then is a good thing. It is also expressed in his Preamble to the Declaration of Independence. Jefferson regarded human rights as "natural" and primary, and saw institutions as tools, machines, means to an end that could be adjusted, redesigned, or overthrown when they failed to serve human needs or, worse, when they violated human rights. Since we cannot engineer institutions to make them fully self-adjusting so that they automatically keep up with ever-changing human needs, we have to maintain the right of revolution, violent or otherwise. Built into the political order is the moral and, one might say, biological excuse for its disruption in the name of human rights. As both a moral and a natural being, man should not and need not let institutions stunt his growth. Morality and science, the rhetorical and the experimental, are tidily combined in such an assertion, because the right of revolution involves both moral judgments and natural facts indissolubly joined in the definition of human nature and human rights. The logical difficulties this kind of argument may involve should not cause us to underrate its ethical appeal in an age of experiments.

Jefferson's blending of experimental politics and political moralism is again evident in his call for freedom of thought and expression. The right to express one's ideas without governmental restraint was one of the great causes to which eighteenth-century thinkers rallied. It was championed by philosophes as diverse as Voltaire and Rousseau, and was at the center of the controversy over the publication of the *Encyclopedia* in France. In

America, the issue of free expression was dramatically argued with reference to freedom of the press during the Revolution.[8] And during this period Jefferson emerged as a leading spokesman for liberty of inquiry and expression, which he considered not only a basic right but also a necessary condition for social progress. He expressed his position best in his appeal for religious freedom in Query 17 of his *Notes on Virginia.* "Reason and free inquiry," he declared, "are the only effectual agents against error. Give a loose to them, they will support the true religion by bringing every false one to their tribunal, to the test of their investigation. They are the natural enemies of error, and of error only." He believed that it "is error alone which needs the support of government. Truth stands by itself." (Significantly, he illustrated this by citing an example from the history of science: Galileo was forced to abjure his theory that the earth actually moves; but the earth continued to move, nonetheless, and the truth eventually won out.) Jefferson had a profound faith in reason as a faculty not only for finding the truth, but also for exposing error. He was aware, nevertheless, of the social context of truth. He knew that, if truth is to be found, rational inquiry must be freed from external authority. Society is under the moral obligation to permit the critical intellect to operate without restraint, since free inquiry is a right of man as a rational creature just as freedom of one's person is his right as a moral creature. More than this, it is inexpedient for society to stifle free thought and expression, for truth will out eventually, and truth—and the elimination of error—is the best guarantee of social progress. The technological advances that have taken place since the Dark Ages have resulted from the free exchange of ideas. Jefferson's argument may be reconstructed this way. Error is unnatural. It cannot stand by itself, but must be supported by coercion. Remove coercion and the liberated reason will seek out and destroy error in the open public forum. This will accelerate the advancement of knowledge and ultimately serve the public good. In the Jeffersonian frame of reference the critical spirit and the right of free and open debate of all matters join to promote the general welfare. In his *Notes on Virginia* Jefferson advocated giving the "experiment" of religious freedom "fair play" in the new republic. It seems reasonable to extend this by suggesting that the ideal of intellectual fair play animates his entire social ethic: His hopes for religious freedom were an expression of his wider faith in the freedom of thought.

Jefferson's sentiments on natural rights and freedom of expression are noble ones, and worthy of respect. But they are not without their shortcomings, one of which concerns the open-ended character of natural rights as Jefferson conceived of them. It has often been observed that he thought of natural rights negatively rather than positively—as something the state should not interfere with rather than something it should actively promote.[9] The ideal Jeffersonian state would liberate the active intellect as well as the entrepreneurial initiative, but it would do little to encourage or compensate those in whom years of social injustice arrested the intellect or destroyed initiative. Furthermore, his vague enumeration of human rights—"life, liberty, and the pursuit of happiness"—though unquestionably stirring rhetoric, has weaknesses as well as strengths, especially when we inquire into the meaning of "happiness." It is clear that by "happiness" Jefferson did not mean purely sensual gratification, for he was no voluptuary, or even a hedonist. Nor did he mean the possession of wealth, for if he had, he could very well have repeated Locke's well-known formula, "life, liberty, and property." Certainly his own formula contained a recognition of the legitimacy of private interests and satisfactions over against (but not necessarily in conflict with) the good of society: He did not speak of "public happiness" nor of the "general welfare," but simply of happiness. It seems evident that Jefferson was thinking of happiness in the grand sense suggested by his Epicurean ethic. Happiness is the byproduct of an active, useful, and disciplined life, the satisfaction of soul that is the reward of virtue. Happiness is to develop one's mental and moral capabilities and to live as a fully functioning person. The idea is usefully vague and confines no one within a moral straitjacket (as Jefferson and others accused the Calvinists of doing in *their* notion of happiness). Because it was so vague, however, the idea of happiness was easily perverted into an ethical license to plunder, to rampage a continent and exploit every opportunity in the restless pursuit of wealth. As James Truslow Adams put it, referring to the situation in the late nineteenth century:

> The really great and noble American dream, the dream
> of a better and fuller life for every man, had become a
> good deal like the stampede of hogs to a trough.[10]

Obviously, we cannot blame Jefferson for this perversion of his ideal. It must be said, however, that Jefferson was an aristocrat who read the future of the republic with the eyes of an aristocrat. His ideals were unconsciously intended for men like himself or for those who aspired and stood the chance to become like him. The good life, for Jefferson, was a life of gentility, probity, culture, disinterested public service, and high-minded endeavor. "Happiness is the aim of life. Virtue the foundation of happiness." Projecting his own ideals into the public realm, Jefferson in effect gave a rising democracy the aesthetic and ethical standards of an aristocracy to live up to, and thus unwittingly contributed his share to the disparity between "high ideals" and "catchpenny realities" (to quote Van Wyck Brooks from more than a century later) that gave American civilization in the late nineteenth century its morally lopsided character.[11]

In Jefferson's defense of freedom of expression we find limitations that are similar to those attending his natural rights theory. He certainly was aware of the influence of "prejudices" and "bigotry" on the public mind, but he was still disposed to suggest that error was unnatural, unable to stand by itself. To be sure, as the years passed, he became less sanguine about the cleansing effects of open public debate. Bigotry and prejudice are sustained by more than governmental coercion, and Tocqueville was later to show how subtle and pervasive the tyranny, not of a king or dictator, but of the majority can be. The fact is that error flourishes as naturally as truth, and the truth is seldom as sure as Jefferson intimated in his *Notes on Virginia*. Here again Jefferson was drawing on his experience as a Virginia gentleman living in an age when men could take the time to reflect on the issues of the day and imagine that they were coming to a rational judgment on them. Jefferson projected this image on the people generally, putting his faith in their goodwill and rationality— he called it their "virtue and intelligence." More basically, Jefferson's faith rested on the belief that truth is one and that it is discernible by reason. In modern capitalistic and democratic society, it turned out, ideas are not only tools for rationally constructing the truth but also weapons for controlling the mind and securing belief. Ideas become ideologies in the broad Marxian sense, intellectual excuses for vested interests rather than factual foundations for sound reasoning.

We should not be surprised that his Virginia experience set the limits within which Jefferson would operate when he turned his mind to such things as natural rights and freedom of inquiry. Jefferson's aristocratic background did not equip him with the intellectual instincts appropriate to a democratic and capitalistic society, but this only means that Jefferson was an eighteenth-century man whose ideas are not entirely relevant to the modern scene, the kind of thing that could be said about any thinker of any age. A more serious difficulty with the Jeffersonian outlook concerns the form in which his ideas were expressed more than their substantive import. Jefferson was more than a philosopher setting forth abstract theories, more even than a statesman shaping policy and articulating public sentiments. Jefferson was a formulator of the American national creed. In documents like the Declaration of Independence as well as in occasional remarks that were eventually etched in the marble of public monuments, Jefferson helped make natural rights, freedom for all, government with the consent of the governed, human equality, and the right of revolution part of our spiritual heritage, part of the legacy of values and ideals with reference to which we identify ourselves as a people. He helped to refine the slogans of liberation and revolution into the moral basis of our national identity. Henceforth, the American nation would be officially committed to human rights, equality, and the blessings of freedom for all.

All this takes on fuller meaning, and the difficulties in it become clearer, when we realize the important role our public creed and official beliefs have played in the history of American thought. When the Americans declared their independence from England, they possessed little that drew them together into a single political culture. They shared no common folk identity; they had none of the myths, traditions, common symbols, and public rituals that bind a nation together. They did not even have a common religion. They had to design their own flag. Under these circumstances, it is understandable that ideas and the political rhetoric of the age were called upon to provide the basis for a common allegiance. Once enshrined, the ideas and the rhetoric took on that aura of seriousness and solemnity that distinguishes a nation's patriotic rituals and symbols. They were no longer simply theories or slogans but national commitments.

Now, the ideas and rhetoric that became so vital a part of the American identity were taken mainly from the writings of the radical Whigs, in particular, and of the Enlightenment generally. They were revolutionary in their affirmation of human rights over tradition, institutions, the standing order. A new nation was calling attention to these highly volatile ideas in the very act of establishing itself, and was trying to erect a social order on the foundation of a revolutionary faith. Such a strategy could be expected to yield one of two results: Either the nation might be torn apart by internal uprising as the people asserted their rights, or the nation might end up by merely giving official lip service to the rhetoric while largely ignoring its real meaning. What in fact happened is that the nation avoided being torn apart by uprising, and did, indeed, settle for giving lip service to the rhetoric; but the rhetoric remained charged, and provided the moral rationale for American reformers and radicals through the years that followed. The abolitionists of the early nineteenth century, for example, would be able to invoke a "higher law" than the Constitution in indicting slavery. And the civil rights leaders of the twentieth century would be able to point to the contrast between official indifference to equal rights and the promises given in the official creed, thereby charging the establishment with betrayal and hypocrisy. We may conclude, then, that making a revolutionary theory the national creed did not entirely rob the theory of its moral energy. Nevertheless, it was tamed and appropriated to the national interest.

The extent to which the revolutionary theory was tamed becomes evident when we consider the most blatant contradiction to the American creed, the persistence of slavery. Richard Price, the great English dissenter and radical Whig philosopher of the later eighteenth century, was a friend of the American Revolution and saw it as opening "a new era in the history of mankind" and as offering "a new prospect in human affairs." This English champion of American freedom regarded the continued enslavement of the black race as entirely incompatible with the ideals proclaimed by his American ideological kinsmen. Unless slavery is abolished, he declared in his *Observations on the Importance of the American Revolution* (1784), the Revolution will have failed. Many of the American revolutionaries were themselves aware of this contradiction—sometimes painfully so, in Jefferson's case; and if they did not at once abolish slavery, they did leave it mortally crippled, as William Freehling has shown.[12] The fact remains, nevertheless, that racism and the high regard for property rights in eighteenth-century America combined with a commitment to other national priorities to permit the institution to exist for many years after Jefferson had declared "all" men endowed with "inalienable" rights that included "liberty" and the "pursuit of happiness." Jefferson himself, despite his feelings of "moral reproach" over the continuation of slavery, did not manumit his own slaves until his death.

The truth of the matter is that no people can live by high moral principles and social ideals with even the same consistency that it obeys its written laws. Moral idealism cannot be legislated. Yet by making the revolutionary rhetoric the national creed the Americans were trying to do something very much like legislating morality—political morality, in this case. The gap that opened between profession and performance was bound to be obvious and embarrassing. The gap between human expectation and fulfillment—in the case of those Americans who ranked low on the list of national priorities—would be tragic.

Here is where the limitations of the Jeffersonian outlook (and it is important to remember that we are not placing the entire burden on the man but on the perspective he represents) become strikingly clear. In making the ideals of natural rights, of liberty for all, of human fulfillment into an official creed, the Americans gave themselves what turned out to be a tradition of radical moderation in which, as Richard Chase once observed, we became officially and morally committed to ideals we were temperamentally reluctant to pursue.[13] Radicals could henceforth reprove us for our shortcomings by appealing to the spirit of the American Revolution and the promise of American life. Reactionaries and conservatives, on the other hand, could as easily remind us that dissent is inappropriate in a nation that has so effectively embodied the principles of amelioration in its very institutions. Aware of the repressive capabilities of institutions and the public's short memory where questions of social justice are concerned, Jefferson and others of his generation made the noble effort to incorporate the moral vehemence of Whig and Enlightenment ideals into the American political identity. Such an effort was bound to suffer some frustration and could never be completely successful. The measure of the Jeffersonian success or failure is—as it has always been—the responsiveness of America's institutions and of her public conscience to the needs and the claims of all her citizens.

[9]

JOHN ADAMS AND THE
SCENERY OF POLITICS

IF Jefferson represents the hopeful rhetoric of American republicanism and the Enlightened confidence in man's future prospects, then John Adams seems the appropriate spokesman for those conservative dissenters who stood aloof from their century's optimism and despised anything smacking of utopianism and perfectionism. Often portrayed as a Burkean conservative, Adams was unquestionably distrustful of his country's democratic sentiments. And, having confessed his preference for New England cider over the finest wines of France, Adams certainly was not one to become intoxicated by the philosophes' grander schemes for human progress. Yet he is worth considering in the study of the American Enlightenment, for an Enlightened American he certainly was—even though his perception of things was sometimes strikingly different from that of many of his distinguished countrymen.

John Adams was a most serious man. When he was only twenty-three years old, a friend sarcastically asked him if he intended one day to become a sage. Characteristically, Adams thought of a clever comeback only sometime later. "A sage, no," he would reply if he were ever asked the same question again. "Knowledge enough to keep out of fire and water, is all I aim at." Even if it should turn out to be Adams' fate to live and die "an ignorant, obscure fellow," as he once gloomily predicted, he would at least know enough to come in out of the rain. Adams would never be taken in. If he was not to become a sage, he would nevertheless have the sagacity not to be made a dupe.

It is ironic that today John Adams is widely recognized as a

great American sage precisely *because* of his tough-minded refus-
al to be swindled by the huckster-theorists who tried to sell him
easy answers, grandiose social systems, and double-your-money-
back political nostrums. He was a right Yankee philosophe—
possibly the shrewdest political thinker ever to turn a cold eye on
the hopes and aspirations of a generation. That Adams was often
wrong in his analysis of society in no way diminishes the impact of
his intuitive misgivings about his nation's progress and his age's
expectations.

Indeed, Adams' social analysis was often quite wrong. He could
impose an almost medieval picture of social classes on the
relatively mobile and flexible American social scene, and argue
with a straight face that it is the function of the monarch to see
that a fair balance is maintained between the aristocracy and the
populace. He thought it appropriate to address President George
Washington as "His Highness the President of the United States
and Protector of their Liberties." Returning from abroad in 1788
after spending a decade there on diplomatic assignments in
France and then in England, Adams projected his image of the
European situation on his native land, perceiving the young,
agrarian republic as a civilization approaching the last stage of
moral and spiritual dotage—that of decadence, effeminacy,
licentiousness, defeat. Yet he knew that no social system could
possibly succeed that did not face head-on the facts of humanity's
fallibility, moral frailty, self-deception, and irrationality. He
knew that no one group could be trusted to place the nation's
welfare consistently above its own. And he knew that, for all the
talk about human equality, *inequality* not only of talent but of
opportunity was part of the nature of social life and could never
be wished away. Adams, in sum, was a silly, serious, pathetic,
perceptive, comical, heroic man. He *was* a man. His philosophy
was informed by his humanity—more than most people's. This is
what makes him perhaps the most interesting spokesman for the
American Enlightenment.[1]

The striking thing about Adams' political thought, despite the
seriousness and pedantry of the treatises he wrote on the subject,
is its personalism. Adams' ideas spring from his emotions as well
as from his understanding. Often he would respond to a political
situation in intensely personal terms, as when his personal

antagonism toward Governor Thomas Hutchinson of Massachusetts fired his patriotic rebellion against English rule in America. More important, Adams' vision of society reflects his image of human nature, which in turn reflects his honest reading of his own character. This is most evident in his understanding of the motives that drive political man, which derives from Adams' own struggle for fame.

Born in Braintree (Quincy), Massachusetts, in 1735, the son of a farmer, Adams graduated from Harvard College in 1755 and, after doing some school teaching in Worcester and studying law with Rufus Putnam, was admitted to the Massachusetts bar in 1758. He became politically active in 1765 in response to the Stamp Act, although he had become concerned about the colonial question as early as 1761. From 1774 to 1778, when he sailed for France, Adams was a member of the Continental Congress. He served as America's first Vice President from 1788 until 1796, and as our second President from 1796 until 1800, when he was defeated by Jefferson after a particularly bitter campaign that left lasting scars on the thin-skinned New Englander. Through his entire career as lawyer and politician, and into a retirement that lasted a quarter of a century, Adams was preoccupied by the quest for recognition and fame.

His diary shows that, as a young man, Adams lusted after reputation, was driven by a desire to distinguish himself, and, conversely, was obsessed with the dread that he might pass his days an obscure person. "May I blush whenever I suffer one hour to pass unimproved," he solemnly wrote in 1756. "I will rouse up my mind, and fix my Attention." Reputation, he decided a few years later, "ought to be the perpetual subject of my Thoughts, and Aim of my Behaviour." There is a note of desperation in his concern: "How shall I gain a Reputation! How shall I Spread an Opinion of myself as a Lawyer of distinguished Genius, Learning, and Virtue!" His ambition and his self-doubt troubled his sleep: "I had an aching Void within my Breast, this night," he wrote in 1759:

> What is it? I feel my own Ignorance. I feel concern for Knowledge, and fame. I have a dread of Contempt, a quick sense of Neglect, a strong Desire for Distinction.

He berated himself when he slept past sunrise, having thereby wasted precious time.

Many young lawyers before and since Adams' time have lost sleep worrying about their careers. What makes Adams' case interesting is the way he probed his own consciousness, good Puritan that he was, and read in his own emotional agitation a lesson about human motivation generally. Adams came to the conclusion that all men were driven by passions similar to his own. He went a step further and decided that the essence of the moral life is the harnessing of these passions, as one harnesses a massive energy source, putting them in the service of one's better impulses. Envy and the desire for fame, he confided to his diary, along with the passions associated with love,

> should be bound fast and brought under the Yoke. Untamed they are lawless Bulls, that roar and bluster, defy all Controul, and some times murder their proper owner. But properly inured to Obedience, they take their Places under the Yoke without Noise and labour vigorously in their master's Service.

To accomplish this, we must see to it, Adams believed, that our actions primarily originate "from a sense of the Government of God" and "a Regard to the Laws established by his Providence." For John Adams the moral law was not some abstract principle of ethical theory, but an intimately felt necessity of the interior life, an essential instrument for governing the passions that in turn drove him and urged him on. The moral government of God was a vitally real aid to self-government among men.

Unfortunately, morality, though indispensable, is not enough. Man is morally frail, constitutionally incapable of fully governing himself. This moral weakness makes human government necessary. More: Vice and folly, he noted in 1760, "are so interwoven in all human Affairs that they could not possibly be wholly separated from them without tearing and rending the whole system of human Nature, and state." Civil magistrates, lawyers, tradesmen, preachers—all these people function as they do because of man's moral limitations. Moral perfection, in other words, is not only theoretically unattainable and practically impossible: It is socially inconceivable. Society, as we know it, would cease to exist if there were no sin. Before John Adams ever entered politics his conservative perception of human nature and of the function of government had been shaped. He would look critically at all utopian schemes not because of philosophical principles or theological reservations about building the heavenly city here on earth, but because he knew in his very bones that utopias would not work. He needed only to consult his own consciousness to remind himself how weak man really is.

After retiring from public life, Adams, in 1805, added an interesting postscript to a letter to his friend Benjamin Rush, the great Philadelphia physician. "I admire [Napoleon] Bonaparte's expression 'The Scenery of the Business,' " he observed:

> The scenery has often if not commonly in all the business of human life, at least of public life, more effect than the character of the dramatis personae or the ingenuities of the plot.

He meant by this that public events are often determined more by effective staging and by spectacle than by the character of the men participating in them or the logic of history. "Was there ever a *coup de théâtre*," he demanded, using one of his favorite phrases, "that had so great an effect as Jefferson's penmanship of the Declaration of Independence?" Adding to his list of unwritten works, Adams expressed the desire "to write a book on 'The Scenery of the Business.' "

Surely Adams might have produced a most instructive guide to the "scenery" of politics. His use of the term actually suggests several things about him and his perception of political life. First, it suggests his own resentment over the fact that, during and after his years on the public stage, others seemed consistently to capture the public imagination, not because their performance was inherently superior to Adams' own, but because of their personal appeal and glamor, their flair for the dramatic, or their lucky appearance at just the right time. Adams resented what he considered the overblown reputations of Franklin and Washington. He envied Jefferson his popular following. And, above all, he begrudged Thomas Paine, for whom he had no use in the first place, his celebrity as a great revolutionary hero because of his *Common Sense.* The diligent, industrious, honest John Adams, hardworking and thoughtful player in one of the greatest dramas in human history, was forever being upstaged by more glamorous stars who invariably received all the applause. These others were getting the rave notices while Adams scarcely got his name spelled right. He was in France, for instance, when everyone was talking about Paine's anonymously published *Common Sense.* People believed the pamphlet had been written by Samuel Adams, John's cousin. Are you the "famous Adams"? John was asked. Alas, no. He was not famous. Adams was no Tom Paine. He was not even a Sam Adams! Performing in an essential role, poor Adams was yet treated as an inconsequential bit-player.

Second, Adams' idea of scenery of political life expresses his reading of history. In an age when many thinkers were at last beginning to hope that politics, as Hume put it, may be reduced to a science, and some, like Condorcet, were coming to suspect that they themselves were perhaps the Newtons of that science, John Adams was saying that events may outflank our rational faculties. The hand is quicker than the eye. We think we understand what is happening and about to happen when, suddenly, with a crash of cymbals, a flash of light, and a puff of smoke the stage is transformed. Political events do not move according to some simple plot that the mind can quickly grasp. There are too many unexpected, irrational things happening, too many independent variables in the equation. More than this, what captures our attention is often not what really moves events. The American Revolution, Adams told Jefferson in 1815, actually occurred in the hearts and minds of the American people some fifteen years before the first shots were fired. The war itself was a great spectacle, but it was only part of the revolution, indeed, more a consequence of it than anything else. Would historians one day see beyond the spectacle and tell the real story of the American Revolution? Would they ever get beyond the scenery of the business? Perhaps. But Adams had his doubts. For Adams, history—like human experience itself—is ultimately mysterious. This mystery, however, should not cause the rational man to give up and despair of ever understanding his society. Rather, it has to be taken into account: It ought to make us a bit more humble when it comes to proposing solutions to history and the human condition.

This leads to a third and final point. Aware of the disparity between illusion and reality, appearance and actuality, Adams knew well that we pursue shadows through much of our lives, chasing "empty but glittering Phantoms rather than Substances." In our individual lives this causes much waste and regret. In our social life it can be disastrous. It is essential, therefore, that we exert our critical faculties not only to demolish the illusions and superstitions of others, but also to correct our own errors and discard our own chimeras. Adams, in effect, called on his generation to exercise its sociological imagination responsibly. The ethics of belief apply to our personal convictions. Adams knew he lived in the age of experiments, and he was as committed to the experimental method of reasoning as anyone of his generation. But for Adams "experiment" was not the same as mere innovation or the crackpot conviction that any scheme is worth trying at least once, just for the sake of seeing how it works out. Adams' experimentalism was precise, cautious, realistic. It was realistic in the sense that we are seriously to entertain no social scheme that depends for its success on a change in human nature or that is founded not on fact but on postulate. Adams' marginal notes in his copies of the writings of Rousseau, Condorcet, Mably, and other philosophes illustrates this critical second sight of his. "Reasonings from a state of nature are fallacious, because hypothetical," he commented in Rousseau's case. "We have not facts. Experiments are wanting."[2] If he deserves to be called a sage, it is because, in a time when the liberation of the human mind tempted many to speculative extravagance and political wishful thinking, Adams resolutely kept his head. In an age that brought Rousseau's totalitarian suggestion that a good citizen should be not only orderly and cooperative but *sincere,* Adams held onto his conviction that we cannot expect too much from human nature, and we have no business legislating a state of mind or a change of heart. If there is to be progress in human affairs, that progress must be solidly founded on constants in the human equation. If the eighteenth century really were an "age of reason," as Paine called it, it would have been reasonable enough to recognize and take account of the passions and lunacies that drive men about their business. For Adams' money, his age—whatever else it succeeded in doing—fell short in the area of truly critical thinking. Adams perhaps judged his age harshly. But we are bound to admire him for his independence of mind, his willingness to take account of his own baser instincts, and his fine sense of intellectual responsibility when it came to assessing his century's noblest dreams. Like his great-grandson Henry, a century later, John Adams was willing to acknowledge his own bewilderment over his times. He had the courage of his confusions.

Adams set forth his political philosophy in letters to friends, in essays written for publication in newspapers, and in one three-volume work, published in the late 1780's, defending the state constitutions and the American system of government against foreign critics. Though a large work, Adams' *Defence of the Constitutions of the Government of the United States of America* consists mostly of long quotations from a number of writers, with Adams' comments inserted here and there, as though he were carrying on a conversation with authorities on history and government from Herodotus to Hume. This was a favorite technique of Adams' who apparently lacked the time and the patience to compose a formal treatise on government, and found it convenient to insert his own thoughts as responses, so to speak, to the theories and opinions of others. But though Adams never produced a systematic treatise on politics, he, in fact, had one of the most coherent and well-thought-out political philosophies of all the Americans of the revolutionary generation. It is set forth in his brief *Thoughts on Government* (1776), his *Defense of the Constitutions* (1787), and his controversial *Discourses on Davila* (1791), which he originally intended as Volume Four of his *Defense.*

Adams was greatly influenced by the English and Scottish political theorists of the radical Whig tradition, and makes frequent references to James Harrington, Algernon Sidney, Milton, Locke, Henry Neville, and Benjamin Hoadly. Adams was also in debt to Adam Smith, whose theory of human emotions provided a basis on which to bring his own thoughts on the subject together. To Adams, it appears, the British thinkers represented sound judgment and sanity—a sanity not always in evidence among the eighteenth-century philosophes on the Continent, whose skepticism, infidelity, and irreverence, Adams feared, could produce only social chaos. Never enthusiastic about the French Revolution, Adams considered the influence of French rather than British thinkers on that event a bad portent. In 1790 he wrote grimly to Richard Price:

> I know that encyclopedists and economists, Diderot and D'Alembert, Voltaire and Rousseau, have contributed to this great event more than Sidney, Locke, or Hoadly, perhaps more than the American revolution; and I own it to you, that I know not what to make of a republic of thirty million atheists.

From the British writers, Adams received, above all, a commitment to republican government as a government "of laws, and not of men"—a government where the influence of the arbitrary human will is reduced to a minimum. Always aware of man's moral fallibility and of his passionate nature, Adams wanted a government that was so carefully engineered that human passions could be effectively brought under the yoke, as it were, harnessed—just as an individual's passion must be, but by man-made rather than by moral law—and put to the service of the public good. Good government serves the public by producing what Adams called "social Happiness." This service can be performed best in a government that is as well balanced, as law-bound, as the Newtonian world-system. Like many others of the revolutionary generation, including many of the framers of the American Constitution, Adams was a political Newtonian who wanted to establish, in the political realm, something of the order that Newton had revealed in the physical cosmos.

How could this be done? How could such order be achieved in the very unpredictable social realm where, as Adams certainly knew, it is often the irrational forces that shape events and move men? Is not Adams the greatest utopian of them all for even considering such a scheme?

Adams would reply that he is not a utopian dreamer, for two reasons. First, he never hoped for anything approaching perfect fulfillment of his scheme—he sought not the Ideal Society but the better society, the more nearly perfect union. Second, he began by accepting human beings as the fallible wretches they are, not by postulating some inherent, natural goodness in man that awaits only the opportunity—the proper political circumstances—to reveal itself. Man is not virtuous by nature, Adams knew, but under the right political conditions he might be made to *behave* virtuously—even though his heart remains corrupt. These right political conditions include a careful balance of power within government, and a system in which each individual would find it to his own self-interest to see to it that each other individual behaved himself. Adams acknowledged that it would be difficult to prove it, but he wondered out loud whether a republic "cannot exist even among highwaymen by setting one rogue to watch another; and the knaves themselves may in time be made honest men by the struggle."

It is rightly contended that Adams' political thought changed during the 1780's, and that, although he had never been a naïve optimist, he came to have less confidence in his country's political virtue and to rely more and more on a well-balanced constitution to ensure America's republican future. It is also rightly charged that Adams imposed on the American political environment his own antiquated theory of sovereignty, viewing government as the place where the forces of democracy, aristocracy, and monarchy come together. He regarded the American President as serving as, in effect, an elected monarch whose job it was to maintain the balance of power between the aristocratic and democratic elements, "the few and the many." Adams believed that aristocracy was a natural part of any society, and even though his analysis was based on the political circumstances of a passing era, his reading of human nature and his speculations on the social implications of man's moral fallibility provide food for thought even today.

Following the reasoning of Adam Smith as set forth in the *Theory of Moral Sentiments* (1759), Adams maintained that man is motivated not only by feelings of "benevolence" and other "generous affections," but also by various "selfish passions," among them the "passion for distinction," which expresses itself in a desire to excel, which Adams called "emulation," and a quest for power, or "ambition." These passions are too strong to be effectively checked by our benevolent impulses, and so government becomes necessary—government in the broadest sense, including not only the political mechanism by which society is run, but also the internal order of that society, including its social hierarchy.[3] The goverment of society involves the setting up of instruments "of order and subordination," through which feelings of esteem, sympathy, admiration, and so forth are stimulated and encouraged. Rank, nobility, status—these are not accidents of history or artificial impositions on the social order. They are natural and necessary parts of any orderly society. Those who suppose that rank and aristocracy are going out of fashion could not be more mistaken. Social hierarchy cannot be dismantled so that all are reduced to a condition of equality. A society without rank, Adams maintained, is as unthinkable as a vertebrate without a ganglion. If there is to be justice, however, rank must be regulated—the interest of the few being balanced over against the good of the many. And in a nation's political life this may be done by establishing a two-house legislature, one house representing the Lords and the other the Commoners, and placing a strong executive in between to wield his decisive veto with the authority of a fair-minded monarch.

Adams' theory, needless to say, created quite a stir among those Americans who saw in the American Revolution the opportunity to strike off the shackles of ancient tyranny and remove "artificial" distinctions from the new republic. The Republican press attacked Adams throughout the 1790's as a monarchist and an apologist for aristocracy. The radicals were, of course, right and Adams was wrong. America managed to do rather well without noble lords or a monarchical President—however, the exigencies of the twentieth century seem to have led us in the direction of the latter, though not perhaps in the way Adams had in mind. But if Adams' political theory was wrong, his basic insight was not. For, putting aside all his theory and his misreading of his times, we find in Adams a man whose Puritan distrust of power and whose recognition of the basic irrationality of politics allowed him to offer an effective counterstatement to the Age of Reason. We come to understand him best, however, not in his political treatises, but in his personal letters—where we encounter not just his theories but the forthright character of the man himself.

The eighteenth century was a great age of letter writing. To be sure, letters had been important to the intellectual culture of western Europe since the Renaissance, but in the eighteenth century a significant change took place. Back in the days of Erasmus, letters served mainly as a vehicle for the exchange of scholarship, much as our professional journals do today. Personal observations on the changing scene were plentiful, of course, but the kind of shared intimacy we associate with personal correspondence was lacking. It was the eighteenth century—with its new emphasis on the importance of the inward life and the interior consciousness—that gave rise not only to the art of familiar correspondence, but also to that of conversation, diary keeping, and intimate biography.[4] In literature, the novel, as we know it, took its form in the eighteenth century in the work of Samuel Richardson, who used the device of intimate correspondence to reach a new level in revealing the emotional life of his characters. An intensely personal man like John Adams is best met, not in dry treatises or public documents, but in the warm exchanges he had with others through the medium of private correspondence. It is one of the misfortunes of our present age that the art of letter writing has passed. In losing that skill, we have also lost much of our capacity meaningfully to communicate with one another about the really important things in life.

During his long years of retirement at Quincy, Adams corresponded with many prominent men of his age, among them Benjamin Rush and Thomas Jefferson. In the opening years of the nineteenth century, Adams was able to reflect on human nature, on society, and on the century that had just passed. In these letters, in sustained conversation with intimate though distant friends, we meet Adams not as a remote political thinker and statesman but as a man whose ever-active mind responded to the major issues of his age with intellectual emotion and a passion to understand the workings of his world.

MAN

It is frequently observed that Adams, a conservative, distrusted human nature and took a dim view of man. It is certainly true that

Adams took no stock in the notion that man is naturally good and is corrupted only by the social institutions about him. For Adams, the human condition is something like the government of an unruly province. Reason and conscience, the governors, are sent from on high to keep the barbaric emotions under control, to harness their energy and put it to good use. By themselves, the benevolent emotions that dwell in the province are not strong enough to restrain their fiercer countrymen. Adams' view of human nature, in other words, is a dynamic one, one that places emphasis on conflict and tension. Life is a continual moral struggle, a fight for rational self-control. Given this view of things, it stands to reason that Adams would have little regard for those who glorified man, flattered human nature, and championed the perfectibility of the race.

To Rush, Adams professed not to understand what is even meant by the perfectibility of man. What is this "perfectibility"? he demanded in 1806. Is it ultimate immortality here on earth? Elimination of all disease? Eventual omniscience? If so, he snorted, perfectibility is something that is impossible and the doctrine is "pure nonsense." Or does it mean "the continual amelioration of the condition of man in this world"—man's moral, material, political improvement? If *this* is what they mean—these philosophes who rant about perfectibility—it is surely no original idea, but only common sense. Everyone hopes for improvement, and the belief in such improvement is "nothing to excite the gaping wonder of a vicious mob, nor the ignorant admiration of superficial philosophers." If Condorcet wants to attach his name to this doctrine, Adams shrugged, he is welcome to the honor.

Adams enjoyed doing this sort of thing. He enjoyed exposing the pet philosophies of his time—or what he considered the pet philosophies of his time—as either nonsense or a superficial rewording of common opinion. Truly an intellectual conservative, Adams believed that basic human convictions do not change much, though methods of thinking may change greatly—as witness the impact of the scientific method. Beliefs about human nature and destiny, however, remain fairly constant, though they may be dressed up in the latest fashions and paraded about as modern discoveries, celebrities of the hour. It was all part of the scenery of the business, and harmless folly until this "latest cause" is taken up by the mob, until the slogan of the day becomes a war cry. This is exactly what had happened in Adams' own age: Man's most ancient hopes were reduced to slogans and politicized. The results were bizarre and perverse. "Helvétius and Rousseau preached to the French Nation *Liberty,* till they made them the most mechanical Slaves," he wrote to Benjamin Waterhouse in 1821, "*Equality* till they destroyed all Equity; *Humanity* till they became Weasels, and African Panthers; and *Fraternity* till they cut one another's throats like Roman gladiators." Human nature being what it is, it is dangerous to translate man's noblest dreams into popular catchwords and political rhetoric. For it takes very little to unleash man's savage, more diabolical passions.

Adams distrusted human nature but did not despair of it. In 1806 he commented on man's brutality to Waterhouse, taking note of the pleasure people seem to derive from watching pain being inflicted, as when they beheld "the delicious spectacle of the Guillotine" in revolutionary Paris. Still, he said, we must not hate or despise the human condition, "but make the best of it, and believe it on the whole to be better than nothing. Nay, we must on the whole believe it to be social and benevolent in grain." We must "on the whole" cast our vote with the party of humanity. A doubter, Adams yet retained this sense of on-the-wholeness, ultimately siding with those who believed that, whatever the hazards, men must stand free, finally confiding to Jefferson that on the whole the eighteenth century was "most honorable to human nature."

SOCIETY

It is not in his misgivings about human nature, but in his view of society and politics, that Adams' insight was most penetrating. Many of Adams' generation wanted to engineer a better future by redesigning society's institutions. While by no means against such a project, Adams nevertheless insisted that before tinkering with social institutions we fully understand the principles on which they operate. It was Adams' sad conclusion that his generation was deficient in its knowledge of society and, worse, was unwilling to take the time to acquire knowledge. "Awakenings and Revivals are not peculiar to Religion," he wrote in 1815. "Philosophy and Policy at times are capable of taking the Infection." The French Revolution was the primary example of the kind of political "Distemper" that seizes the people and drives them beyond the bounds of political sanity. "The human understanding is very well in the ordinary affairs of life," he wrote to Benjamin Rush. In architecture we plan intelligently, studying our needs, taking the environment into account, puzzling over the relation of form to function. But in government we seem to be "destitute of common sense. The nature of men and things is laid out of the question. Experiment, which is admitted in all other arts and sciences is wholly unheeded in this." The age of experiments was not experimental enough when it came to politics.

Adams was a stickler for recognizing the limitations of political activity. Through politics we govern human behavior, but we really do not change human nature. Similarly, politics allow us to modify social institutions but not to transform society. Adams' outlook is well illustrated in his famous exchange with Jefferson in 1813 over the "natural" aristocracy. Jefferson maintained that "virtue and talents" are the basis for natural aristocracy, but that there is "an artificial aristocracy," founded not on virtue and talents but on "wealth and birth." In a free society, he argued, we must so arrange things that the natural aristocracy comes to the top—that society's leaders be those whose talent and virtue equip them for that position. One way of doing this, Jefferson believed, is through the educational system, which should train all in the basic skills and can function as a selection agency to choose the most talented for higher education and positions of leadership. The American experiment in republican government, Jefferson said, and the rise of science and spread of ideas, have caused "rank and birth" to fall into contempt in the course of the past hundred years, while the people have grown more courageous in defending their rights. The age of aristocracy has passed, and the democratic era is at hand.

Now, whatever his enemies thought, no one hated aristocracy more than John Adams, and no one was more eager to affirm that the days of feudal privilege were past. Adams agreed with

Jefferson about the need for a "natural aristocracy." He agreed in all but one crucial point. To Adams, the "natural" aristocracy included not only virtue and talents, but "Beauty, Wealth, and Birth," too. These things are natural to society—that is, inequality is natural to society. The man who can command one vote besides his own is *in fact* an aristocrat. The man of wealth, the man with good connections and a good name, the man whose public image is attractive, commands votes—even if he is a bit short on virtue and talent. To dismiss these assets as "artificial" is simply self-delusion. Whatever happens of necessity in a society is, in fact, natural to it. What we can and must work against are efforts to give the natural aristocracy a legal foundation—through hereditary titles and so forth. But we are only fooling ourselves if we believe we can base social distinctions exclusively on virtue and talent. We must not let our egalitarian rhetoric blind us to the hard facts of social life.

Of all political thinkers, Adams was harshest in his estimation of the philosophes or, as he called them, the "encyclopedists and economists." He had carefully studied the works of Rousseau, Voltaire, Condorcet, and Helvétius, and he had met and mostly liked Condorcet, Turgot, and the Duke of Rochefoucauld, but he accused the whole lot of a "blind infatuation to a chimera." "The truth is," he wrote to James Madison in 1817, "that none of these gentlemen had ever had any experience with a free government." Worse still, they had never really studied government empirically—through history or comparative studies. The philosophers were merely theorists and system builders. Kierkegaard once accused the Hegelians of erecting a magnificent castle of thought then crawling into the doghouse beside it. Adams' attack on the philosophes is as withering:

Erect a house of a cubic form, one hundred feet square at the base, without any division within into chambers, parlors, cellars, or garrets; would not this be the simplest house that ever was built? But would it be a commodious habitation for a family? It would accommodate nothing but a kennel of hunter's hounds. These gentlemen all affect to be great admirers of nature. But where in nature do they find the models of their adored simplicity?

Again and again, Adams accused the philosophes of the worst intellectual crime imaginable from their own point of view—unscientific thinking. They were quacks and dreamers who lacked the patience to study society before plunging into the fascinating job of demolishing and rebuilding it. Brilliant they undoubtedly were, but they lacked common sense, and this deficiency rendered their intelligence dangerous. The French Revolution and its Napoleonic aftermath, Adams believed, were the awful fruits of the philosophes' labors. For they had undermined political sanity.

Though Adams' judgment on the philosophes expresses a stereotype that was to haunt them ever since, it is not entirely unjust. As Isabel Knight has shown in her admirable study of the thought of Condillac, Enlightenment thinking moved about two poles. At the one end we encounter the search for simplicity, the love of universals, the spirit of system, and the desire to integrate man into the Newtonian order and explain him in terms of the laws of mechanics. At the other end we find an emphasis on complexity, diversity, and irregularity, and the drive to preserve man's uniqueness and moral identity.[5] Now the philosophes were not as addicted to the spirit of system as Adams and others of their critics liked to charge. But when their ideas were used to feed the blazing political rhetoric of the late eighteenth century, when the philosophe's hope for progress became the Jacobin's demand for heaven on earth, when the skepticism of a Voltaire became the licentious blasphemies of the Parisian mob, it did indeed seem that the philosophes' theoretical contribution to the lunacy of the times was as obvious as their practical contribution to the betterment of humanity was doubtful. Their experimental and critical side was dismissed or downgraded as mere skepticism. Their rhetorical and moral side was exposed as the most irresponsible kind of pipe dreaming and slogan mongering. Adams realized that he lived in an age that was rapidly—perhaps too rapidly—becoming politically conscious. His conservative instincts told him that, in such an age, it was the duty of the intellectual to exert responsible and restraining leadership. What were needed were not more orators to inflame the mob, or system-builders to design shimmering new utopias, but men of thought who would seriously engage in the empirical study of society. What were needed were not superficial observers who were content to admire the scenery of politics, but restless probers who were willing to delve into the actual workings of the social order. Although Adams agreed that his age had contributed much in the areas of science, technology, art, and philosophy, it fell sadly short in the area of responsible social thought.

THE AGE OF REASON

The Age of Reason, Adams wrote Benjamin Waterhouse in 1805, had been ludicrously misnamed. The best symbol for the age, he believed, was surely not the goddess of Reason, whose role had been played by a Parisian whore at the ridiculous ceremony at Notre Dame—renamed the Temple of Reason—in 1793. Nor was the central character of the age Voltaire or Diderot. The age is best represented, Adams believed, by Tom Paine, that rascally, alcoholic journalist whose superficial writings contributed so little to the action and so much to the spectacle of the period. "I know not whether any Man in the World has had more influence on its inhabitants or affairs for the last thirty years than Tom Paine," Adams wrote:

> There can be no severer Satyre of the Age. For such mongrel between Pigg and Puppy, begotten by a while Boar and a Bitch Wolf, never before in any Age of the World was suffered by the Poltroonery of mankind, to run through such a Career of Mischief. Call it then the Age of Paine. He deserves it much more, than the Courtezan who was consecrated to represent the Goddess in the Temple at Paris, and whose name, Tom has given to the Age. The real intellectual faculty has nothing to do with the Age [,] the Strumpet [,] or Tom.

In the final analysis, however, Adams was more charitable to his age and more optimistic about its contribution than this outburst would suggest. In 1816, when Napoleon had fallen from power and the melodrama that had so involved the moral imagination of the Western world had at last ended, Adams could write to Jefferson that, all things considered, the passing age was not so bad after all. If writers did not study politics as closely and as carefully as they should have, at least they drew attention to political life. Moreover, the number and variety of experiments made in national constitutions, beginning with America's and spreading through western Europe and Hispanic America, mark the awakening of the political intelligence of Western civilization. "And I have no doubt," Adams went on,

> that the horrors we have suffered in the last forty years, will ultimately terminate in the Advancement of civil and religious Liberty, and Ameliorations, in the condition of Mankind. For I am a Believer, in the probable improvability and Improvement, the Ameliorabi[li]ty and Amelioration in human Affairs; though I never could understand the Doctrine of Perfectibility of the human Mind.

It was just like Adams to add that last clause, as it was like him to declare himself a believer in man's "probable improvability." Adams was committed to the program of the Enlightenment. But his commitment retained that note of probability and on-the-wholeness that makes him distinctive. Adams turned the critical faculty on the age of criticism itself.

John Adams is an interesting amendment to the story of the American Enlightenment. It would be wrong to call him more realistic than James Madison or more practical than Jefferson, for Madison's realism was hard even to match, and Jefferson knew how to confine his speculations to his private hours and to meet the business of life on its own terms. It would be wrong to group Adams with the forces of anti-Enlightenment, for he was an enthusiastic supporter of the new learning and warmly applauded the freeing of the Republic of Letters from the restraits of superstition and despotism. Though a pessimist, moreover, Adams was on the whole a believer in progress, and was willing to accept change. It is more a matter of personality that finally distinguished Adams. Self-conscious, thin-skinned, ambitious, honest, blunt—Adams could not blink away the moral blemishes he saw in himself and others. More than this, he could not bring himself to accept shadow for substance. Any age, no matter how grand its contribution to human advancement, has its show, its display, its parade. While the real work of an era goes on, our attention is often diverted by the ceremony and the fireworks, and we often confuse clever political staging with real change, spectacular events with significant developments. Adams, burning with a sense of his own undeserved obscurity, forced to watch the parade go by without him, was able to see that it *was* only a parade after all. "Politicks and War are transient as the Waves of the Sea," he advised his friend Waterhouse. "Health, and Nature, and Science, and Morals, and Religion, are permanent, and will be perpetually interesting." What makes history happen? Adams was rationalist enough to believe that politics are a natural phenomenon and, as such, can be studied scientifically and understood by the mature intellect. And yet, although history is no divine mystery, Adams had to conclude that we can never entirely unravel its riddle. For behind the display and show, behind all the rhetoric, behind the scenery of politics, is that mysterious realm not of the supernatural but of human nature. And, when it came to human nature, Adams was political scientist enough to know that there ar some mysteries science will never completely solve.

[10]

POLITICAL MECHANICS
AND THE NEW CONSCIOUSNESS

PRESENTING the Common Sense of the matter in the famous pamphlet of January, 1776, Thomas Paine had charged that the time was ripe for the American people to declare their independence. Appealing to the reader to "divest himself of prejudice and prepossession," he advocated going to war. "By referring the matter from argument to arms," he prophesied, "a new era for politics is struck—a new method of thinking has arisen." He declared it to be "repugnant to reason, to the universal order of things, to all examples from former ages, to suppose that this continent can long remain subject to any external power."

The announcement that a "new era" has dawned, the recognition of "a new method of thinking," and the appeal to reason, history, and the "order of things"—cunningly brought together by Paine in this most successful of propaganda pieces—make use of some of the favorite assumptions of the eighteenth century and set the tone for subsequent reactions to the American Revolution. By 1791-92, when Paine published his *Rights of Man*, the French and American revolutions together seemed a fulfillment of his earlier prophecy. He could appeal directly to events themselves to establish his argument:

> The opinions of men, with respect to government, are changing fast in all countries. The revolutions of America and France have thrown a beam of light over the world, which reaches into man. . . . And though man may be *kept* ignorant, he cannot be *made* ignorant.

Paine identified a new consciousness that marked the new era in politics. He insisted that the process, once begun, is irreversible, for a man cannot "*unknow* his knowledge, or *unthink* his thoughts." It is "not difficult to perceive that spring is begun."

What was this new consciousness? As Paine described it, it was a new political awareness, a spirit of criticism and testing, a denial that the *status quo* is beyond human amendment. It was, consequently, a determination both to understand the workings of society and to gain control of them. It was the experimental method of reasoning applied to the body politic. The new consciousness brought freedom from tradition and recognition of what Paine called "the right of the *living* " over the "manuscript-assumed authority of the dead." Once possessed of this new consciousness, people would study government scientifically and no longer stand in a kind of religious awe of it. Once the principles of government were learned, man could manipulate and direct his society—just as mankind, in mastering the laws of mechanics, was learning to modify and control the physical environment. Paine argued that, in the political and social—as in the natural—world, the advancement of science means the advancement of technology: Social science and social engineering arise together. Government, far from being some sacred institution, is a tool, a device, an instrument. Government is "nothing more than a national association acting on the principles of society." And the great "laws of society are laws of nature." In mastering these laws man becomes the master of his political destiny.

Several implicit and explicit themes in Paine's outlook deserve special emphasis. We shall set forth four of these, then examine each in turn. The first takes us to the center of the new consciousness, and concerns the abolition of mystery in our thinking about government and society. The second, a consequence of the first, involves applying the rational will to the body politic—designing society intelligently just as an engineer designs a machine. The third, following from the first two, suggests a new view of history and historical change, and leads to a theory of progress. The fourth describes America as an experimental model available to the world to illustrate the new consciousness mobilized, fully operative, and performing remarkable feats.

Although these four themes are all suggested in Paine's *Rights of Man*, they are hardly original with him. They represent a consummation of Enlightenment social thought in the late eighteenth century, particularly with reference to events in the United States.

Before worthwhile social thought can take place one has to be persuaded that society can really be understood. Society, that is, has to be treated as a natural phenomenon, susceptible of observation and subject to law, in the sense that social behavior is seen to exhibit a measure of regularity and predictability. Among American thinkers, the one who most clearly articulated the theme was, of all people, the canny John Adams, who, despite his distrust of naïve rationalism, liked to think of America as a society openly and rationally governed. The American colonists, he wrote in his *Dissertation on Canon and Feudal Law* (1765), "knew that government was a plain, simple, intelligible thing, founded in nature and reason and quite comprehensible by common sense." He sounded the same note more than twenty years later in his *Defence of the Constitutions of the Government of the United States of America* (1787): The thirteen state governments were founded, he observed, "on the natural authority of the people alone, without a pretense of miracle or mystery." These governments "were contrived merely by the use of reason and the senses." The metaphor of the social contract takes on new meaning in this context. It suggests not only the volitional element in political association but also the historical—as opposed to the miraculous and extratemporal—roots of that association. However old the political society may be, it is a manmade contrivance and not, like the Mosaic Law, a divine gift to be cherished and preserved unchanged forever. A fairly common way of expressing it was to point out that the social *principle* is divinely ordained—man being by nature a social being—and government is necessary, considering man's aggressive nature (like clothing, government is the badge of lost innocence). Nevertheless, no particular *form* of government is divinely sanctioned, and, most importantly, no existing government is to be considered more than a human enterprise. What is new here is not the idea but the attitude—as when a young person, who has always known that automobiles are machines that run according to natural rather than supernatural principles, at last feels he or she has begun to grasp those principles and is able to handle one of those machines.

By removing miracle, mystery, and the aura of divine authority from existing societies, the way to rational social control was open. Alexander Hamilton proudly proclaimed at the outset of his first Federalist Paper that it is the mission of the Americans, "by their conduct and example," to decide "whether societies of men are really capable or not of establishing good government from reflection and choice, or whether they are forever destined to depend for their political constitutions on accident and force." The first American nationals, thinkers like Adams, Hamilton, and Madison, saw themselves as participating in an experiment that was both historic and historical: They were putting social principles and theories to the test. James Madison declared in 1791 that Montesquieu was a Bacon rather than a Newton in politics: He showed the way to the science of society but established no "immortal system." He suffered the disadvantage "of having written before these subjects were illuminated by the events and discussion which distinguish a very recent period." Revolutionary Americans quarreled with Montesquieu not only over his adulation of the British constitutional system, but also over his assertion that a republic must remain small, like Switzerland or the ancient Greek city-states—that an extensive republic would necessarily suffer either disunity or the collapse of its republican government. Responding to this charge in the fourteenth Federalist Paper, Madison set forth the assumptions on which the American "experiment" was based:

> Is it not the glory of the people of America, that whilst they have paid a decent regard to the opinions of former times and other nations, they have not suffered a blind veneration for antiquity, for custom, or for names, to overrule the suggestions of their own good sense, the knowledge of their own situation, and the lessons of their own experience? To this manly spirit, posterity will be indebted for the possession, and the world for the example of the numerous innovations displayed on the American theatre, in favor of private rights and public happiness.

Having mastered history, the Americans believed they were no longer mastered by it. Like expert mechanics who understood the machinery before them, they were guided by good sense, clear understanding of their job, and practical experience, not by custom, tradition, and legend.

The mastery of history brings not just the hope for progress but the very idea of progress. The story of the rise of the idea of progress in the modern period is lengthy and involved. What is important for our purposes is to remember that the linear view of history—which perceives history as a kind of one-way highway that might possibly lead somewhere—appeared only recently in its secular form, although it is part of the Judeo-Christian tradition. It is the thinkers of the Enlightenment above all who broke free from both the providential history of Christianity, which interprets history in terms of the events and prophecies of Scripture, and of the cyclical history of the classical world, which treats the rise and fall of empires as something analogous to the growth and decay of living organisms.

As long as history is seen as a hopeless story of degradation or as endless repetition, there is no room for the idea of progress. One version of Christian theory, which places the Second Coming of Christ *after* the occurrence of the glorious millennium prophesied in the Bible, offers something that comes close to the idea of progress, since the Christian watches for signs of improvement as an indication of the nearness of the End. This "post-millennialist" thinking, as it was called, was common among American Protestants in the eighteenth century. But the idea of progress as it finally emerged at the end of the century is something quite different from the Christian millenarian hope. It centers on the concept of the rational will, man exerting intelligent control over his social and natural environment, modifying it to suit his purposes. It suggests purpose that is not implicit in the historical process nor imposed on it from above by a benevolent deity, but is worked out through history by men acting deliberately, coming to decisions and devising the means of implementing them. In America, this idea of linear history-as-opportunity came into its own in the latter part of the eighteenth century.[1] A common interpretation—set forth by Thomas Paine—saw the American Revolution as marking the opening of a new era, a fresh start for mankind, the Year One. (The French, of course, literally acted this out in their revolution, by creating a new calendar.) Jefferson exulted to Joseph Priestley in 1801:

> We can no longer say there is nothing new under the sun. For this whole chapter in the history of man is new. The great extent of our republic is new. Its sparse habitation is new. The mighty wave of public opinion which has rolled over it is new.

In a tone more moderate but a frame of mind perhaps even more adventurous, Jefferson, Adams, and Franklin placed the American Revolution in a wider perspective, tracing their new age back to the invention of printing, the Reformation, or the development of gunpowder. In any case, the birth of the new republic was viewed as a lesson in history, an opportunity to study social change, and a historic event, a culmination, and a decisive turn in human affairs. The older interpretations of history were not swept entirely away. Christian millenarianism remained on the scene; and the cyclical view, combining with a decidedly biological interpretation of society and of the historical process, still haunted the imagination. Side by side with the older views, however, there was now a new idea of social change and a new vision of human possibility, and America seemed the embodiment of both. James Wilson, a great American jurist and revolutionary figure who is perhaps too little known in an age of great men, summed the matter up nicely in his address to the Pennsylvania ratifying convention in 1787:

> Governments, in general, have been the result of force, of fraud, and of accident. After a period of six thousand years has elapsed since the creation, the United States exhibited to the world the first instance as far as we can learn, of a nation, unattacked by external force, unconvulsed by domestick insurrections, assembling voluntarily, deliberating fully, and deciding calmly, concerning that system of government, under which they would wish that they and their posterity should live.

The fourth and final theme—concerning America as a working model of the new consciousness—is now obvious. Back in the seventeenth century Jonathan Winthrop had described the Massachusetts Bay Colony as a "city upon a hill," an example to all the world. Now the entire nation was so situated, presenting itself as an example, if not of Christian piety, at least of rational government. Following the Revolution, as Peter Gay has remarked, America changed its status from importer and consumer of Enlightenment ideas to producer and exporter.[2] What America produced, to be accurate, was not so much ideas as a fusion of theory and practice that resulted in a political society established from "reflection and choice" rather than "accident and force." The American production that most attracted attention overseas came not from the act of revolution itself but from the constituting of a new government once independence had been achieved. It was the social contract actually performed on the stage of history, the United States Constitution. The intellectual significance of that document is suggested in the arguments offered for its ratification, particularly the widely read *Federalist Papers*.

Hamilton, Madison, and John Jay are the authors of the eighty-five essays, published in the New York newspapers in 1787 and 1788, which have come to be known as *The Federalist Papers* or simply *The Federalist*. As was customary, they were published anonymously under a classical pseudonym—"Publius," in this case. Although these papers constitute only a segment of the material written for and against the new Constitution, they have become classics and have stirred widespread interest in Europe and Latin America as well as in this country. Rather surprisingly, to one interested in political philosophy, this collection—except for a paper here and there or an occasional generalization— seems remarkably dry and matter-of-fact, full of historical analogies and technical discussions of revenue policy, national defense, and the mechanics of the new government, but lacking in theoretical daring. As an example of the political philosophy of the Enlightenment, *The Federalist* lacks the glamor of Rousseau's *Social Contract*, the analytical probing of Hume's political essays or of Adams' *Defence of the American Constitutions*, or the encyclopedic range of Montesquieu's *Spirit of the Laws*. Indeed,

The Federalist would seem to bear out Hannah Arendt's claim that the American Revolution produced no political science, and that the Constitution-makers were informed more by "experience" than by reason or theory—that they took their lesson more from the variety of covenants, compacts, and agreements they lived under as colonists, than from the political thinking of the Enlightenment.[3] The question to ask, then, is this: In what way is *The Federalist*—if indeed it is—an instructive example of the thought of the Enlightenment?

The best answer is the most obvious and common one. *The Federalist* is useful to us precisely because it exhibits the cautious practicality of mainstream American political thought at the end of the eighteenth century. By this is meant not only that *The Federalist* is *in fact* cautious and practical, but that it was contrived to give that *appearance*. In this respect, it is effective propaganda because it sanely tries to give the impression of political sanity. The tone is set in the first paper, where Hamilton takes pains to acknowledge the "upright intentions" of many who oppose the new Constitution, and admits that perverse motives may influence those on both sides of the issue, slyly observing that such a major political innovation is bound to excite "passions and prejudices little favorable to the discovery of truth." Above all, Hamilton appeals to rational men to "take an enlarged view of the subject," to wage the debate on the public issues themselves, and not to impeach one another's motives: "My motives must remain in the depository of my own heart," Hamilton declared. "My arguments will be open to all, and may be judged of by all." While by no means denying the play of "interests," "prejudices," and "passions"—those forces that secretly energized the eighteenth-century psyche, just as repressed sexual desires energized (and enervated) the Freudian psyche of a later day—Hamilton called for a public dialogue that was rational and empirical. He wanted the debate confined to real issues over which good men might legitimately disagree, and to which refutable evidence might be brought to bear. There is no attempt to politicize the interior life of the mind by demanding total and selfless dedication to a general will—the kind of demand that ultimately led Robespierre to associate "virtue and terror." Instead, we have the picture of rational men sensibly deliberating the hard political issues and putting secret reservations and hidden motives aside. The actual debate over the Constitution was passionate, sometimes shrill, and hardly as cool-headed as Hamilton's words may lead us to believe. Nevertheless, the *mood* of rationality and sweet reasonableness was carefully cultivated. It is captured in Jefferson's flattering account (he, of course, was in France at the time) of the Convention in Philadelphia:

> We are yet able to send our wise and good men together to talk over our form of government . . . with the same *sang-froid* as they would a subject of agriculture. The example we have given the world is single, that of changing our form of government under the authority of reason only, without bloodshed.

In cultivating a tone of rational deliberation, the authors of *The Federalist* never lost sight of the irrational and selfish motives that influence political behavior. Quite the contrary. They constantly referred to what Hamilton called the "momentary passions" and "immediate interests" that have throughout the centuries excluded mankind from "the happy empire of perfect wisdom and perfect virtue." In his famous tenth paper, Madison frankly acknowledged that, human nature being what it is, the *causes* of factiousness cannot be removed, but he insisted that the *effects* can be controlled. This is precisely what the new Constitution had been designed to do. Madison cleverly pointed out in the thirty-seventh paper that, given the limitations of human nature and intelligence, given the enormous complexity of political life, it is scarcely short of miraculous that the constitutional convention performed so well in sacrificing "private opinions and partial interests to the public good." It was as though, against all odds, the lucky combination had been struck for once in history: Fallible men had pooled their limited capacities to produce a document that was greater than the sum of its moral parts. It was now up to the rest of the nation to bestir itself to look beyond narrow interests and base passions in ratifying the new Constitution. This was a remarkable demand to make in the political turmoil of what one historian has labeled "an Age of Passion."[4] Madison himself conceded that men find it hardest to be objective and dispassionate at times when these qualities are most needed.

"The genius of American politics," observes Robert Paul Wolff, "is its ability to treat even matters of principle as though they were conflicts of interest."[5] Here is an important key to *The Federalist*. To be sure, the writers regularly refer to the highest principles—like the public good or the value both of personal "liberty" and of social "order"—and assume that all men of goodwill support these. Presupposing general agreement at this level, and avoiding a too precise definition of the terms involved, the writers seem to follow a pattern of reasoning that goes like this: The proposed Constitution effectively accomplishes what all right-thinking citizens want—it promotes the public good and protects basic liberties while preserving the peace; those who oppose it, therefore, are either misinformed about the facts or misled by "passion" or a too narrow view of their own best "interests." From this point, the authors could move into a detailed discussion of the facts and could concern themselves with explaining how the new Constitution effectively serves the best interests of all. Though based on a careful analysis of human motivation and a Newtonian calculation of the political balance needed to regulate and control the passions that govern social beings, *The Federalist* does not present anything approaching a systematic political theory. This is not because such a theory seemed needless, but because, under the circumstances it would have been impolitic. Rather than probing the principles involved in the debate, it was wiser—indeed, politically healthier—to shift attention to operational details and to the question of private interest *versus* the public good.

This was an effective tactic in political propaganda (*The Federalist*, after all, was a propaganda piece), but it was much more besides. The fact is that the American people were deeply divided among themselves in the late 1780's. The authors of *The Federalist* were themselves far apart on basic political principles. A thoroughgoing public debate over principles would have been at best inconclusive and quite possibly disastrous for the republic. If matters were shifted from the realm of principle to that of interest, disagreement would thereby be made possible—interests, for Americans, being a more debatable topic than principles. We today may have a problem appreciating the positive significance in all this, because our idea of "interest" derives from the progressive era and suggests a conspiracy of the rich and powerful against the public welfare. Although the idea of interest did have this darker meaning to eighteenth-century thinkers—as when one speaks of "narrow" self-interest or when Madison defined "faction" as a group united by a common "passion" or "interest" that is "adverse to the rights of other citizens"—it also had a more neutral, even positive meaning. The "public interest," as one would expect, was always a good cause. *The Federalist* also distinguishes between a person's "immediate" interest and his "true" interest, suggesting that even the most self-serving individual may be persuaded that a sound policy is really to his best interests, and hence lend his support to it.[6] The issue is complicated, somewhat, because in the eighteenth century the idea of interest was often closely connected with the idea of property: Madison himself traced the interest of faction to the "unequal distribution of property." We cannot doubt that those who supported the new Constitution were often very much concerned about the protection of property—which they regarded as the most vulnerable of rights in a republic. What we must avoid doing, it seems, is reading backward into this concern for property issues that took shape only later, in the business civilization of the nineteenth and twentieth centuries. In the early modern period, as the individual began painstakingly to distinguish himself within the corporate society in which he lived, he found in the customs and laws concerning property an important, legally definable basis for his new identity. Now, since the industrial revolution, and especially since the time of Marx, it has become common with some to see property as potentially a dehumanizing force and to regard property rights as antithetical to human rights. Since the early nineteenth century various writers have warned that our business ethic turns man into a commodity while our machinery turns him into a thing. Although in our industrial-capitalist society property unquestionably does present us with serious problems, and human rights and dignity are often threatened by it, it would be putting the cart before the horse to criticize seventeenth- and eighteenth-century thinkers who defined "rights" and "interests" in terms of property for contributing to the dehumanization of man. The idea of the individual's humanity and intrinsic worth was new in those days. It was what these thinkers were groping toward, and the concept of property provided them with one conceptual device for giving such a notion something approaching legal meaning and protection. We are thus led to the final point, that by the eighteenth century the legitimacy of private interest and the right to pursue one's personal happiness were finally receiving recognition. As the twentieth-century psychologist Erich Fromm analyzes it, self-interest (as distinct from base "selfishness") is not only to be expected in people, but is, in fact, an important part of any healthy and normal person's total orientation toward life.[7]

By treating matters of principle as matters of interest the writers of *The Federalist* were able better to avoid head-on collision in the public debate over the new Constitution. Federalists and Antifederalists alike, for example, agreed on the need for both "liberty" and "order" in society. But they defined these things differently, radically so in some cases. So, instead of debating this kind of thing directly, on the theoretical level, one argues instead over the best *means* of securing these (undefined) blessings; and when one's plan meets with opposition, one responds to the critic not by questioning his principles (on these consensus is assumed) but by referring him to his own "true" (as opposed to his imagined) interest. This tactic helps avoid a stalemate or possibly violence. But it presents a problem of its own. For although the idea of interest was supported by much of the prevailing psychological theory of the eighteenth century, and was receiving the sanction of political philosophy as well, nevertheless private interests may conflict with the public interest, and may thus threaten the social good. No society has the resources, furthermore, to serve the interests of all its members. How, then, may a society keep the self-interest of its members from tearing it apart, without instituting a repressive and arbitrary government? How may self-interest and the public good *both* be given maximum protection?

This was a challenge *The Federalist* met directly. It did so on two levels. First, on the moral and rhetorical level, *The Federalist* makes a moral appeal to all Americans to transcend narrow self-interest and rise to the cause of the "public good," addressing itself to the good sense and the patriotism of the American people. Second, on what may be called the mechanical level, *The Federalist* demonstrates how the new Constitution provides a form of government that counterbalances private interests, protects basic rights, and ensures social order, thus showing that a political society can be intelligently engineered to achieve maximum moral efficiency.

First, on the mechanical level, the problem of the mechanics of government received thorough treatment throughout the pages of *The Federalist*. At times it appears that the writers thought of the new government as a political and psychological version of the Newtonian world system, with each department and function of government set in perfect gravitational relation to one another. The political apparatus would be so designed, Madison declared, that ambition would be made to counteract ambition, and the private interest of each person would serve as a sentinel to protect the public interest. Both Hamilton and Madison liked to think in terms of establishing a correct balance between what the former called the "energy of government" and the "security of private interests," explicitly comparing the axioms of politics to those of geometry. Madison, who referred to representative government as a "great mechanical power," was particularly prone to sound more like an engineer than a politician. An efficiently designed government, he said, must have power sufficient to the work it is expected to perform, but not so much power as to operate detrimentally to the public good. The critics of the new Constitution, he charged, in expressing misgivings about "the extensive powers of the government," show that they

> have very little considered how far these powers were
> necessary means of attaining a necessary end. They
> have chosen rather to dwell on the inconveniences
> which must be unavoidably blended with all political
> advantages and on the possible abuses which must be
> incident to every power or trust, of which beneficial use
> can be made. . . . The purest of human blessings must
> have a portion of alloy in them; and the choice must
> always be made, if not of the lesser evil, at least of the
> GREATER, not the PERFECT, good; and in every
> political institution, a power to advance the public

happiness involves a discretion which may be misapplied and abused.

As is the case with any machine, the efficiency of government must be judged according to its actual mechanical advantage.

The mechanics of the new government, including both the details of its operation and the engineering principles behind it, are the primary concern of *The Federalist*. Treating differences of principle as differences of interest leads discussion away from fundamental policy and to the techniques of implementation. Still, the broader moral and rhetorical appeal of *The Federalist*, while perhaps less prominent—or more easily overlooked—should not be ignored entirely. While assuring the American people that their "rights" and "interests" would be adequately protected under the new Constitution, the writers of *The Federalist* constantly urged their readers to take a larger view of things, to consider the good of the country as a whole. It must become "a deep and solemn conviction in the public mind," Hamilton wrote, "that greater energy of government is essential to the welfare and prosperity of the community." The American Revolution, he noted, inspired "a zeal for liberty" in the public mind, a zeal that is at times "more ardent than enlightened." If the principles of nearly anarchic liberty become "the popular creed," he warned, "they would utterly unfit the people of this country for any species of government whatever." Making the usual allowances for Hamilton's dread of anarchy, and acknowledging the fact that many of the Federalists were troubled by the democratic stirrings at the state and local level during the Revolutionary period, we must nevertheless look closely at this concern over the "public mind" and the "popular creed." For the writers of *The Federalist*, it was important not only that behavior be controlled by mechanical devices, but also that public sentiments and attitudes be cultivated, that the people be taught to take "an enlarged view" of things, as Hamilton put it. To appreciate the significance of this moral appeal, we must look beyond *The Federalist* itself—which, of course, had the limited goal of defending the new Constitution—into the events of the 1780's and 1790's. *The Federalist Papers*, to put it another way, have to be seen in a wider context, one that transcends the debate over the Constitution, in fact one that ultimately goes beyond politics.

The American Revolution did more than separate America from Britain and stir up a zeal for liberty among the people. On one level, as Barnard Bailyn has shown, it served to legitimize developments that had been taking place throughout the colonial period, developments that included a growing authority of the colonial legislatures, greater popular influence on the government through a broadening franchise, the abolition of legal privilege and the withering or increasing irrelevance of such imported feudal institutions as entail and primogeniture, and the breakdown of the authority of established religion.[8] Those things that the French revolutionaries had to fight for bitterly came much more naturally in the social environment of North America. On another level, the American Revolution stirred great expectation in the minds of some Americans, partly because of the enthusiastic way some Europeans, especially some Frenchmen, reacted to it. We have the picture of Jefferson developing a more revolutionary ideology—turning, as R. R. Palmer puts it, from "a Lockean into a Rousseauist"—during his visit to France in the 1780's.[9] We may put the entire matter this way: The revolutionary spirit was more a consequence than a cause of the American Revolution, and a rather indirect consequence at that. Furthermore, this revolutionary spirit manifested itself in a time when there was at least as much concern for securing the nation and reestablishing social order as there was for completing the job of freedom that was called for in the rhetoric of 1776. Radical ideals and conservative impulses were oddly blended in the American temper of the late eighteenth century.

Historians have vehemently disagreed in their interpretations of the 1780's and 1790's. They have seen these years as a time both of securing the revolution and of selling it out, both of triumphant moderation and of opportunity lost. Much testimony has been introduced in evidence, on the one hand, to show that the politicians of the time stirred unrealistic fears among the people for self-serving ends, and, on the other hand, to prove that the republic really was in danger, if not from revolution from below then from a Federalist coup at the top, perhaps from both.

The historians disagree in part because the witnesses themselves fail to agree. Federalists warned of impending anarchy not just to get elected, but because they were really fearful. Their Anti-federalist and, later, Jeffersonian opponents, for their part, really were afraid for their liberties and alarmed about a central government that could generate too much Hamiltonian "energy." At times the Americans could sound bravely confident, especially when they were reassuring overseas friends. But anxiety ran deep among both radicals who feared betrayal of the revolution and conservatives who feared its excesses. More fundamentally, the American people were as a whole anxious over the future of the new republic and the course it would take.

Events in France in 1789 and following had a profound influence on the American scene. On the positive side, the French Revolution could be viewed as further evidence that a new era was at hand. This was Tom Paine's reaction in *The Rights of Man.* The American Revolution had served as a demonstration model of the principles of republican revolution: They could now be applied in France, where the forces of oppression had been operating for centuries. Ultimately, they would triumph everywhere. To some, the French Revolution at first looked like the triumph of the American Dream in Europe.[10]

As the French Revolution progressed, its ugly side became increasingly apparent. A mounting crescendo of violence killed Jefferson's early hopes that bloodshed could be avoided or limited. By July, 1794, with the fall of Robespierre and the coming of the counterrevolution following a bloody Reign of Terror, the misgivings of many were confirmed. The reaction against international Jacobinism had already begun in America, and the ensuing years would see mounting conservative fears of radicalism and infidelity. Ultimately, the French Revolution and its aftermath would serve Americans for generations to come as a symbol of the hazards facing a republic and of what happens when a society tries to be at once free and freethinking. "I know not," Adams said of the situation in France in 1790, "what to make of a republic of thirty-million atheists."

We are now in a position to see what happened to the revolutionary spirit in America and to show the relation between this and the fate of the American Enlightenment. The Americans fought in 1776, expecting more than independence. Reacting not only to Parliamentary taxation but also to domestic circumstances, many Americans came to feel that independence was the only way to preserve themselves from the corruption of manners and (for some) the religious indifference that seemed increasingly evident around them. Many came to believe that England was not only conspiring against colonial liberties and rights, but that it was also spreading this corruption: The corruption of English politics, of morals, and of religion was advancing westward through the Empire. The Declaration of Independence would do more than strike away the chain of political bondage: It would serve the prophylactic function of a moral and spiritual quarantine. It would preserve the faith and virtue of the American people from overseas infection.

What happens, however, once independence is achieved? May not America, once free of moral contamination, become like the woman who drove a demon from her house only to find that seven more had taken its place? Sound public morality requires positive as well as negative action: It must be provided with positive principles and not merely protected from corrupting influences. What these positive principles might be was a matter of some disagreement. For a New England Puritan like Ezra Stiles, these principles were provided by Christianity. To secure the future of the nation, he said in 1783, we must dedicate ourselves afresh to God and His holy experiment in the New World:

> We must become a holy people in reality, in order to exhibit the experiment, never fully made in His hallowed part of the universe, whether such a people would be the happiest on earth.

For the more secular Jefferson, these principles arise from an agrarian way of life, which encouraged him, in his *Notes on Virginia*, to recommend pastoralism as a kind of political ideology:

> Those who labor in the earth are the chosen people of God, if ever He had a chosen people, whose breasts He

has made His peculiar deposit for substantial and genuine virtue.... Corruption of morals in the mass of cultivators is a phenomenon of which no age nor nation has furnished an example.

We must discourage domestic manufacturing—"let our workshops remain in Europe"—and devote all our energies to agriculture, whose precious byproduct is public and private virtue.

John Adams offered still a third alternative in his *Thoughts on Government* (1776). Alluding to Montesquieu, Adams notes that different forms of government are said to be founded on different moral and psychological principles. That is, despotism is founded on fear, aristocracy is founded on honor, and republicanism is based on virtue. Virtue, as Montesquieu described it (making it clear that he meant "political virtue," as distinct from moral virtue), is an internal principle of self-regulation that protects a free people from the fatal political consequences of avarice and ambition. Adams reworked Montesquieu's theory, taking virtue in its broadest sense as the normative principle of *all* good government. All governments, that is, *should* be founded on virtue. Since virtue is more natural to a republic, where its practice is regularly encouraged, it follows that the republican principle itself is the best one on which to establish a virtuous society. Reversing Montesquieu's formula, Adams in effect made the cultivation of national virtue into a problem of political mechanics. A political form—namely, republicanism—was declared the best means of producing a moral condition. Adams' *Thoughts on Government* are devoted mainly to the task of describing the best structural arrangement—with a bicameral legislature, an executive, and a judiciary, all independent of one another—to ensure both the stability of government and "the morals of the people." Adams helped make republicanism into what Gordon Wood brilliantly describes as a "republican ideology."[11]

The trouble with virtue is that it is always being threatened and potentially compromised. Whether it is founded on religious faith, on the agrarian way of life, or on the mechanics of good government, virtue is constantly in jeopardy; and any threat to faith, to the supremacy of agriculture, or to sound government becomes a threat to the nation's moral identity. When we call the Americans of the last two decades of the eighteenth century "anxious," we use the term advisedly. Anxiety, as the theologian Paul Tillich describes it, is fear without a clear object: It is the threat of nonbeing, the feeling that one's very identity (not merely one's life) is in peril; it is the gripping recognition of one's finitude.[12] How does this apply to the infant American republic? A nation, like a person, develops an identity that may be as seriously threatened as that of an individual. The people of a country come to think of themselves in a certain way, and when this self-estimate is called into question, the result is a widespread feeling of uncertainty and self-doubt and a vague dread of the future. A young nation—still unsure of itself and in need of self-esteem—is particularly vulnerable to this kind of distress, although any nation passing through a profound moral crisis may suffer from it. The Americans of the late eighteenth century—cut loose from Europe and concerned about their moral identity as a people—were going through such a period of anxiety.

In the colonial period, the Americans, seemingly isolated from the corruptions of Europe, had come to value highly their innocence and moral integrity. Innocence of the corruptions of civilization is one of the few things of which those on the outskirts of civilization can boast. An intellectual vogue in Europe at the time, extolling "natural" simplicity and goodness over "artificial" refinement and corruption, further encouraged the Americans to cherish their wholesome moral circumstances in the New World. As American society grew up economically, socially, demographically—and it grew enormously in the eighteenth century—and as American life became more complicated, sophisticated, and materially comfortable, the resulting change in American manners and morals had a troubling effect. People were developing a taste for a refinement and luxury that many regarded as a disturbing sign of the end of America's virtuous simplicity. It may be too strong to say that the Americans became obsessed with their virtue, but they certainly suffered something deeper than normal concern over changing standards of conduct. The Revolution presented the opportunity to recover an earlier purity and dedication. As a war of national liberation, one that marks the birth of a nation, the Revolution both freed the Americans from the "corruptions" of English society and presented them afresh with the question of their identity as a people. Thus the act of recovering an earlier virtue took on added meaning: The quest for virtue merged with the question of the American national character. Virtue was not only indispensable to the stability of republican government, but was also the most important basis for distinguishing Americans from others, namely, from Europeans. To put the matter in Montesquieu's terms, political virtue and moral virtue joined; and a nation was born whose identity is determined by its righteousness and whose virtue bears the burden of its national identity. Add to this the eschatological rhetoric, both sacred and secular, surrounding the revolutionary events—identifying the American Revolution as the dawning of a new dispensation, a new moral epoch, a new era in human history—and we may agree that the Americans had good reason to be anxious. The most vulnerable of principles, virtue, was at the core of American nationality while a weak and uncertain new nation bore the awful responsibility of mankind's political redemption. Political mechanics worked only up to a point. The principles of sound constitutional government can help to balance the demands for freedom over against those for order, but they cannot save a nation's soul nor guarantee that it will fulfill its historic destiny. It seems clear, then, that certain of the new nation's difficulties were deeply psychological or spiritual in nature, and had to be settled in the realm of beliefs and values, in a battle for the hearts and minds of the American people.

IV

THE ENLIGHTENMENT AS AN
AMERICAN INSTITUTION

[11]

THE CRITICAL PERIOD IN AMERICAN INTELLECTUAL HISTORY

A revolution cannot be confined to one or two limited objectives. No exception to this rule, the American Revolution did more than establish an independent nation. It gave rise to a host of aspirations and desires, including a desire to distribute widely the benefits of freedom throughout society, and a desire to knock off the shackles, as Jefferson put it, of all those tyrannical laws and customs that restrained human thought and expression. The first set of aspirations—we may call them *democratic* aspirations—were most evident at the various state levels in the 1780's and 1790's, and greatly alarmed Federalists like Hamilton, who feared that a too ardent zeal for liberty would destroy the people's capacity for government. The second set of aspirations are more vague and elusive. They were expressed in the demand for freedom of religion, of speech, and of the press—the subjects of the First Amendment to the Constitution—but they go beyond this rather limited formula. They were inspired by the intellectual adventurousness of the Enlightenment, a spirit of searching inquiry and a determination to free the mind from the shackles not just of government censure but of habit and "prejudice" as well. These *intellectual* aspirations, let us call them, were most stridently voiced in the last decade or so of the century. The 1790's mark the critical period in American intellectual history. The events of that decade were to determine the course of American thinking for years to come.

The political significance of the last decade of the eighteenth century has long been obvious. These are the years not only of the formation of the new government but of the rise of an American party system out of a particularly bitter political contest. In histories of this decade, thought is eclipsed by politics in spite of the fact that the 1790's and the decade immediately preceding are commonly regarded as marking the crest of the American Enlightenment. Even intellectual histories of the period are written with an eye on the political forum. This is understandable when we recall that the 1790's were at the very center of what John Adams called "an age of revolutions and constitutions." Indeed, politics—though not necessarily in the narrow, partisan sense of the word—play a major role in the intellectual life of the time. Still, our interest in the political realm should not cause us to overlook a significant development in the intellectual. To state the matter as tersely as possible: The 1790's shaped the American mind through the containment and appropriation of Enlightenment thought.

In order to contain the Enlightenment, it was necessary to organize resistance to its more dangerous ideas. The single most important event around which this effort was mounted was the French Revolution. The Americans interpreted the French Revolution in the light of their concern for the future of the American republic and for the preservation of American virtue, those traits of national character considered so essential to the preservation of social order in an open society. Principally, containment involved mounting a crusade against deism, infidelity, and what was often referred to as "licentious speculation." It went hand-in-hand with a growing distrust of rationalism and a political assault on the intellectual. It set a pattern of defensiveness, conscious provincialism, and anti-intellectualism that was to harden into a tradition in the course of the nineteenth century.

At this point a note of caution should be sounded. Agreeing that a young nation might have been troubled by the situation in Europe, how realistic were American fears over speculative and radical ideas? Obviously, the 1790's were marked by intense political rivalries and by fundamental disagreements over both domestic and foreign policy—disagreement, that is, that went beyond mere partisan bickering and involved the very principles of American government and the determination of the country's political destiny. Although it was an intensely political decade, in other words, it was a time when basic issues were at stake and ideological divisions among the nation's leaders threatened the domestic tranquillity. The Federalists in power, moreover, were very nervous over the threat of anarchy or of further popular uprisings, and the rise of an increasingly determined opposition together with the appearance of Jacobin clubs in this country did nothing to put their minds at rest. Moving beyond the political sphere, however, how widespread and vital were speculative and skeptical philosophies in America? What chance did infidel philosophies really have of seducing the public mind and thereby, presumably, undermining national character? The record is confusing.

In support of the thesis that freethinking and its intellectual cohorts, skepticism, deism, infidelity, atheism, and licentious speculation, were actually rampant in America in the 1790's we have primarily two sets of testimony. First, the culprits themselves, the deists and others like them, were exhilarated by the prospect of making America a nation not only of free men but of free minds. The call was sounded from overseas by Thomas Paine, who had become the literary hero of the Revolution, in his two-part tract *The Age of Reason* (1794, 1796). Although presented as his "own opinion" on religious matters, a kind of personal confession of faith, the work was addressed to the people of the United States and proclaimed deism the only suitable faith for free men, since it is based solely on reason and the scientific study of nature. *The Age of Reason* denied all ecclesiastical authority, condemned "Mystery, Miracle, and Prophecy" as a technique for duping mankind, and openly ridiculed Scripture— making fun of the Old Testament, denying the divinity of Christ, and dismissing the Apostle Paul as "that manufacturer of quibbles." Holding that the energetic use of reason is "the most formidable weapon against errors of every kind," Paine affirmed his belief in one God ("and no more") and asserted that "My mind is my own church." This pamphlet, which was soundly condemned by most Christian spokesmen in America, effectively ended Paine's career as an American hero.

The Americans produced some home-grown freethinkers. Our own Ethan Allen (1739-1789), leader of the legendary Green Mountain Boys in the Revolution, published his own deistical work, *Reason the Only Oracle of Man, or a Compendious System of Natural Religion,* in 1784. Of greater influence was Elihu Palmer (1764-1806), a militant deist and admirer of Paine, who was active especially in Philadelphia and New York in the 1790's and early 1800's organizing deistical societies and even establishing a deistical journal. Palmer and others like him argued vociferously that free religion was the only appropriate faith for the new republic, and they confidently predicted its eventual triumph in the United States.

The second source of testimony supporting the contention that freethinking was a significant influence in America comes from its opponents. In his study of American deism in this period, *The Religion of the American Enlightenment,* G. Adolf Koch, in fact, relied mainly on anti-deistical writings—which are as abundant as they are at times shrill—to document his argument that deism really did enjoy widespread (if short-lived) success in the United States.[1] According to these reports, infidelity was rife in all the colleges, libertines and self-proclaimed philosophes were stridently holding forth on every street corner, and deistical societies were springing up all over the place like onion grass after a spring rain. Emphatic though such testimony is, most of it comes from reminiscences made years later. And, as Martin E. Marty maintains, in trying to find actual proof of all this deistical activity, historians "have dragged magnets through the evidence and come up with few significant filings."[2] For evidence of even a short-lived triumph for free thought, then, we are left with the inflated hopes of its advocates and the panicky reactions of its enemies. What *is* evident is the fearfulness free thought generated among the pious and the vehemence of the American reaction to it.

Several features of American free thought in the 1790's should be brought out clearly. First, it was anticlerical rather than speculative in origin. That is, writers like Allen and Palmer, and Paine, were stirred more by a resentment of religious authority—a prominent feeling in France at the time—than by the intellectual urge to think out their personal faith. Furthermore, their attack was directed not only against the "priestcraft" of Roman Catholicism (always a fair target among Protestants) but against all clergymen who spoke in the name of revealed truth: The freethinkers, in other words, challenged Christianity in general.

Second, the new deism was militant and assertive, expressive more of anger than of curiosity, resolute inquiry, or even mischievous irreverence. This was hard-line deism, often oversimplifying issues and villifying its opponents in its ideological battle against "superstition" and "bigotry." Third, the new freethinking directed its appeal not to the patrician class, men of learning and leisure, but to the people. Earlier in the century, speculative religion had been largely the philosophical amusement of the gentleman or the scholar (or an occasional leather-apron intellectual). The deism of the 1790's was intended as a popular creed, a new religion for the masses. Anticlericalism, militancy, missionary zeal. Combine these with infidelity, and, no matter how meager the actual number, the new deists might well be seen as a potentially deadly enemy. Intellectual speculation had become politicized. Here was the real menace of the new deism. The defenders of the Christian faith quite correctly saw that they were engaged in an ideological battle.

It was a widely (though not universally) held conviction in the eighteenth century that religion is essential to social order. Certainly many besides John Adams found it hard to imagine a republic of atheists. In a republic, the reasoning went, where the external controls are minimal, public order demands a kind of internal regulation. This kind of self-regulation depends, in turn, on sure moral principles, which are themselves mostsecurely grounded in firm religious belief. An attack on belief, then, is ultimately an attack on society. It was alarming enough when philosophes questioned the truth of basic Christian doctrines. To encourage the great mass of people to indulge in this kind of speculation was out and out madness. The enemies of freethinking drew terrifying pictures of how, unchecked by religious principle, the mob would erupt in savage fury, pillage and burn property, violate pure womanhood, and gibbet the master of the house on the nearest tree. This picture took on increasingly lurid detail between the 1790's and the mid-nineteenth century. To the enemies of freethinking, the issue here was not one of freedom of thought versus coercion and intellectual oppression, as Jefferson presented it in his *Notes on Virginia.* The issue was authority and social order. The merry skepticism of the idle gentleman, bad in itself, was now the blatant profanity of society's "lowest order," at least this was how it seemed. When Jefferso defended freedom of thought, he had in mind and he evoked the image of Galileo facing the Inquisition with the knowledge that the earth really did move. When the enemies of deist infidelity condemned licentious speculation, they had in mind not daring thought but disorderly conduct, and they evoked the image not of a great scientist but of the town drunk. In the 1820's the great American Evangelical Lyman Beecher was to apply the term "political atheism" to the kind of freethinking that implicitly denies the authority of God's moral government, thereby threatening all decency and order.[3] It was as though the intellectual and the political principles of Jeffersonianism were at odds with each other. If we are to set men free, we dare not free their minds as well: Political democracy and the spirit of intellectual criticism do not seem to get on well together.

Instead of the governmental repression Jefferson hated, the reaction to deism and the host of intellectual immoralities associated with it came in the form of voluntary association. To be sure, the evidence is abundant that certain Federalists in the 1790's were quite willing to use the government to stifle dissent and put an end to radical speculation. Nevertheless, after the triumph of the Jeffersonian "faction" in 1800, it became clear that the government was too weak to coerce opinion, even if such a thing were considered desirable; and, in any case, the government could too easily be taken over by the enemy. No, a republic is animated by the principle of virtue, not of fear, and virtue is promoted by education, exhortation, and persuasion, rather than by force. The schoolroom, the pulpit, and the lecture hall, supplemented by the moral tract and the religious leaflet, became the chief means for preserving the faith, establishing sound ethical principles, ensuring virtue, and saving the republic. These means were employed not by the government but by private citizens acting in concert, voluntarily associating together in the performance of their Christian and patriotic duty.

This effort, which began in the late 1790's, has been called by Dixon Ryan Fox the "Protestant Counter-Reformation," a crusade initially against religious liberalism and skepticism in the interest of true belief and of moral and social reformation. In the first three decades of the nineteenth century, this effort—stimulated by the nationwide religious revivals beginning in 1799 and reinforced by a similar development in England—gained strength, resulting in what Fox describes as a "vast web of societies and other agencies of propaganda," ranging all the way from Sunday school unions and missionary societies to antislavery organizations. Thanks to the untiring efforts of Evangelical Protestantism, the American republic was to be preserved as a Christian culture.[4]

While the forces were gathering to preserve America from the skeptical excesses and violent implications of Enlightenment thought, the thinkers themselves were coming under attack. The daring speculations of the philosophe had always been suspect, but by the close of the 1790's names like Voltaire, Rousseau, Diderot, and—alas—Tom Paine were presented as a kind of intellectual rogues' gallery. Intellectual "superficiality" and the rise of the "infidel philosophy" were among the things that saddened Samuel Miller in 1803, when he wrote about the century that had just ended. In the light of the fires lit by the French Revolution, the philosophes began to look more and more irresponsible, like delinquent juveniles whose wanton destruction of old certainties had somehow brought on the holocaust. By the 1800's their infamy, in America and abroad, had been established for at least the next half-century. In 1817 the French philosopher Victor Cousin cried the lament of the new generation: "Let us acknowledge with freedom and with grief," he confessed,

> that the eighteenth century applied analysis to all things without pity and without measure. It cited before its tribunal all doctrines, all sciences; neither the metaphysics of the preceding age, nor the governments with their ancient authority, nor the religions with their majesty,—nothing found favor before it. . . . The eighteenth century let loose tempests. Humanity no more progressed, except over ruins. . . . The philosophy of the eighteenth century has left us with a vacuity for an inheritance.[5]

Two particular charges in this indictment—that the Enlightenment philosophy "let loose tempests" and that it "left us with a vacuity for an inheritance"—are characteristic of the reaction to the Enlightenment. The philosophes, with their reckless criticism of everything (a result more of their superficiality than of outright malice, it seems), produced a kind of moral vacuum, like the low-pressure hush that immediately precedes the hellish whoosh of a tornado. Can a thinker be both superficial and dangerous? Yes, if his superficiality causes him to belittle fundamental religious and moral principles, principles on which the social order must stand. As long as such thinking is confined to the philosopher's study, it is inconsequential—as harmless as the raving of a confined lunatic. But let it loose in the body politic and its effect is disastrous. Taking this line, their critics could at once ridicule and condemn the philosophes, taking them to task for their wicked influence while withholding from them even the grudging admiration one sometimes has for evil masterminds. The philosophes had enervated their culture with their own philosophical impotence.

The relevance of this to America should be clear. Although America produced no intellectual celebrities to rival Voltaire or Rousseau, the American philosophe was considered every bit as pathetic as and even more dangerous than his overseas counterpart. He was more dangerous because his ideas were less easily confined in a free society, and their corrosive effect was even more deadly. More than this, the American philosophe was dangerous because, in a republic, he might hope to attain political power. This is precisely the tack taken against Jefferson during his bids for the Presidency in the 1790's. Mr. Jefferson, wrote one Federalist pamphleteer, is a "theorist" in politics "as well as in philosophy and morals." He is "a *philosophe* in the modern French sense of the word." Joseph Dennie, of all people, accused Jefferson of being "a man of letters": "His closet, and not the cabinet, is his place." Ensconced in Monticello, he may "harmlessly examine the teeth of a non-descript monster, the secretions of an African, or the almanac of Banneker." But in political office Jefferson's brand of "metaphysico-politics" are either "nugatory or noxious." Besides, Dennie sneered, his principles are too prominently seasoned with "French garlic" and are bound to offend the American public. Richard Hofstadter, in his commanding study of the subject, correctly sees in the politics of the 1790's the origins of anti-intellectualism in American life.[6] It was of course intellectuals who brought America through the turmoil of revolution and established the American government. By the 1790's, as Hofstadter says, these statesmen-intellectuals were bitterly divided among themselves and, in struggling against one another, exploited the fears generated by the French Revolution. Jefferson, with his notorious versatility, was an easy target for an anti-intellectual assault. His open admiration for French culture, his many intellectual pursuits, his speculative temperament and religious liberalism—all these now looked like a threat to sane government and public virtue, before one even got to his democratic sentiments. As it turned out, Jefferson could not be contained. He was elected and reelected President of the United States in 1800 and 1804. Nevertheless, the days of the man of letters as political leader were numbered. The first generation of American intellectuals was to be enshrined as the Founding Fathers and remembered with an attitude approaching reverence. After the Presidency of John Quincy Adams, however, the American statesman-as-intellectual was to become a rare and endangered species. Jefferson was not contained, but Jeffersonian intellectualism was.

It should perhaps be noted at this point that American anti-intellectualism as it emerged in the 1790's was not confined to the political arena. Sidney Mead traces, from this period, a similar development in religious thought. Through much of the eighteenth century Evangelicals and rationalists could cooperate with and even respect each other, the "civil friendship" between George Whitefield and Benjamin Franklin being a case in point. A staunch defender of orthodoxy, like Thomas Clap, might consider himself both enlightened and Enlightened, being proud both of his intellectuality and of his modernity. Many of the New Light Evangelicals who followed in the theological footsteps of Jonathan Edwards were as hungry for the New Learning as were their religiously liberal opponents. The 1790's brought an end to all this. Following the political and social turmoil of the decade,

American rationalism and American pietism parted company, and Evangelical Protestantism became increasingly suspicious of the intellectual life. The direction was set for the century ahead.[7]

In the 1790's, then, the American Enlightenment was contained in two ways. First, its speculative and critical temper came under suspicion, especially when its political potential was understood. Public virtue, it was found, could not withstand persistent and universal critical inquiry. Second, its intellectual leadership was discredited—at least the job was begun during the decade under consideration. The philosophe was dangerous when he was on the loose and a deadly menace in public office. The example of the French Revolution, the anxiety about America's moral identity, the domestic political instability of the 1790's gave rise to a defensive and insular frame of mind that was to prove resistant to the more caustic acids of intellectual criticism. Henceforth, mainstream American thought would display that happy mediocrity that Franklin attributed to American society. The events of the next few decades confirmed all this. During these decades, as Hofstadter observes, the rising forces of popular democracy broke free of the "restraining hand" of America's patrician leadership—that class which best represented learning and Enlightenment in eighteenth-century America. With the political decline of what must pass for the American aristocracy, the most effective and reliable institutional support for the American Enlightenment crumbled. Meanwhile, Evangelicalism produced its own moral and organizational apparatus to implement the mood of the 1790's. The hysteria, of course, eventually passed. But it left behind a wariness and, more, a resolve to blockade the American mind from the likes of speculative unruliness that had—as seemed obvious to many— destroyed Europe.

The word "blockade" may seem too strong, but this is the kind of language frequently used in the early nineteenth century to describe intellectual relations between America and Europe. The Harvard philosopher Francis Bowen voiced a common concern when he spoke, in his Lowell Lectures of 1849, of the need for the clergy and the educated laity to work together "to erect a barrier against the licentious and infidel speculations which are pouring upon us from Europe like a flood." When we speak of a barrier or a blockade, however, we must be careful not to suggest a system of censorship or a kind of American Iron Curtain. The blockade that would protect America's public virtue was moral and internal rather than logical and political in nature. The man of character is not easily seduced, nor is the nation that is governed by sound principles. Right thinking and high ethical standards would protect our shores from infidel speculations. So, instead of the postal and the customs inspector, the preacher, the educator, and the Christian philosopher would be the ultimate protectors of American virtue. It was they who would erect her moral and mental defenses against European corruption.

When all is said and done, the fact remains that the Enlightenment could be contained but not extinguished. We cannot unthink our thoughts, as Thomas Paine said. If the philosophe was the object of contempt, it was only because his real accomplishments were conveniently overlooked. Confidence remained high in the new science and in the experimental method of reasoning, although the latter was to come under sharp attack by some of the romantic thinkers of the nineteenth century. The truth is that the Enlightenment was more than a passing intellectual vogue. It amounted to more than the irreverent chatter of the fashionable *salon,* the polemical wit of the philosophe, and the slogans heralding a new "age of reason." The Enlightenment marked, as we noted at the outset, a significant stage in the coming of modernity, the application of the techniques and assumptions of the new science in areas of metaphysics, ethics, and social thought. It was part of the wider culture's assimilation of the scientific revolution. *This* inheritance of eighteenth-century philosophy, clearly, was not a "vacuity." No "barrier" would be able to contain it. The rationalism of the Enlightenment could be ridiculed and condemned, but its rationality one just had to learn to live with. For the Christian thinker, for all right-thinking Americans, in fact, who were concerned about infidelity and skepticism, this meant that the Enlightenment had to be appropriated to the cause of faith and morals. Enlightenment thinking had to be used as a weapon against its own extremes.

[12]

JOHN WITHERSPOON
AND THE EDUCATION OF THE
PUBLIC CONSCIENCE

THE American appropriation of the Enlightenment required two things. First, that portion of the intellectual community that could be trusted or made trustworthy had to be brought into public service—enlisted, that is, in the cause of sound thinking and high principles. Second, philosophy had to be made to serve the public good by being used to defend and declare, rather than criticize, fundamental truths, by giving scholarly support to the basic tenets of the American public faith. These developments took place in the early nineteenth century, but their roots go back to the 1790's.

Enlisting the support of the intellectual was the first priority. It would be a mistake to regard American anti-intellectualism in this period as a blockheaded contempt for all thinkers, the kind of neo-Neanderthal mentality H. L. Mencken so savagely derided in the 1920's. Joseph Dennie (1768-1812), the Federalist writer who ridiculed Jefferson's interest in fossils and French philosophy, was himself a man of letters and took almost extravagant pride in the fact. America in the 1790's was still a deferential society in which people looked to the members of its upper classes for leadership and wisdom. Of all Americans, these were the men best able to afford good education and fine libraries and most representative of that neoclassical ideal of political sagacity, public spirit, and learning that Gordon Wood calls "civic humanism."[1] Thus, although Jefferson's philosophical vagaries made him vulnerable to the satire of his political enemies, Jefferson himself was a member of a class from which examples of erudition and intellectual curiosity were not unexpected, though not as frequently forthcoming as one might suppose. The learned gentleman in politics was not yet the butt of jokes, as he would increasingly be after the triumph of Andrew Jackson. Still, the handwriting was on the wall. Those very men who ridiculed candidate Jefferson for his intellectualism were already complaining in the 1790's of the boorishness of their fellow Americans. These men sensed, even in these early years, that as American democracy emerged, the quality and tone of America's public and cultural life would decline.

The Federalist man of letters, although his political fate was sealed, left an important legacy to his society. He believed that, in a republic, where political power is widely distributed, there is always the possibility that the people will be guided more by their immediate passions, appetites, and whims than by sound judgment. The political dangers of this were foreseen and met in the new Constitution, with its checks and balances, its geographic dispersion of power, and its intricate system of representation. But what of the more subtle dangers to the standards of good taste and sound morality? What is to keep political democracy from spilling over into cultural or moral democracy, where the vote of any clod or reprobate would count as equal to that of the most civilized and scrupulous citizen? How could the young and impressionable American civilization be saved from what one Federalist writer called "promiscuous equality"? Obviously, it was up to men of breeding to guide their country through her delicate early years. The Federalists' gift to American democracy would be to save it from itself. Looking to Britain for literary guidance, the Federalist writers of the 1790's gave shape to a cultural tradition that would be of great importance in the century following, and was eventually to be identified as the genteel tradition. This intellectual contribution of Federalism is often regarded only incidentally or treated negatively. The Federalists, it is said, lost political power in 1801, never to regain it; henceforth, they exerted their conservative influence only in America's cultural life. By examining the Federalist years from the standpoint of intellectual rather than of political history, however, it seems clear that the Federalists' retreat into the cultural sphere involved more than the surrender of political territory. Cultural criticism was part of the Federalists' continuing effort to stabilize and preserve the tone of American life, and was not only a kind of intellectual compensation for political impotence. These men wanted to give their country the best they had to offer—their own high ideals of gentlemanly taste and refinement and of the public responsibility of the man of letters. Their passion for restraint, their literary moralism and didacticism, and their Anglophilic reliance on imported standards of taste—disagreeable though these look in retrospect—were expressive of a sensibility that produced Jefferson and Adams as well as Joseph Dennie and Joseph Stevens Buckminster. This sensibility harked back to Cicero as an exemplary man of letters and promoted what Buckminster called a tutelary spirit in the service of the nation's civic virtue and cultural integrity.[2]

Thus, at the highest cultural level, the intellectual (if a term so closely identified with literary misfits and rebels is not too anachronistic) was conscripted into public service. He would see to it that political liberty did not lead in the direction of moral and aesthetic libertinism. Other fortresses of reliable intellectuality were also established. The clergy, naturally, contributed its share of educated, scholarly men who were willing and able to defend public faith and morals against the onslaughts of skepticism and infidelity. This was particularly true of the New England clergy, who still wielded considerable authority in their region at the end of the eighteenth century, and who had behind them a tradition of theological erudition extending back to the days of the Puritans. By the beginning of the nineteenth century some denominations were incorporating Enlightenment ideas into their thinking. The Episcopal church, for example, was beginning to assimilate Lockean theories of the preceding century into their official theology by 1810, blending them with sixteenth-century Elizabethan doctrines.[3] With the Second Great Awakening in 1799, however, and the subsequent democratization of American Evangelical Protestantism, the course away from Enlightened Pietism was set. Evangelicalism and rationalism went their separate ways. The lingering mark of Enlightenment thought on mainstream Protestantism—aside from the various retreats it demanded in matters of doctrine—was perhaps the continuing appeal to the wonderful design of the natural world as evidence of God's existence and benign Providence.

The appeal to the design in nature as an aid to faith was a tactic favored by many besides theologians. Even Thomas Paine believed that nature attested to the wisdom and goodness of its Creator. Many came to regard nature as highly for the religious instruction and inspiration it offered as for its intricate regularities and curious artifacts. This seems particularly true in the United States in the decades after the Revolution. In the introduction to his lectures on the *Science of Nature* in 1800, which were intended to drum up public support for his museum, Charles Willson Peale emphasized the religious and moral, as well as the practical benefits of studying nature. As we study "the precision and character" and "the beautiful uniformity" of all things, Peale rhapsodized, "our astonished souls are elevated as it were to a converse with the great Moving Power, who governs worlds!" As to moral uses, nature "teems with the most striking examples which the Moralist can desire." Peale's idea was not a new one, but his ecstatic tone suggests the feeling of the time. Jefferson, at the end of his life, might be avidly following the latest experiments on the function of the nervous system in vertebrates, but at the level where the intellectual meets the public, the natural world was approached not primarily in a spirit of inquiry and curiosity—as Franklin approached it—but rather in a spirit of religious awe and moral didacticism.

The most pertinent and important example of the co-opting of the intellectual at the end of the eighteenth century is in the area of philosophy. The 1790's brought into prominence a new breed of American intellectual, the academic philosopher, more specifically, the college professor as moral philosopher. Actually, moral philosophy was a very old academic subject, both in America and Europe. In America, however, it gained new life in the half century or so following the ratification of the Constitution. As it was taught then, moral philosophy included not only ethics but virtually every subject that concerned itself with man's social behavior and motivation, including psychology, political science, sociology, anthropology, economics, and jurisprudence. By the mid-nineteenth century the subject was taught, along with a related course on "mental philosophy"—which combined philosophy and psychology—in nearly every American college. By then it was usually a required senior course, frequently taught by the college president himself and designed to bring together everything the student had learned and to put it in proper moral perspective. The course in moral philosophy became the center of a system of higher education that Stow Persons has called "Protestant scholasticism," and correctly described as "a synthesis of seventeenth century religious ideas with those of the Enlightenment."[4] This particular effort to join faith and reason, though in one sense expressive of a traditional Christian concern, seemed especially necessary in an age committed to the new science yet longing for the assurances of an ancient faith. It has special relevance, also, to a society that seemed so much in need of well-grounded religious and moral principles. If our modern intellect has threatened our faith, and if faith is essential to the well-being of the republic, what better public service can the learned class perform than to train the intellect to respect faith by demonstrating that there is really no conflict between them? It would be inaccurate to say that Protestant scholasticism arose in the 1790's. Nevertheless, the concerns of that decade remained long after deism and infidelity had ceased to be real threats: People alive in those years, people like Timothy Dwight (1752-1817), president of Yale, left behind a rhetoric of moral and political anxiety by means of which later generations would describe the ever-present menace of unbelief. In his influential book *The Nature, and Danger, of Infidel Philosophy* (1798), Dwight, a Congregationalist and Federalist, exposed the dangers of rationalism and skepticism to the republic. The man whose work most clearly portends the rise of Protestant scholasticism, however, is not Dwight but the president of Princeton, John Witherspoon.

John Witherspoon (1723-94) was born and raised in Scotland and educated at the University of Edinburgh, where he studied divinity. He was ordained a Presbyterian minister in 1745. In 1768, partly through negotiations with Benjamin Rush, Witherspoon was persuaded to come to America to assume the presidency of what was then known as the College of New Jersey. In this country, Witherspoon was active in the American

Presbyterian church as well as in political affairs. Besides being a member of the New Jersey constitutional convention in 1776, he was a delegate to the Second Continental Congress and was one of the signers—the only clergyman among them—of the Declaration of Independence. As president of Princeton, back in the days when college presidents were more than just administrators and public relations men, Witherspoon taught not only the course in moral philosophy, but history, rhetoric, Hebrew, and French as well (in those days, too, college professors were not nearly as specialized as they are today). Although his name is unfamiliar to most modern Americans, Witherspoon is important to our story for several reasons. He was, first of all, a man of some influence in his own time, having trained many men destined for national prominence, among them James Madison. Second, as we shall see, he represents what was to be an important influence in American thought during the first fifty years of the nation's life—the Scottish philosophy. Third, Witherspoon displays in his intellectual personality that blending of flexibility and orthodoxy that characterizes the final years of the American Enlightenment and that was to remain characteristic of mainstream American thought for years to come. Finally, Witherspoon serves as a symbol of the intellectual in a new office—that of college professor and public moralist.

Without stretching things outrageously, we may distinguish three types of public intellectuals in eighteenth-century America: the clergyman, the politician, and the academician. "Intellectuals" refers to people who are thinkers and who are most comfortable in the world of ideas. A public intellectual is the intellectual as public figure or, better, the intellectual in office. According to this definition, Franklin, though he was an intellectual and a public figure, was not a public intellectual, because his intellectual life was not a part of his official life. By contrast, the preacher-theologian, the politician-philosopher, or the professor-moralist combine their intellectual life and their official duties. Edwards would qualify for the first category, Jefferson and Adams for the second, and Witherspoon for the third. We may go further and suggest that, in the last half of the eighteenth century in America, each of these figures had his period of special prominence. Before the Revolution the clergyman was still the leading public intellectual, to be replaced (though never completely) by the politician in the 1770's. By the late 1790's the academic philosopher's star was on the horizon and would continue to rise in the decades following. These three figures all have one thing in common: Though men of thought, they put their thinking into public service. They did this, further, not merely in the sense of "serving the public," as, say, a government scientist does, but in a more immediate and direct way of coming forth as a source of wisdom and moral admonition, of guiding the nation in its choice of principles and ends and not only in its implementation of policy or even formation of policy. These men were not the government "experts" or brain trusters of their day; they were the moral and spiritual leaders of their society. Their function was hortative and judgmental rather than advisory or administrative. They represented the American public conscience.

The 1790's demonstrated the need for the public intellectual to assert himself forcefully in the name of basic moral and religious principles and of social stability. The clerical intellectual, of course, remained effective until well into the nineteenth century, despite the damage done to his spiritual and intellectual authority respectively by the two Great Awakenings and by the critical mentality of the Enlightenment. The intellectual politician, too, would continue to exert influence, although his authority was weakened by the political bitterness of the 1790's and would be further weakened as politics became more and more democratized in the early nineteenth century. The academician, who would never enjoy as great and direct an influence as the pastor and the politician, would nevertheless exert considerable indirect influence by being the one who instructed society's leaders and trained its educated class. Above all, this group would protect America's public virtue by setting forth the philosophical argument for what was called the "first truths of religion and morals." This philosophical argument constitutes the second major tactic in America's appropriation of the Enlightenment.

The second step, then, in the American appropriation of the Enlightenment, that of putting philosophy into community service as a support rather than a challenge to the public faith, was largely the work of philosophers, like John Witherspoon, who taught in the nation's colleges. The chief instrument employed in this reconstruction in philosophy was the so-called Scottish philosophy of common sense. Here again, the example of Witherspoon is instructive. Witherspoon was one of several academic innovators in the 1790's—including Timothy Dwight at Yale and David Tappan at Harvard—who were responsible for the rise of Scottish common-sense philosophy in America. But whereas Tappan and Dwight are best known for their theological efforts, Witherspoon is remembered particularly as a moral philosopher.

Scottish philosophy was influential in America long before the 1790's. The works of Francis Hutcheson and of Henry Home seem to have been particularly well thought of in colonial times. So influential was Scottish thought in this country, in fact, that Herbert W. Schneider, the historian of American philosophy, has claimed that the Scottish Enlightenment was perhaps "the most potent single tradition in the American Enlightenment." And Perry Miller, speaking of the early nineteenth century, called the commonsense philosophy "the official metaphysic of America" for roughly half a century. It would indeed seem that Scottish philosophy had a considerable impact on American thought.[5]

Scottish philosophy is by no means a monolithic system of ideas, and, in fact, it reflects many different points of view. Although this is not the place to elaborate on the intricacies of eighteenth-century Scottish thought, we may at least point out one or two common features and significant variations. First, it is fair to say that Scottish philosophy was particularly concerned with the empirical dilemmas presented by Locke's epistemology. If all our knowledge comes through our experience in the form of "ideas," how do we know our "ideas" really conform to the external objects they purport to represent? A second look at the object before us only provides us with a second idea or set of ideas. We may never compare our ideas with the object itself. Here was an epistemological problem that Locke never solved and that one Scottish philosopher, David Hume, suspected was insoluble by the empirical method. All this, of course, was a philosophers' conundrum and of little concern to the average person. Nevertheless, in an age when so much was in doubt, it was disturbing to think that the philosophers themselves—those who presumably are dedicated to the love of wisdom—were not even sure about the independent existence of the external world and of the objects people take most for granted, much less of such things as moral law, the soul, the life everlasting, and God! Again, if our ideas derive from our senses, as Locke maintains, what authority do our moral ideas have? Is Right whatever feels right to me? Is the Good whatever gives me pleasure? What is the source of our uniquely moral ideas, ideas of obligation and justice, for example? Is our sense of duty connected with our tastebuds or our optic nerve? Here again was a philosophers' muddle, but the social implications seemed enormous. Just when former restraints were collapsing and religious faith was coming under attack, the philosopher was apparently informing the world that he, of all people, did not know the difference between right and wrong, good and evil. It is little wonder that Victor Cousin accused eighteenth-century philosophy of leaving a "vacuity for an inheritance."

All of the Scottish philosophers were concerned about the ethical implications of the new philosophy, although not all of them addressed themselves to the subtle epistemological problems it presented. Hume, who was concerned with both sets of difficulties, offered a theory of ethics that, in the final analysis, was based on the emotions (pity for others) and on calculations of expediency; and Hume's theory of knowledge, as we have seen, seemed to compound rather than solve the problems raised by Locke. It was partly in reaction to Hume that Thomas Reid (1710-96), James Beattie (1735-1803), and Dugald Stewart (1753-1828), alarmed over the philosophical, moral, and social consequences of the empirical method of reasoning, and persuaded that their Scottish predecessors had either done too little or had taken a wrong path in their well-meant efforts to put things aright, set forth what came to be known both as Scottish Realism and the Scottish commonsense philosophy.

The basic assumption of Scottish Realism is that the world that we perceive is the world that really exists. Locke and others had gotten into philosophical trouble because they had atomized human experience into tiny quanta called ideas, and had then tried to reconstruct knowledge, using these ideas as building blocks. Each idea was like a hastily scribbled message slipped to a prisoner in a dark dungeon and supposedly containing some bit of information on events on the outside. The prisoner is left unsure how to put these fragments of information together; indeed, he is not even sure whether some well-meaning friend or a sadistic jailer has written the notes in the first place. This was all wrong, Reid and the others declared. Instead of discrete, irreducible particles of information, our senses provide us with an entire package of data that may be checked against itself, much as one checks a press release for plausibility, consistency, and coherence. The human mind is not like a prisoner in a dungeon. Rather, the mind is like an informed citizen in a free society who reads all the newspapers and follows public events closely. He may still be duped. (Reid and the others never denied the possibility of error.) But he could be at least reasonably confident that he understood what was happening about him. This elaborate analogy, of course, demonstrates nothing; and this is precisely the charge that critics of the commonsense philosophy have brought against it. Although the Scottish Realists did not use this exact analogy (it was Locke who had compared our mental world to a "dark room"), their reasoning was on the whole more analogical than logical, which is perhaps why they are not better known today. But in their day they had wide appeal in Europe and America, in part, one suspects, because they seemed to do what Locke had originally set out to do: They made a case for philosophical sanity, freeing thought from the chains of scholastic logic but not, in the process, losing their link with reality. They said, in effect: Our knowledge is reliable; the common sense of mankind cannot be universally deluded; and the burden of proof properly lies with the skeptic who denies all this, and not with the right-minded philosopher who merely acknowledges what everyone knows. Such a statement might not completely satisfy a Hume or a Kant, but it would make good sense to a practical man like Jefferson, who wrote to Adams in 1820:

> A single sense may indeed be sometimes deceived, but rarely; and never all our senses together, with their faculty of reasoning. They evidence realities, and there

are enough of these for all the purposes of life, without plunging into the fathomless abyss of dreams and phantasms. I am satisfied, and sufficiently occupied with things which are, without tormenting or troubling myself about those which may indeed be, but of which I have no evidence.

By appealing beyond the analysis of ideas to the common sense of mankind, the Scottish Realists set the stage for the reaffirmation of all the old verities. To James Beattie, the propositions "I exist," "the sun rose today," "the angles of a triangle equal 180°," "there is a God," and "ingratitude is evil" were all equally true because he could not imagine them to be otherwise. The same internal certainty that restores chairs and tables to the philosopher's study also reestablishes the moral order of things and returns God to His heaven, making all things right with the world. There is a kind of intellectual ritual to all this that transcends logic and is hard to appreciate today. For centuries people had gone about their business leaving the really deep questions to philosophers, pretty certain that they would be dealt with, but not really caring much one way or the other. Now, just when the authority of philosophy was really needed, it offered only timidity and confusion. The Scottish Realists served an important cultural function of their age: Wearing the philosopher's robe, they yet told people what they wanted to hear, just as philosophers had done since the fall of Rome. Here were important thinkers at famous European universities, and for once they were saying what everyone knew to be true. To an age still unsure of itself—still in need of some kind of commanding intellectual authority—this was no small consolation.

The Scottish Realists offered more than philosophical horse sense to a world that demanded practical reassurance. They were not, like the Wizard of Oz, artful confidence men who could make a scarecrow intelligent by equating intelligence with schooling and then presenting it with a diploma. They were right to challenge Locke's analysis of mind and to insist that no philosopher can logically blink away the universe (though they were wrong to believe that they could logically blink it back again). More, they were committed to empiricism, to the experimental method of reasoning; and, like Locke and Hume, they too wanted to set forth a "science" of the mind. "The way of experiment and observation," Reid maintained, is the only way to study nature, including human nature. What the Scottish Realists did was to effect a kind of compromise between the new methods and assumptions of the Enlightenment and the old truths of religion and ethics. Studying what he called the anatomy of the mind, Reid justified the duality of spirit and matter, asserted the authority of the conscience in establishing man's moral obligation, maintained the authority of a transcendent moral law, and reaffirmed belief in a Supreme Being. If his compromises did not withstand the sober second look of later philosophers, it permitted many to accept new ideas without jettisoning old faiths. Nowhere was this compromise more successful than in the United States.

Witherspoon is usually credited with bringing the common-sense philosophy to America, a claim that should be qualified at least with the observation that Witherspoon's philosophy was not purely of the school of Reid; it was far more eclectic and open-ended. Nevertheless, Witherspoon must surely get credit as the most significant figure in the coming of Scottish Realism to the American colleges. And, though eclectic, his philosophy has some of the essential traits of the commonsense philosophy. We find, first of all, the commitment to the empirical method and the faith in the new science generally. There is the didactic moral concern, second—the effort, not only to elaborate an ethical theory, but to set forth and defend a highly practical morality that the student is admonished to follow. Finally, Witherspoon, like Reid and his followers, begins with the conviction that the study of morality must start with the study of human nature, particularly the human mind—analyzed into its various "faculties" of reason, emotion, and volition. Witherspoon's position was set forth in his posthumously published *Lectures on Moral Philosophy* (1800).

Witherspoon began his moral philosophy with the question of our duty: What ought we to do? Our duty, he found, is revealed in human nature, for the moral law is written in the human soul. Man is possessed of a "moral sense" or "conscience" (Witherspoon used the terms interchangeably), a "sense and perception of moral excellence, and our obligation to conform ourselves to it in our conduct." The moral sense, Witherspoon maintained, furnishes us both with a feeling of obligation—to do what is right and avoid what is wrong—and a feeling of gratification and moral delight when we have obeyed its dictates.

So much for how we come to know our duty: Why ought we perform it? Why should we do what is right? What obliges us to live a virtuous life? This question of moral obligation was a troublesome one in the eighteenth century. Although various philosophers fought vigorously for different answers to the question, Witherspoon genially lumped together a number of different solutions. The question of moral obligation or the "obligation of virtue," he said, involves "all the following particulars":

> A sense of its [virtue's] own intrinsic excellence—of its happy consequences in the present life—a sense of duty and subjection to the Supreme Being—and a hope of future happiness, and fear of future misery from his decision.

We should be virtuous, then, because virtue is good in itself, because it will make us happier, because God wills it, and because of the promise and threat of the afterlife. While some philosophers would consider this an example of logical overkill (if virtue is good in itself, is it not worth doing regardless of whether it also makes us happy or pleases God?), Witherspoon's concern was more didactic and hortative than logical. As an American college professor he was training his society's future leaders. He was not teaching a course on theories of ethics: He was inculcating his students with high moral principles. In this regard, it is noteworthy that, after setting forth the theoretical basis for ethics in the first few lectures, Witherspoon goes on to spend three-fourths of his lectures on matters of "practical" morality—dealing with the nature of our duty under three heads, Ethics (personal duties to others, God, and ourselves), Politics, and Jurisprudence.

Witherspoon's moral philosophy seems remote and musty when we read it today. Perhaps a professor's lectures should be buried with him, and not be left around to do greater disservice to his memory with each passing year. Witherspoon's ideas, however vermiculate they may seem to us, were nevertheless once fresh and vital, especially at conservative Princeton. To teach moral philosophy independently of religion was considered an innovative, even daring, step in some quarters. Witherspoon knew this, but he pressed on. If Scripture is true, he said, the "discoveries of reason cannot be contrary to it," so there is no cause for alarm. The application of the new science to moral philosophy was another innovation. Again Witherspoon faced the challenge. The great advances in "natural philosophy" have promoted religion rather than hurt it, he maintained: "Why should it not be the same with moral philosophy, which is indeed nothing else but the knowledge of human nature?" Having established the theological independence and scientific status of moral philosophy, Witherspoon was in a good position to amaze his students when he showed them that man, objectively and scientifically studied, was a moral being, endowed by his Creator with a moral sense in order to guide him in a life of virtue. The new science, turned on man, merely reaffirmed the old faith. Witherspoon had put the Enlightenment to the service of sound morality and traditional values. We can appreciate his importance, therefore, in his own age. Beyond all this, Witherspoon's *Lectures on Moral Philosophy* display a generous humanity and rational openness to new intellectual possibilities that should have some appeal in any age.

This was the trend academic moral philosophy was to follow for the next fifty or more years. Although it may not be entirely accurate to say (as Perry Miller did) that Scottish Realism was the "official metaphysic" of the period, since most American academicians amended it to suit their own philosophical inclinations, it was nevertheless an important source of inspiration to those who provided the Americans with their official philosophy. By the mid-nineteenth century virtually all educated Americans were trained in the principles of moral philosophy. They were taught that morality is not a matter of personal preference but of dedicated obedience to a higher "moral law"— a law as real as science's natural law—whose dictates are inscribed in human nature. They were taught that they were possessed of a conscience that allows them to know their duty, and that they were under the sternest obligation to perform it. They were taught that the virtuous life, which also meant the life of Christian piety, was something to be cultivated with the assiduity with which a virtuoso or professional athlete masters his skill. They were taught, finally, that the future of the republic depends on the "virtue and intelligence" of its people, and that they—the nation's educated class—have the duty to serve as sterling examples. Franklin's "art of virtue," now the "science" of morals, was placed at the center of the American public philosophy.

John Witherspoon represents more than the ascendancy of moral philosophy: He represents the rise of education—at all levels—as a fundamental republican institution. The American people had always had great confidence in education, whether we take the term to mean parental guidance of children, self-improvement with the help of books and pamphlets, religious instruction, or formal schooling at whatever level. With the birth of the republic, education seemed more necessary than ever. The importance of education in the republic was discussed in 1786 by the American philosophe and physician Benjamin Rush (1745-1813), a man of catholic interests, a close friend of Adams and Jefferson, and the one who did more than any other single person to bring Witherspoon to America. Beside providing students with the necessary practical and intellectual skills, Rush maintained, education—especially in ethnically diverse Pennsylvania, where Rush lived—will help make the "mass of the people more homogeneous, and thereby fit them more easily for uniform and peaceable government." He believed sound religious principles should be inculcated in youth (although he spoke in behalf of Christianity, Rush claimed to be amenable to any religious system, including Muhammadanism, that acknowledged a Supreme Being and the life after death). Without religious faith of some kind, he said, "there can be no virtue, and without virtue there can be no liberty." The purpose of all this intellectual and moral training, Rush said, is "to convert men into republican machines," something which "must be done" if we "expect them to perform their parts properly, in the great machine of the government of the state." The modern reader winces at this talk of turning men into machines. The totalitarian overtones of the French Revolution have long been apparent, and the fascination in revolutionary America as well as France with the self-denying patriotism of Roman republicanism reminds us of the fascism of a later day. Still, we must remember that in this preindustrial era of our history the machine was not yet the symbol of oppression and mindless obedience it has since become. In fact, in the eighteenth century the machine most frequently suggested the precision of a fine instrument and the ingenious contrivance of the Newtonian world system. Rush's implication is clear, nevertheless. Education will make Americans more alike and implant in all a common set of moral principles and a common devotion to country. What was done by coercion or out of habit in the monarchies and aristocracies of Europe had somehow to be put on a voluntary basis in America. Education— moral as well as intellectual—was the best means of making free men, of their own volition, regulate themselves and work together in harmony. The moral mechanics of education were the counterpart of the political mechanics of Federalism in ensuring social stability. In the final analysis, the American reaction to the Enlightenment was not suppressive but pedagogical. The crisis of the 1790's brought religious and moral revival and a strenuous educational endeavor rather than military force or political despotism. However grudgingly, the Federalists accepted their own political defeat in 1800. Ultimately, their influence was to be moral and literary rather than political. More broadly, the American people would react to the intellectual tempests of the eighteenth century by erecting, in the century following, an educational system in the broadest sense that would contain and guide the intellectual life—that would make it serve the national interest.[6]

This effort involved myriad voluntary associations as well as public schools, lyceums as well as académies, and editors and preachers as well as schoolteachers and college professors. If liberty depends on public virtue, then the practical-minded Americans would see to it that the conditions needed to sustain public virtue would be maintained, just like any other indispensable public work. Such an important thing as public virtue should not be left to chance or to the fortunes of history.

The American appropriation of the Enlightenment, however,

included more than the shaping of a public philosophy and the effort to educate and direct the citizens of the new republic. It also involved the inward life of persons, the more intimate aspects of thought and experience, the yearnings and strivings of the individual heart and mind. In the early nineteenth century the effort was made not only to educate the American conscience, but also to cultivate the interior nature, the spiritual sensibility of an alert and literate people who suffered the doubts and uncertainties attending the coming of modernity. This effort is part of the complicated story of the fate of higher thought in an increasingly democratic culture.

[13]

WILLIAM ELLERY CHANNING AND THE INWARD ENLIGHTENMENT

SUMMARIZING Samuel Miller's 1803 summary of the eighteenth century, we may call it an age of science, of communication, and of speculation and criticism. It was the dangerous speculation and criticism that most nineteenth-century critics had in mind when they attacked the Enlightenment and its representatives for corroding belief and destroying sound philosophy. The science of the Enlightenment—that is, its wide application of the scientific method—was frequently forgotten or dismissed as superficial or coldly rationalistic. Too often passed over entirely was the advancement in communications that took place in the course of the eighteenth century. Here we should include all the things that Miller listed in the conclusion of his *Brief Retrospect of the Eighteenth Century*—the enormous increase in printing and in the publishing and distribution of books, the rise of literary and philosophical societies to exchange ideas, the linguistic studies and the number of translations undertaken, and the general spirit of free inquiry that prompted people not only to examine all things but to announce their findings to the world at large. Though often overlooked by friends and foes of the Enlightenment alike, this spirit of communication is what gives Enlightenment science and criticism their cultural impact. The eighteenth century was the age of the popularization of science—when names like Galileo and Newton were casually used by people who had only a fuzzy notion of what these men really did to earn their reputations. It was an age, as well, of the popularization of criticism, if we may put it thus, when to some it seemed that the skeptical philosopher was not content to enjoy the private satisfaction of his doubt, nor even to declare it to other philosophers, but was determined to persuade the world to join him in his unbelief. More than spreading trust in science and distrust of authority, however, the advances in communications contributed to and signaled a profound transformation in Western society and culture, a transformation that Alexis de Tocqueville described as an "irresistible revolution advancing century by century over every obstacle."[1] This transformation was the rise of democracy in the Western world, meaning not only the broader distribution of political power among the population, but the establishment of what Tocqueville calls general equality of condition in society.

When we bring all this together, we begin to appreciate the significance that democracy and the Enlightenment had for each other. To be sure, the Enlightenment was an elitist (though not an aristocratic movement)—theoretically welcoming all free and inquiring minds, but, in fact, limited to those with the talent and opportunity to participate in the intellectual life. Though desiring to liberate and enlighten the people, the philosophe was, in most cases, no champion of democracy and egalitarianism. Even Jefferson, though committed to democratic principles, wrote of democracy with all the instincts of the gently bred aristocrat he was. For most European philosophes the ignorance and wretchedness of the great mass of people made any notion of practical intellectual equaliy and community among men virtually unthinkable. Yet the fact remains, in their persistent efforts to communicate and diffuse knowledge, the thinkers of the eighteenth century contributed to the rise not just of political but of cultural democracy. Their real contribution, in this respect, was not so much what they did as it was the spirit they nurtured. It was not, in other words, that the philosophes eradicated illiteracy or educated the masses, but they made it seem vital to the welfare of their civilization that these things be done. The philosophes left us an ethic of education and enlightenment that is today an essential part of our concept of democracy. They made it seem "natural" to later generations that, in the normal course of things, every citizen should become enlightened, should be made intellectually aware of his world. Thanks to them, the "informed citizen" became the irreducible particle of liberal democratic society.

In the United States, where democracy—if we may accept Tocqueville's assessment—was more advanced than anywhere else in the Western world, the "informed citizen" was soon to be more than just a literate, politically conscious voter. The intellectual culture itself was influenced by democracy, that is, by the general equality of condition. In the democratic context, ideas became less the precision instruments philosophers used for investigating and understanding themselves and their world, and more tools for moving public opinion, weapons for fighting error and superstition, sedatives to allay people's spiritual anxieties, and commodities to be hawked and sold in the public forum. The intellectual life itself was popularized. In response to this popularization and democratization of the intellectual life there arose a new kind of thinker. This new intellectual was as different from the eighteenth-century philosophe as he was from the cloistered scholar of the Middle Ages. He saw himself as the cultivator of his society's moral and cultural sensibility. It was his goal to keep the best and noblest productions of the higher culture always before the public mind, preserving democratic society from its own egalitarian excesses by trying to raise the standards of public taste and judgment. His vehicle was the spoken and printed word, and though he stood for freedom of thought and independence of mind, he regarded himself as being constructive rather than destructive in his criticism. Although he was committed to the use of reason, he believed that reason should be balanced by piety and good sense and should not wantonly undermine people's beliefs. Such a thinker—be he a writer, editor, clergyman, or professor—represents the afterglow of the Enlightenment, the effort to join the experimental method of reasoning with a regard for what he considered the basic human values that are shared by men of goodwill. Though opposed to superstition, prejudice, dogma, and blind obedience to authority, he tried to support and nurture rational faith, and sought to reassure people as well as challenge them. In this country, such a thinker was the great Boston Unitarian William Ellery Channing (1780-1842), whose career, personality, and thought suggest what happened to the more intangible aspects of the Enlightenment in America's democratic culture.

Channing, who was reared in Newport, Rhode Island, graduated from Harvard in 1798 and taught school for a few years before accepting a call to the Federal Street Unitarian Church in Boston, where he spent his professional life. In the early nineteenth century, Channing not only was the most representative figure in Bostonian religious life, but was acknowledged as a thinker and a man of letters as well. After his death in 1842, Channing's reputation continued to grow both in America and overseas. He became, in fact, one of the most revered and respected Americans of the nineteenth century. He represents official American culture, if not at its best, at least at its most characteristic.

Like many of his contemporaries, Channing considered himself Enlightened, though he rejected the skeptical excesses of the Enlightenment. While he was a student at Harvard, he found his own theology being altered as a result of his exposure to the thinking of his century. He moved away from the moderate Calvinism in which he had been raised and in the direction of moderate liberalism and Unitarianism, which at the time stressed the oneness of God without necessarily denying Christ's divine attributes, and which above all emphasized man's free will and moral responsibility. During this period Channing was particularly influenced by English and Scottish thinkers. He read and admired the social ethics of the Scottish philosopher Adam Ferguson and was struck particularly by the ethical theories of Francis Hutcheson, Joseph Butler, and Thomas Reid—all of whom, in different ways, stressed the centrality of the conscience to the moral life. It is indeed significant that these writers who influenced the young Channing are all best known as moral philosophers. For, though a clergyman, Channing became better known and more respected for his moral teaching than for his theology. The French writer Ernest Renan, who dismissed Channing's theology as "Franklinesque," nevertheless greatly praised him for his moral philosophy and for the "decorous fervor" he brought to his moralism. Channing was a man who could move forward with the times intellectually, accepting new ideas and amending traditional beliefs, but at the same time he could express, in his own character, a reassuring moral stability and loyalty to fundamental values and principles. His contribution to his age lay not in the substance of his philosophy but in his ability warmly and honestly to express what so many wanted to hear: that one need not renounce the modern world in order to preserve one's moral sanity, and conversely that one need not abandon faith in order to be a modern and Enlightened man.[2]

Channing was generally optimistic about his age, seeing it as a time of immense opportunity as well as of danger. The eighteenth century, he believed, had ended disastrously as "men's minds were convulsed, old institutions overthrown, and old opinions shaken." The ruinous course of events in France that preceded the rise of Napoleonic despotism he saw as the legacy of the worst excesses of the Enlightenment: France lacked "that moral preparation for liberty," he contended in his famous essay on "Napoleon" (1827-28), "without which the blessing cannot be secured." France was "too corrupt for freedom." How could anyone believe, he demanded, "that a liberty of which that heartless scoffer, Voltaire, was a chief apostle, could have triumphed?" Yet, in spite of these typically Federalist sentiments, Channing—like John Adams in his old age—thought that the preceding century had mainly been honorable to human nature. Above all, he applauded the spread of science and technology, and the application of the experimental method of reasoning in new fields, including philosophy and religion. Like Samuel Miller, Channing emphasized and celebrated the great advance in communications since 1700 and the "revolution" in the "intellectual culture" of the West, by which knowledge and ideas were widely diffused. He perceived the connection between this general diffusion of knowledge and the democratization of politics, about which he was also hopeful. All the progress, of course, had its price, and Channing estimated this price in terms of the rise of skepticism, utilitarian morality, "insensibility to God," and "practical atheism." It was necessary to see to it that the blessings of modernity were not blighted by the very excesses they encourage. This, Channing believed, was the task of the ministry of his day.

"The state of the world, compared with the past, may be called enlightened," he announced in 1824, "and requires an enlightened ministry." It is no longer enough just to proclaim the gospel, he said at the ordination of Ezra Stiles Gannett in Boston. The minister today must have the intelligence and knowledge to demonstrate God's work in nature and to reveal the harmony between nature and revelation. To this extent the minister must be an empiricist and scientist. Channing went on to say that, as old institutions and authorities prove unreliable in sustaining faith, it becomes one of the minister's duties

> to search deeply and understand thoroughly the true foundations and evidences on which the religion stands. Now it seems to me, that just in proportion as the human mind makes progress, the inward evidences of Christianity, the marks of divinity which it wears on its own brow, are becoming more and more important. I refer to the evidences which are drawn from its excellence, purity, and happy influences; from its adaptation to the spiritual wants, to the weakness and the greatness of human nature. . . . The historical and miraculous proofs of Christianity are indeed essential and impregnable; but, without superseding these, the inward proofs of what I speak are becoming more and more necessary, and exert greater power in proportion as the moral discernment and sensibilities of men are strengthened and enlarged.

Our knowledge of God grows as the human mind develops, he continued, and as our "moral constitution" grows: for here is our greatest source of spiritual knowledge.

It is to the "inward evidences" and "inward proofs" that Channing ultimately directed people. In effect he had internalized natural theology, putting his emphasis not on the design in nature but on the design in human nature, particularly man's "moral constitution." In proposing what may be called this natural theology of mind, Channing was making perhaps his single most important contribution to his age. To be sure, this was not really an original approach. It was favored by Cotton Mather over a century earlier and extends back to St. Augustine and, beyond him, to the early Christian Platonists. Moreover, a number of eighteenth-century deists, Shaftesbury among them, preferred to approach God through the study of man's moral nature rather than through the natural environment. Channing, nevertheless, perceived that the conditions were right in his day for a renewal of this tradition and a revision of it. Armed with the knowledge gained by the new science of the mind, and realizing that vital religion can neither ignore the new physics nor survive as a kind of theological appendix to the mechanical philosophy, Channing was determined to find a path to spiritual truth that was at once Enlightened and fervent, scientific but still inspiring. He combined the fire of Augustinian pietism, the analytic precision of experimental psychology, and the dedication of Enlightened moralism. In doing this Channing felt that he was meeting his age's two most pressing spiritual needs: its need for a credible faith, an Enlightened religion; and its need for a religion of the heart, faith that was deeply lived and not merely the cold intellectual assent of belief.

Channing showed his generation that man's moral nature not only prompts him to behave himself or to sympathize with others: It urges him on and on, making him transcend himself, leading him inexorably to that divine Source of all Good. God is not to be found in nature, he said, but "in our own souls." Within us is a "moral principle" that "brings God nigh to us as no other can." This divine nearness is experienced whenever we struggle to overcome evil, to realize the good. To be sure, God might have made us incapable of sin or evil, but then we would not be human either. It is our constant struggle to overcome evil and to practice virtue that makes us fully human: Where would we be, Channing asked, without "the discipline of virtue?" We would be incapable of the highest happiness possible. He continued:

> Force of moral purpose makes us happy. Happiness does not consist, as men are too apt to imagine, in passive enjoyments. It is found in the strenuous use of our best affections. . . . There is a constant satisfaction attending the vigorous exercise of conscience. . . . There is an exhilaration, a hope, a joy, springing up within us when we *will* with power what we see to be

good. . . . Moral energy inspires an unconquerable resolution, and fills us with rare delight.

On some other occasions Channing offered more serene definitions of happiness—describing it once as "a very demure lady" who smiles benignly "but seldom laughs." But, as he expresses it here, happiness is the delight experienced by the moral athlete, the kind of joy sought, in quite different ways, by Edwards, Franklin, and Jefferson. It is, furthermore, a happiness warmed by piety—a piety that harks back to Edwards in some ways, only with man left in full control of his will and his cosmic destiny. Ernest Renan was correct in this respect: Channing's pietism, if not his theology, was Franklinesque. The Federal Street Unitarian preached a gospel of responsibility and ability: Man is a child of God but also a partner with God in effecting his own salvation. But it was not salvation that most concerned Channing. Rather, it was the task of living a life of virtue and piety—the effort rather than the reward—that his preaching emphasized. It was what Channing called the aliveness to God's all-pervading presence as one aspires onward and upward that captured Channing's imagination. He spent his life trying to communicate that sense of aliveness to his generation.

We see, now, how Channing used the legacy of the Enlightenment—the experimental method of reasoning—to reach beyond indifferent, arid reasoning and skepticism. Beginning with the empirical study of man's moral nature, Channing made an eloquent case for a life of strenuous virtue and resolute piety. It was a life, moreover, energized and comforted by cosmic emotion—the feeling that God is as close as one's heartbeat, the joy in realizing that one's effort takes place in the center of a caring universe.

It is little wonder that Channing was a much-admired preacher and that his influence remained strong throughout much of the nineteenth century. He told his age what it so much wanted to be told: that despite the awful intellectual crimes committed in its name, science was not the enemy of faith and morals, but their handmaid. Religion, on the other hand, was not assent to a lifeless creed, or fear and trembling before an angry God, but a temper of mind that was man's highest and noblest happiness. People were assured that the eternal truths were still eternal no matter what the philosophers claimed; and they were assured that, no matter how disorderly human society might be in a time of profound change, the moral government of God remained stable and unchanging, holding absolute jurisdiction over the heart and mind of each individual. Such news was comforting and reassuring to people emerging from an era of criticism, an age of experiments.

Like the other figures we have considered, William Ellery Channing is representative of the direction his age's thinking was taking. In a democratic as opposed to an aristocratic soiety—as we have used these terms—thought is no longer confined, no longer contained among a tiny portion of the population. Since the Reformation, the social importance of ideas had become increasingly clear, all the more so after the expansion of printing and of general literacy produced for the first time in the history of the world a reading public. What people thought and believed affected their conduct, public as well as private. "Licentious speculation" could destroy society. There is more to it than that, however. It is said that Voltaire, seeing an old peasant woman in prayer, asked himself whether he would not forsake all he knew in order to gain her simple joy and devotion. He decided he would not. The truth is, he *could* not. We cannot unthink our thoughts, we cannot recapture the innocence of lost ignorance. Knowledge, however, makes us more sensitive to life and more vulnerable to the agony of doubt and uncertainty. Channing addressed himself to this vexation of spirit and personal yearning of the private man, providing a newly sophisticated culture with a justification for the right to believe. Late in the nineteenth century, Charles Sanders Peirce, in an essay on "The Fixation of Belief" (1877), put his finger on the problem. Doubt, he said, is a form of pain, and people cannot tolerate it. In former ages— more primitive times—this doubt could be overcome by appeals to authority: the authority of the Church, or of the Scriptures, or of the ancient sages. Since the scientific revolution, this means of overcoming doubt has become ineffective for thinking people. Only truth can put doubt to rest, and in modern times the measure of truth is increasingly the method of science. A scientific philosophy, Peirce contended, is the only effective way of overcoming doubt.[3]

Channing, like other nineteenth-century thinkers, used philosophy to serve what amounted to a psychological function. The concern was not really to seek truth (as popular mythology interprets the aim of philosophy), but to permit belief. Since we can believe only what we regard as true, however, and since science is the measure of truth, the scientific philosophy was put to the task not of criticizing but of reassuring, vindicating, justifying. To put it another way, the democratization of the Enlightenment philosophy changed it from a critical to an apologetic instrument. The overriding concern was not to eradicate error or clarify thought but to defend the faith. This was done because people wanted it and needed it. A Voltaire might indeed resist the temptation to return to ignorance in order to regain faith. But what of the peasant woman herself? Were she, by some means, to become Enlightened, would she choose to remain so? Or would she, if given the chance, be willing at least to compromise her new insight for the sake of repossessing at least a portion of her former trust? Such a compromise would involve self-delusion, for there can be no compromising with the truth. But if the delusion is offered persuasively and eloquently enough, perhaps she can overcome her reservations, particularly if she is in the company of many others exactly like herself.

The implication of this is that Channing helped his generation delude itself. To draw such an inference would not be fair. It is entirely possible that thinkers of the eighteenth and nineteenth centuries—including Voltaire—placed too much confidence in the scientific philosophy in the first place. It is certainly true, as Whitehead pointed out in his criticism of the philosophes, that man cannot live on criticism alone, however important and necessary that function is. The point to be made, rather, is that, in America at least, the combination of Enlightenment thought and literate, democratic society served to alter the function of philosophy—indeed, of so-called higher thought generally—putting it to the task of banishing doubt and supplying people with the intellectual tools they need in order to sustain themselves morally and emotionally in an uncertain universe.[4] After the Age of Enlightenment, American thought was drawn into the service of the people—in the public realm, in shaping a national creed and, on the personal level, in offering consolation, hope, and reassurance to people in their quest for certainty. In the process, the American intellectual would feel himself torn between two responsibilities, one to the truth and to his own critical sensibilities, and one to the demands of his age, the needs of his society, and—most of all—to what he regards as his own humane sentiments. If there is tragedy here, it is precisely in the fact that one must be forced to make such a choice.

[14]

THE AMERICAN ACHIEVEMENT

EARLY in the nineteenth century the French writer and diplomat François René de Chateaubriand wrote about his travels in America in the 1790's. Although historians have raised questions about the veracity of many of Chateaubriand's reports, some of his observations remain valid and illuminating. One in particular is worth pondering. He called the formation of the American constitutional republic "one of the greatest political events in the world," because, he said,

> That event has proved . . . that there are two kinds of practical liberty. One appears in a nation's infancy: she is the daughter of mores and virtue—and is the liberty of the first Greeks and Romans, and of the American savages. The other is born of a nation's old age. She is the daughter of enlightenment and reason—and is the liberty of the United States, replacing that of the Indian. Happy is the land which, in the space of less than three centuries, has passed without effort from one liberty to the other, and by a battle lasting no more than eight years.

Whatever the future brings, Chateaubriand predicted, liberty will never completely die in America. This is the advantage that enlightened liberty has over the liberty of virtue and mores. The latter is the liberty of a young, unsophisticated people; it is the liberty of innocence and naïveté, the most fragile kind of liberty. Such innocent liberty, the liberty of political immaturity, must decay after succumbing to "centuries of pomp and display." It is corrupted and is eventually replaced by despotism. Liberty, daughter of enlightenment, on the other hand,

> shines on after the ages of oppression and corruption; she advances with the principle that preserves and renews her. The enlightenment of which she is the effect, far from weakening with time . . . fortifies itself with time. Thus it does not abandon the liberty it has produced. Always in the service of that liberty, it is at the same time her generative virtue and inexhaustible source.

The liberty of enlightenment is the liberty not of naïve youth but of intelligent planning and mature judgment. It is not subject to the historical laws which govern the growth and decay of less conscious societies. Though chronologically a very young republic, America yet enjoys this sophisticated kind of liberty.[1]

How had this come about? How had the Americans become immune to the course of empire, the cycles of history? How did they become able to harness and direct that elusive spirit that animates liberty? Probably, as many have said, because from the beginning the Americans had to be pragmatists and had to learn to contrive all things including things spiritual. They came, in fact, to take a manipulative attitude toward the spirit, as though the psyche could be budged or hoisted. Theirs was the problem-solving mentality of an engineer, regardless of whether they were building a canal or teaching the art of virtue. Thus the Americans were willing to try to seize control of their own political life cycle.

There is more to it than American pragmatism and ingenuity, however. As we have seen, the Americans were aware how vulnerable a republic is, and this awareness became acute in the 1790's. They were aware—and the French Revolution only dramatized this—that a republic must be sustained by a public virtue grounded in sound principles and beliefs. In 1762 Rousseau called for a "civil religion" to support public virtue (Franklin had similarly called for a "Publick Religion" in 1749), an official "profession of faith" that consists not so much in "religious dogmas" as in "sentiments of sociability" sustained by official belief in a Supreme Being and in the rewards and retributions of an afterlife.[2] Belatedly and pathetically, Robespierre had even tried to institute such a civil religion amid the French Terror. Whatever handicaps Robespierre suffered, civil religion was something that could be engineered, providing certain conditions prevailed. It could not be simply declared by the fiat of some dictator of the hour. That would be against all the principles of good political mechanics: A free society cannot start its career by having a code arbitrarily imposed on it. America's civil religion had to begin with voluntary consent, just as the American government did. This agreement had to be secured by persuasion and education, not by force or threats. These were exactly the tools the Americans had come to rely on during the colonial period. There had been religious establishments and coercive laws, to be sure. But these had never been entirely effective even locally and had proved useless at the intercolonial level. The things that had proved most successful, locally and intercolonially, stemmed from efforts at cooperation and persuasion: founding colleges, raising militias, undertaking public-works projects, establishing networks of scientific correspondence, instigating philanthropic projects, and—above all—promoting revivals of religion. None of these things had come easily or without bickering and factionalism. Nevertheless, the Americans had learned how to live with the problems of voluntarism. The colonial experience had provided them with just the right background to make the job of creating a public spirit, a common sentiment of sociability, feasible.

We should mention one final thing that helped place the Americans in a position to guide their own political destiny. As an outgrowth of colonial circumstances, the intellectual and the public realms were never far apart; the intellectual was always involved in the common life. This meant, in Chateaubriand's terms, that liberty, daughter of enlightenment, and liberty, daughter of mores and virtue, were always very close. By most European standards, the American philosopher was never aloof from popular mores, and the people were extraordinarily enlightened. America may have been a very young republic, but its people were not naïve, unlettered innocents whose virtue was at the mercy of historical fortune. Her philosophers' activities, directed toward the building of a new society, were not—as had often been the case in the ancient world—the herald of the end of that society's innocence. Further, in spite of the heterogeneity of its population and the diversity of its beliefs, if ever a republic were in a position consciously to commit itself to a set of common principles, the United States would seem to have been that republic. Pluralism, in fact, made a common commitment possible and perhaps necessary: A diverse people, coming together to form one nation, was quite willing in the public interest to offer its allegiance to a set of general principles that seemed to transcend local and sectarian loyalties. Thus, the diversity of its population, combined with the close correspondence between its intellectual life and its common life, made it possible for America to substitute "enlightenment" for "mores," as it were, to rely more on a conscious acceptance of common guiding principles and skillful political planning than on the good habits and wholesome practices that are among the happy advantages of a nation's youth. The American Revolution had indeed inaugurated a new era, abrogating the natural laws of society, freeing at least a portion of mankind from the melancholy cycle of youth-maturity-decay that had formerly governed the life of republican liberty.

So much for the principles involved. What of the substance of the matter? From where were the elements of America's public commitment to come? Here is where the Enlightenment, joined with the principles of Protestant Christianity, comes into the picture. The ideals of the Enlightenment, modified to conform to the Christian faith and the dictates of common sense, provided the Americans with a national credo that was up-to-date, rational, and universal in its appeal. Commitment to human rights—including the rights of life, liberty, and property (as set forth in the Whig tradition)—renunciation of all "superstition," trust in the natural sciences, confidence in rational morality, belief in individual freedom balanced by a concern for public welfare, an empirical attitude toward politics that was not burdened by undue respect for custom and authority: These ingredients went into the formation of an American faith. Combined with this, always, was that unshakable American belief in the efficacy of belief—confidence, that is, in a broad cultural commitment to basic religious truths that presumably all sects share in common and that stand as the basis of public virtue. Liberty, daughter of enlightenment, was, in fact, the daughter of the Enlightenment joined in marriage with sound "Publick Religion." These parents would nurture their offspring in the nation's public school and in the church of their choice.

By the early nineteenth century the Americans had achieved a moral consensus that was to serve them well for generations. The thinking of the Enlightenment was embodied in American institutions and mores, the latter having become a matter of public interest and no longer merely a reflection of changing social circumstances. Republican liberty would thus outlive the disappearance of Jefferson's pastoral society and survive into an urban and industrial age. Yet in the very process of institutionalizing and making public property of these ideas they were compromised, amended, and obscured. Instead of a political science or a new theory of politics, America over the years gave the world a unique working example and a growing list of accomplishments. What remained of Enlightenment thinking was generalized into the public philosophy, which upheld many of the moral *principles* of the Age of Reason but retained little of its critical and experimental *method*. The method having been assimilated into our institutions, we were left with an official allegiance to high ideas that were universal but vague, inspiring but all-too-difficult to practice.

The men of the American Enlightenment dedicated themselves and their nation to a number of moral propositions that they and their countrymen failed to pursue. They committed themselves to the task of creating a society where human potential would at last be fully realized, where human rights and the dignity of all would seem like self-evident truths, and where practical liberty would be not just a happy accident of history but the result of enlightened social planning. This commitment was real and important to the men of the American Enlightenment, and it has remained important to Americans ever since. But it proved extremely difficult to translate our national commitment into effective public policy: Our enthusiasm for it was perhaps more rhetorical than experimental. If the Americans have not always lived up to their national ideals and official beliefs, however, the moral legacy of the Enlightenment is such that they have not been able to forget them either. Like God's blessing on the children of Israel, our national ideals are at once our pride and our curse.

Notes

INTRODUCTION

[1]Samuel Miller, *A Brief Retrospect of the Eighteenth Century, Containing a Sketch of the Revolution and Improvements in Science, Arts, and Literature During that Period,* two vols. (New York: T. & J. Swords, 1803), II, pp. 330-31.

[2]*Ibid.,* pp. 410-42.

[3]On the meaning of "philosophe," see Peter Gay, *The Enlightenment: An Interpretation,* two vols. (New York: Alfred A. Knopf, 1966, 1969), I, pp. 3-19.

[4]See Daniel J. Boorstin, "The Myth of an American Enlightenment," in *America and the Image of Europe: Reflections on American Thought* (New York: Meridian Books, 1960), pp. 65-78.

[5]David Hume's centrality to the Enlightenment is discussed in Alfred Cobban, *In Search of Humanity: The Role of the Enlightenment in Modern History* (New York: George Braziller, 1960), pp. 133-38; Basil Willey, *The English Moralists* (New York: W. W. Norton & Co., 1964), pp. 248-68; and Peter Gay, *The Enlightenment,* I, pp. 401-19.

[6]Howard Mumford Jones, *O Strange New World. American Culture: The Formative Years* (New York: Viking Press, 1964), p. 393. *See also* John Clive and Bernard Bailyn, "England's Cultural Provinces: Scotland and America," *William and Mary Quarterly,* 11, Ser. 3 (1954), pp. 200-13.

[7]Louis Hartz, *The Liberal Tradition in America* (New York: Harcourt, Brace and Company, 1955), pp. 3-66.

[8]John Francis McDermott, "The Enlightenment on the Mississippi Frontier, 1763-1804," *Studies on Voltaire and the Eighteenth Century,* 26 (1963), pp. 999-1018.

[9]Henry F. May, "The Problem of the American Enlightenment," *New Literary History,* 1 (1970), pp. 201-4.

Chapter 1

RELIGION AND THE EXPERIMENTAL METHOD OF REASONING

[1]On Hume's skepticism and its reception in the eighteenth century, *see* especially Richard H. Popkin, "Scepticism in the Enlightenment," *Studies on Volatire and the Eighteenth Century,* 26 (1963), pp. 1321-45.

[2]On deism the following works are of particular interest: Leslie Stephen, *History of English Thought in the Eighteenth Century,* two vols. (New York: Harcourt, Brace Jovanovich, 1962; originally published in 1876), esp. I, pp. 62-234; Norman L. Torrey, *Voltaire and the English Deists* (Hamden, Conn., Shoe String Press, 1967);

Arthur O. Lovejoy, "The Parallel of Deism and Classicism," *Essays in the History of Ideas* (New York, G. P. Putnam's, 1960; 1948), pp. 78-98; Alfred Owen Aldridge, "Shaftesbury and the Deist Manifesto," American Philosophical Society, *Transactions*, Ser. 2, XLI, Part 2 (1951), pp. 197-385; Gerald R. Cragg, *From Puritanism to the Age of Reason: A Study of Changes in Religious Thought within the Church of England, 1660-1700* (New York: Cambridge University Press, 1950); and Peter Gay, ed., *Deism: An Anthology* (New York: Van Nostrand, 1968), Introduction, pp. 9-26.

³*See* Robert H. Hurlbutt, *Hume, Newton, and the Design Argument* (Lincoln, Nebr., University of Nebraska Press, 1965).

Chapter 2
JONATHAN EDWARDS AND THE
REALITY OF THE UNSEEN

¹Richard Hofstadter, *America at 1750: A Social Portrait* (New York: Alfred A. Knopf, 1971), pp. 243-44. On the debate over the modernity of Edwards, *see* Peter Gay, *A Loss of Mastery: Puritan Historians in Colonial America* (New York: Vintage Books, 1968; 1966), pp. 88-117; Claire McGlinchee, "Jonathan Edwards and Benjamin Franklin, Antithetical Figures," *Studies on Voltaire and the Eighteenth Century*, 56 (1967), pp. 813-22; Perry Miller, *Jonathan Edwards* (New York: Meridian Books, 1959; 1949); and Vincent Tomas, "The Modernity of Jonathan Edwards," *New England Quarterly*, 25 (1952), pp. 60-84.

²Shaftesbury's ethics and aesthetics are perceptively analyzed by John Andrew Bernstein, "Beauty and the Law: Shaftesbury's Relation to Christianity and the Enlightenment," (Unpublished doctoral dissertation, Department of History, Harvard University, 1970). *See also* Roland A. Delattre, "Beauty and Theology: A Reappraisal of Jonathan Edwards," *Soundings*, 51 (1968), pp. 60-79, and his *Beauty and Sensibility in the Thought of Jonathan Edwards: An Essay in Aesthetics and Theological Ethics* (New Haven and London: Yale University Press, 1968).

Chapter 3
FROM PIETY TO MORALISM

¹William G. McLoughlin, *New England Dissent, 1630-1833: The Baptists and the Separation of Church and State,* two vols. (Cambridge, Mass.: Harvard University Press, 1971), I, pp. 330-31.

²On "supernatural rationalism," *see* Conrad Wright, *The Liberal Christians: Essays on American Unitarian History* (Boston: Beacon Press, 1970), pp. 1-21.

³Samuel Johnson's *Elementa Philosophica* is found in *Samuel Johnson. President of King's College, His Career and Writings*, Herbert W. and Carol Schneider, eds., four vols. (New York: Columbia University Press, 1929), II, pp. 257-518. On Johnson, besides Schneider's introduction to this collection, *see* Paul Kent Alkon, *Samuel Johnson and Moral Discipline* (Evanston, Ill.: Northwestern University Press, 1967); Joseph John-Michael Ellis, III, *The New England Mind in Transition: Samuel Johnson of Connecticut, 1696-1771* (New Haven and London: Yale University Press, 1973); and

Norman S. Fiering, "President Samuel Johnson and the Circle of Knowledge," *William and Mary Quarterly*, 28, Ser. 3 (1971), pp. 199-236.

⁴Fiering, *op. cit.*, p. 233. *See also* Fiering's "Moral Philosophy in America, 1650-1750, and Its British Context" (Unpublished doctoral dissertation, Department of History, Columbia University, 1969).

⁵Joseph Haroutunian, *Piety versus Moralism: The Passing of the New England Theology* (New York: Harper & Row, Inc., 1970; 1932).

⁶*See* Sydney Ahlstrom, "The Scottish Philosophy and American Theology," *Church History*, 24 (1955), pp. 257-72.

⁷On the fate of theism and of atheism in the modern world, *see* Alasdair MacIntyre and Paul Ricoeur, *The Religious Significance of Atheism* (New York and London: Columbia University Press, 1969), pp. 3-29.

⁸Morton White, *Science and Sentiment in America: Philosophical Thought from Jonathan Edwards to John Dewey* (New York: Oxford University Press, 1972).

Chapter 4
THE CIVILIZED AMERICANS

¹Louis Hartz, *et al.*, *The Founding of New Societies: Studies in the History of the United States, Latin America, South Africa, Canada, and Australia* (New York: Harcourt, Brace & World, Inc., 1964), pp. 3, 11. *See also* Richard L. Merritt, *Symbols of American Community, 1735-1775* (New Haven and London: Yale University Press, 1966), esp. pp. 171-82.

²Carl and Jessica Bridenbaugh, *Rebels and Gentlemen: Philadelphia in the Age of Franklin* (London, Oxford, New York: Oxford University Press, 1962; 1942), p. 314.

³On James Logan, *see* Frederick B. Tolles, *James Logan and the Culture of Provincial America* (Boston and Toronto: Little, Brown, & Co., 1957). On the significance of the virtuosi, *see* Walter E. Houghton, "The English Virtuoso in the Seventeenth Century," *Journal of the History of Ideas*, 3 (1942), pp. 51-73; and Richard S. Westfall, *Science and Religion in Seventeenth-Century England* (New Haven: Yale University Press, 1958).

⁴*See* Brooke Hindle, *The Pursuit of Science in Revolutionary America, 1735-1789* (Chapel Hill, N.C.: University of North Carolina Press, 1956), and Harry Woolf, *The Transits of Venus: A Study of Eighteenth Century Science* (Princeton: Princeton University Press, 1959).

⁵*See* the very readable edition of *Benjamin Franklin's Experiments*, I. Bernard Cohen, ed. (Cambridge, Mass.: Harvard University Press, 1941). *See also* William Martin Smallwood, *Natural History and the American Mind* (New York: 1941).

⁶The idea of literary culture as a "Third Realm" is developed by Lewis P. Simpson in a very helpful article, "Literary Ecumenicalism and the American Enlightenment," *The Ibero-American Enlightenment*, A. Owen Aldridge, ed. (Urbana, Chicago, London: University of Illinois Press, 1971), pp. 317-32. For James Fitzmaurice-Kelly's definition of "literature," see his article on that subject in the *Encyclopedia Britannica* (Eleventh edition, 1910).

⁷On the Americans' use of wholesomeness and naturalness in establishing their moral identity, *see* Charles L. Sanford, *The Quest for Paradise: Europe and the American*

Moral Imagination (Urbana, Ill.: University of Illinois Press, 1961), esp. pp. 114-34.

⁸A good starting-point for information on colonial American colleges is Richard Hofstadter, *Academic Freedom in the Age of the College* (New York: Columbia University Press, 1955).

⁹John A. Garraty, Peter Gay, *et al., A History of the World, II: Towards Modernity* (New York, Evanston, San Francisco, London: Harper & Row, Inc., 1972), p. 196.

¹⁰*See* Carl Bridenbaugh, *Cities in Revolt: Urban Life in America, 1743-1776* (New York: G. P. Putnam's Sons, Capricorn Books, 1955), for a survey of city life in mid-eighteenth-century America.

¹¹*See* Robert Darnton, "In Search of the Enlightenment: Recent Attempts to Create a Social History of Ideas," *Journal of Modern History*, 43 (1971), pp. 113-32.

¹²J. Hector St. John de Crèvecoeur, *Letters from an American Farmer* (New York: E. P. Dutton & Co. Inc., 1957; originally published in 1782), p. 36.

¹³On printing, education, and the expansion of literacy in colonial America, *see* Louis B. Wright, *The Cultural Life of the American Colonies, 1607-1763* (New York and Evanston: Harper & Row, Inc., 1957), pp. 98-175; Daniel J. Boorstin, *The Americans, I: The Colonial Experience* (New York: Random House, 1958), pp. 171-88, 271-90, 319-40; and especially Lawrence A. Cremin, *American Education: The Colonial Experience, 1607-1783* (New York, Evanston, London: Harper & Row, 1970), pp. 365-78, 544-51. But for a contrary view, *see* Kenneth A. Lockridge, *Literacy in Colonial New England: An Enquiry into the Social Context of Literacy in the Early Modern West* (New York: W. W. Norton & Co., 1974). On the growth of a reading public in England and America and the impact of ideas on it, *see* A. S. Collins, "The Growth of the Reading Public During the Eighteenth Century," *Review of English Studies*, 2 (1926), pp. 284-94, 428-38; Arnold Hauser, *The Social History of Art*, four vols.; (New York: Vintage Books, n.d.), III, pp. 38-84; Chester E. Jorgenson, "The New Science in the Almanacs of Ames and Franklin," *New England Quarterly*, 8 (1935), pp. 55-61; Paul Kaufman, *The Community Library: A Chapter in English Social History*, American Philosophical Society, *Transactions*, 57, Ser. 2 (1967); Calhoun Winton, "Addison and Steele in the English Enlightenment," *Studies on Voltaire and the Eighteenth Century*, 27 (1963), pp. 1901-18; J. H. Plumb, "Reason and Unreason in the Eighteenth Century: The English Experience," *Aspects of Eighteenth-Century England*, J. H. Plumb and Vinton A. Dearing, eds. (Los Angeles: William Andrews Clark Memorial Library, 1971), pp. 3-26.

Chapter 5
BENJAMIN FRANKLIN AND THE ART OF VIRTUE

¹Crane Brinton, ed., *The Portable Age of Reason Reader* (New York: Viking Press, 1956), Introduction, p. 17.

²Robert E. Spiller, "Franklin and the Art of Being Human," American Philosophical Society, *Proceedings*, 100 (1956), p. 313.

³Peter Laslett, *The World We Have Lost: England before the Industrial Age* (New York: Charles Scribner's Sons, 1965), esp. pp. 22-52. *See also* Ferdinand Tönnies, *Community and Society*, trans. by Charles P. Loomis (East Lansing, Mich.: Michigan State University Press, 1957; first German edition, 1887), and Philippe Ariès, *Centuries of*

Childhood: A Social History of Family Life, trans. by Robert Baldick (New York: Alfred A. Knopf, 1962), pp. 365-407.

[4]*See* David Levin, "The Autobiography of Benjamin Franklin: The Puritan Experimenter in Life and Art," *Yale Review,* 53 (1963), pp. 258-75.

[5]D. H. Lawrence made his classic criticism of Franklin in his *Studies of Classic American Literature* (New York: Viking Press, 1923), pp. 13-31.

[6]Gladys E. Meyer, *Free Trade in Ideas: Aspects of American Liberalism Illustrated in Franklin's Philadelphia Career* (Morningside Heights, N. Y.: King's Crown Press, 1941), p. 75.

[7]Richard L. Bushman, "On the Uses of Psychology: Conflict and Conciliation in Benjamin Franklin," *History and Theory,* 5 (1966), pp. 225-40.

[8]Alfred North Whitehead, *Adventures of Ideas* (New York: Free Press, 1961; 1933), pp. 69-86.

[9]Bruce Ingham Granger, *Benjamin Franklin: An American Man of Letters* (Ithaca, N. Y.: Cornell University Press, 1964), pp. 19-50.

[10]Paul W. Conner, *Poor Richard's Politicks: Benjamin Franklin and His New American Order* (London, Oxford, New York: Oxford University Press, 1965), pp. 121-48.

[11]*See* Alfred Owen Aldridge, *Benjamin Franklin and Nature's God* (Durham, N. C.: Duke University Press, 1967), for a full discussion of Franklin's religious views.

[12]Peter Gay, *The Party of Humanity: Essays in the French Enlightenment* (New York: Alfred A. Knopf, 1964), pp. 118-26.

Chapter 6
THE ETHICS OF BELIEF AND THE CONDUCT OF THE MIND

[1]For Whitehead's criticism of the philosophes, *see* his *Science and the Modern World* (New York: Free Press, 1967; 1925), pp. 57-74.

[2]The most useful introduction to eighteenth-century British moral philosophy remains L. A. Selby-Bigge, *British Moralists, Being Selections from Writers Principally of the Eighteenth Century,* two vols. (Oxford: Oxford University Press, 1897).

[3]On Joseph Addison and his role as a moralist, *see* Basil Willey, *The English Moralists* (New York: W. W. Norton & Co., 1964), pp. 233-47, and Calhoun Winton, "Addison and Steele in the English Enlightenment," *Studies on Voltaire and the Eighteenth Century,* 27 (1963), pp. 1901-18.

[4]Peter Gay, *The Party of Humanity: Essays in the French Enlightenment* (New York: Alfred A. Knopf, 1964), p. 130.

[5]Whitehead, *op cit.,* p. 59.

Chapter 7
SCIENCE, RHETORIC, AND REVOLUTION

[1]*See* particularly the second volume of Peter Gay, *The Enlightenment: An Interpretation,* two vols. (New York: Alfred A. Knopf, 1966, 1969).

[2]For historical background on the ideas of natural right, natural law, and the social contract, *see* Otto Gierke, *Natural Law and the Theory of Society,* trans. by Ernest Barker

(Boston: Beacon Press, 1957; 1934); Leo Strauss, *Natural Right and History* (Chicago: University of Chicago Press, 1953); and Ernest Barker, *Social Contract: Essays by Locke, Hume, and Rousseau* (New York: Oxford University Press, 1962), Introduction, pp. vii-xliv.

[3] *See* Paul Merrill Spurlin, *Rousseau in America, 1760-1809* (University, Ala.: University of Alabama Press, 1969); and John Dunn, "The Politics of Locke in England and America in the Eighteenth Century" in John W. Yolton, ed., *John Locke: Problems and Perspectives. A Collection of New Essays* (Cambridge: Cambridge University Press, 1969), pp. 45-80.

[4] Bernard Bailyn, "Political Experience and Enlightenment Ideas in Eighteenth-Century America," *American Historical Review*, 67 (1962), pp. 339-51.

[5] *See* Bernard Bailyn, *The Ideological Origins of the American Revolution* (Cambridge, Mass.: Harvard University Press, 1967), pp. 22-54. The thinking of England's "real Whigs" is analyzed by Caroline Robbins, *Eighteenth Century Commonwealthmen* (Cambridge, Mass.: Harvard University Press, 1959). *See also* her article, "Algernon Sidney's *Discourses Concerning Government:* Textbook of Revolution," *William and Mary Quarterly*, 4, Ser. 3 (1947), pp. 267-96.

[6] Perry Miller, "From Covenant to Revival," in James Ward Smith and A. Leland Jamison, eds., *The Shaping of American Religion* (Princeton, N. J.: Princeton University Press, 1961), pp. 322-68. *See also* Alan Heimert, *Religion and the American Mind: From the Great Awakening to the Revolution* (Cambridge, Mass.: Harvard University Press, 1961), pp. 294-350.

[7] Jack P. Greene, "The American Colonies During the First Half of the Eighteenth Century," review of Richard Hofstadter, *America at 1750*, in *Reviews in American History*, 1 (1973), p. 73.

[8] Richard Hofstadter, *America at 1750: A Social Portrait* (New York: Alfred A. Knopf, 1971), p. 193.

[9] Moses Coit Tyler, *The Literary History of the American Revolution, 1763-1783*, two vols. (New York and London: G. P. Putnam's Sons, 1897), Vol. I, p. 8.

Chapter 8

THOMAS JEFFERSON AND THE RHETORIC OF REPUBLICANISM

[1] Adrienne Koch, ed., *The American Enlightenment: The Shaping of the American Experiment and a Free Society* (New York: George Braziller, 1965), Introduction, p. 34.

[2] Karl Lehmann, *Thomas Jefferson: American Humanist* (Chicago and London: University of Chicago Press, 1965; 1947), p. 13.

[3] Richard Hofstadter, *America at 1750: A Social Portrait* (New York: Alfred A. Knopf, 1971), pp. 138-139.

[4] Quoted in Charles S. Sydnor, "The Southerner and the Laws," *Journal of Southern History*, 6 (1940), p. 19.

[5] *See* Charles S. Sydnor, *American Revolutionaries in the Making: Political Practices in Washington's Virginia* (New York: Free Press, 1965; 1957); and Clement Eaton, *Freedom of Thought in the Old South* (Durham, N. C.: Duke University Press, 1940), pp. 3-31.

[6] Alan Gowans, *Images of American Living: Four Centuries of Architecture and*

Furniture as Cultural Expression (New York and Philadelphia: J. P. Lippincott & Co., 1964), pp. 243-54. *See also* William Alexander Lambeth and Warren H. Manning, *Thomas Jefferson as an Architect and a Designer of Landscapes* (Boston and New York: Houghton Mifflin Co., 1913); I. T. Frary, *Thomas Jefferson, Architect and Builder* (Richmond: Garrett & Massie, 1939); Louis Mumford, *The South in Architecture* (New York: Harcourt, Brace & Co., 1941), pp. 43-78; and Desmond Guinness and Julius Trousdale Sadler, Jr., *Mr. Jefferson, Architect* (New York: Viking Press, 1973).

[7] Winthrop D. Jordan, *White over Black: American Attitudes toward the Negro, 1550-1812* (Baltimore: Johns Hopkins Press, 1969; 1968), p. 432.

[8] *See* Lawrence H. Leder, *Liberty and Authority: Early American Political Ideology, 1689-1764* (Chicago: Quadrangle Press, 1968), pp. 19-36.

[9] For example, *see* Daniel J. Boorstin, *The Lost World of Thomas Jefferson* (Boston: Beacon Press, 1960; 1948), pp. 194-204.

[10] James Truslow Adams, Introduction to *The Education of Henry Adams* (New York: Modern Library, 1931) p. ix.

[11] Van Wyck Brooks, *America's Coming-of-Age* (New York: Doubleday & Co., Anchor Books, 1958; 1915), p. 3.

[12] William W. Freehling, "The Founding Fathers and Slavery," *American Historical Review*, 77 (1972), pp. 81-93.

[13] *See* Richard Chase, *The Democratic Vista: A Dialogue on Life and Letters in Contemporary America* (New York: Doubleday & Co., 1958), pp. 120-166.

Chapter 9
JOHN ADAMS AND THE SCENERY OF POLITICS

[1] John R. Howe's *The Changing Political Thought of John Adams* (Princeton, N.J. Princeton University Press; 1966), is an extensive, illuminating treatment of a fascinating subject. Considerably less sympathetic is Edward Handler's *America and Europe in the Political Thought of John Adams* (Cambridge, Mass.: Harvard University Press, 1964), which takes issue with those who consider Adams a great realist and a true conservative. For perceptive shorter discussions of Adams, *see,* particularly, Paul K. Conkin, *Puritans and Pragmatists* (New York and Toronto: Dodd, Mead & Co., 1968), pp. 109-148, and Gordon S. Wood, *The Creation of the American Republic, 1776-1787* (Chapel Hill, N.C.: University of North Carolina Press, 1969), pp. 567-91.

[2] Adams' alert, passionate, often acid marginal comments in his personal copies of the works of some of the leading European *philosophes* are extensively excerpted and discussed by Zoltan Haraszti in *John Adams and the Prophets of Progress* (Cambridge, Mass.: Harvard University Press, 1952).

[3] For a penetrating comment on Adams' *Discourses on Davila* and the view of human nature set forth therein, *see* Arthur O. Lovejoy, *Reflections on Human Nature* (Baltimore: Johns Hopkins Press, 1961), pp. 197-208.

[4] *See* Chauncey Brewster Tinker, *The Salon and English Letters: Chapters on the Interrelation of Literature and Society in the Age of Johnson* (New York: Macmillan, 1915), for a thoughtful discussion of diary keeping, intimate correspondence, intimate biography, and similar developments in the eighteenth century.

[5] Isabel F. Knight, *The Geometric Spirit: The Abbé de Condillac and the French*

Enlightenment (New Haven and London: Yale University Press, 1968), esp. pp. 109-43, 297-99.

Chapter 10
POLITICAL MECHANICS AND THE NEW CONSCIOUSNESS

¹On the changing view of history in the eighteenth century, *see* particularly Stow Persons, "The Cyclical Theory of History in Eighteenth Century America," *American Quarterly*, 6 (1954), pp. 147-63; Alan Heimert, *Religion and the American Mind: From the Great Awakening to the Revolution* (Cambridge, Mass.: Harvard University Press, 1966), pp. 59-94; Hugh Trevor-Roper, "The Historical Philosophy of the Enlightenment," *Studies on Voltaire and the Eighteenth Century*, 27 (1963), pp. 1667-87; and J. A. Black, *The Art of History: A Study of Four Great Historians of the Eighteenth Century* (London: Methuen & Co. Ltd., 1926).

²Peter Gay, "The Enlightenment [in America]," in C. Vann Woodward, ed., *The Comparative Approach to American History* (New York and London: Basic Books, Inc., 1968), p. 38.

³Hannah Arendt, *On Revolution* (New York: Viking Press, 1963), pp. 139-78.

⁴Marshall Smelser, "The Federalist Era as an Age of Passion," *American Quarterly*, 10 (1958), pp. 391-419.

⁵Robert Paul Wolff, "Beyond Tolerance," *A Critique of Pure Tolerance* (Boston: Beacon Press, 1965), p. 21.

⁶*See* James P. Scanlon, "*The Federalist* and Human Nature," *Review of Politics*, 21 (1959), pp. 657-77.

⁷Erich Fromm, *Man for Himself: An Inquiry into the Psychology of Ethics* (Greenwich, Conn.: Fawcett Publications, 1970; 1947), pp. 124-45.

⁸Bernard Bailyn, "Political Experience and Enlightenment Ideas in Eighteenth-Century America," *American Historical Review*, 67 (1962), esp. pp. 344-49.

⁹R. R. Palmer, "A Neglected Work: Otto Vossler on Jefferson and the Revolutionary Era," *William and Mary Quarterly*, 12, Ser. 3 (1955), p. 466.

¹⁰*See* Durand Echeverria, *Mirage in the West: A History of the French Image of American Society to 1815* (Princeton, N. J.: Princeton University Press, 1957), pp. 116-74.

¹¹Gordon Wood, "Republicanism as a Revolutionary Ideology" (1967), in John R. Howe, Jr., ed., *The Role of Ideology in the American Revolution* (New York: Holt, Rinehart, & Winston, 1970), pp. 83-91.

¹²On anxiety, *see* Paul Tillich, *The Courage to Be* (New Haven and London: Harvard University Press, 1952), pp. 32-63.

Chapter 11
THE CRITICAL PERIOD IN AMERICAN INTELLECTUAL HISTORY

¹G. Adolf Koch, *The Religion of the American Enlightenment* (New York: Thomas Y. Crowell Co., 1968; 1933). *See also* Herbert M. Moreis, *Deism in Eighteenth Century America* (New York: Columbia University Press, 1934).

²Martin E. Marty, *The Infidel: Freethought and American Religion* (Cleveland and New York: World Publishing Co., 1961), p. 19.

³Lyman Beecher, *Lectures on Political Atheism and Kindred Subjects,* in *Beecher's Works,* three vols. (Boston and Cleveland: John P. Jewett & Co., 1852), I, esp. pp. 91-139.

⁴Dixon Ryan Fox, "The Protestant Counter-Reformation in America," *New York History,* 16 (1935), pp. 19-35. *See also* Evarts B. Greene, "A Puritan Counter-Reformation," American Antiquarian Society, *Proceedings,* 42, Ser. 2 (1932), pp. 17-46, and Charles I. Foster, *An Errand of Mercy: The Evangelical United Front, 1790-1870* (Chapel Hill, N. C.: University of North Carolina Press, 1960).

⁵Victor Cousin, *Lectures on the True, the Beautiful, and the Good,* trans. by O. W. Wright (New York: D. Appleton & Co., 1854), p. 31.

⁶Richard Hofstadter, *Anti-Intellectualism in American Life* (New York: Vintage Books, 1966; 1962), pp. 145-51. The Dennie quotation is found on p. 149.

⁷Sidney E. Mead, *The Lively Experiment: The Shaping of Christianity in America* (New York, Evanston, London: Harper & Row, 1963), pp. 38-54.

Chapter 12
JOHN WITHERSPOON AND THE
EDUCATION OF THE PUBLIC CONSCIENCE

¹Gordon Wood, ed., *The Rising Glory of America, 1760-1820* (New York: George Braziller, 1971), Introduction, pp. 5-7.

²On the literary legacy of Federalism, *see* Lewis P. Simpson, "Federalism and the Crisis of Literary Order," *American Literature,* 32 (1960), pp. 253-66; Allen Guttmann, *The Conservative Tradition in America* (New York: Oxford University Press, 1967); William Charvat, *The Origins of American Critical Thought, 1810-1835* (Philadelphia: University of Pennsylvania Press, 1936); and Marius Bewley, *The Eccentric Design: Form in the Classic American Novel* (New York: Columbia University Press, 1963), pp. 303-10.

³*See* George Reuben Metcalf, "American Religious Philosophy and the Pastoral Letters of the House of Bishops," *Historical Magazine of the Protestant Episcopal Church,* 27 (1958), pp. 8-84.

⁴Stow Persons, *American Minds: A History of Ideas* (New York: Henry Holt & Co., 1958), pp. 189-94.

⁵Herbert W. Schneider, *A History of American Philosophy* (New York: Columbia University Press, 1946), p. 246; Perry Miller, ed., *American Thought: Civil War to World War I* (New York: Holt, Rinehart, & Winston, 1964), Introduction (1954), p. ix. On the influence of Scottish philosophy in various departments of American thought, *see* Sydney Ahlstrom, "The Scottish Philosophy and American Theology," *Church History,* 24 (1955), pp. 257-72; William Charvat, *op. cit.,* pp. 27-58; Terence Martin, *The Instructed Vision: Scottish Common Sense Philosophy and the Origins of American Fiction* (Bloomington, Ind.: University of Indiana Press, 1961); I. Woodbridge Riley, *American Philosophy, the Early Schools* (New York: Russell & Russell, 1907), pp., 475-563; Douglas Sloan, *The Scottish Enlightenment and the American College Ideal* (New York: Teachers College Press, Columbia University, 1971).

⁶On the importance of education in the early republic, *see especially* Rush Welter,

Popular Education and Democratic Thought in America (New York and London: Columbia University Press, 1962), pp. 3-137.

Chapter 13
WILLIAM ELLERY CHANNING AND THE
INWARD ENLIGHTENMENT

[1]Alexis de Tocqueville, *Democracy in America*, J. P. Mayer, ed., trans. by George Lawrence (Garden City, N. Y.: Anchor Books, 1969; original French edition, two vols., 1835, 1840), p. 12.

[2]*See* Warner Berthoff, "Renan on W. E. Channing and American Unitarianism," *New England Quarterly*, 35 (1962), pp. 71-92. For more information on Channing and his Unitarian background, *see* David P. Edgell, *William Ellery Channing: An Intellectual Portrait* (Boston: Beacon Press, 1955), pp. 56-112; Conrad Wright, *The Liberal Christians: Essays on American Unitarianism* (Boston: Beacon Press, 1970), pp. 22-40; and Daniel Walker Howe, *The Unitarian Conscience: Harvard Moral Philosophy, 1805-1861* (Cambridge, Mass.: Harvard University Press, 1970). On Channing's influence and appeal in the nineteenth century, *see* D. H. Meyer, "The Saint as Hero: William Ellery Channing and the Nineteenth-Century Mind," in Ian M. G. Quimby, ed., *Winterthur Portfolio* (Charlottesville: University of Virginia Press, 1973), VIII, pp. 171-85.

[3]Charles Sanders Peirce, "The Fixation of Belief," *Popular Science Monthly*, 12 (1877), pp. 1-15.

[4]The impact of democracy on American philosophical thought is discussed by Morton White, *Science and Sentiment in America: Philosophical Thought from Jonathan Edwards to John Dewey* (New York: Oxford University Press, 1972), esp. pp. 290-310. *See also* the perceptive review of this work by David A. Hollinger, "The Enemy Within," *Reviews in American History*, 1 (1973), pp. 589-94.

Chapter 14
THE AMERICAN ACHIEVEMENT

[1]François René de Chateaubriand, *Voyages en Amérique et Italie*, two vols. (Paris: Pourrat Frères, 1837), II, pp. 117-20.

[2]Jean-Jacques Rousseau, *The Social Contract*, trans. by Maurice Cranston (Baltimore: Penguin Books, 1968; 1762), Chap. 8.

SELECTED BIBLIOGRAPHY

INTRODUCTION

Primary Works

BERLIN, ISAIAH, ed., *The Age of Enlightenment.* New York: New American Library, Mentor Books, 1956.

BRINTON, CRANE, ed., *The Portable Age of Reason Reader.* New York: Viking Press, 1956.

CAPALDI, NICHOLAS, ed., *The Enlightenment: The Proper Study of Mankind.* New York: G. P. Putnam's Sons, Capricorn Books, 1967.

CROCKER, LESTER G., ed., *The Age of Enlightenment.* New York, Evanston, London: Harper & Row, Inc., 1969.

KOCH, ADRIENNE, ed., *The American Enlightenment.* New York: George Braziller, 1965.

OSTRANDER, GILMAN M., ed., *The American Enlightenment.* University City, Missouri: Marston Press, 1970.

Secondary Works

ADAMS, JAMES TRUSLOW, *Provincial Society, 1690-1763.* New York: Macmillan, 1927.

BECK, ROBERT W., "The Philosophical Concept of Enlightenment" in A. Owen Aldridge, ed., *The Ibero-American Enlightenment,* pp. 58-70. Urbana, Chicago, London: University of Illinois Press, 1971.

BECKER, CARL L., *The Heavenly City of the Eighteenth-Century Philosophers.* New Haven: Yale University Press, 1932.

BLAU, JOSEPH L., *Men and Movements in American Philosophy,* Chap. 2. New York: Prentice-Hall, Inc., 1952.

BOAS, GEORGE, "In Search of the Age of Reason" in Earl R. Wasserman, ed., *Aspects of the Eighteenth Century,* pp. 1-19. Baltimore: Johns Hopkins Press, 1965.

227

BOORSTIN, DANIEL J., *The Americans, I: The Colonial Experience.* New York: Random House, 1958.

CASSIRER, ERNST, *The Philosophy of the Enlightenment,* trans. by F. C. A. Koelln and J. P. Pettegrove. Boston: Beacon Press, 1951; 1932.

CLIVE, JOHN and BAILYN, BERNARD, "England's Cultural Provinces: Scotland and America," *William and Mary Quarterly,* 11, Ser. 3 (1954), pp. 200-213.

COBBAN, ALFRED, *In Search of Humanity: The Role of the Enlightenment in Modern History.* New York: George Braziller, 1960.

CROCKER, LESTER G., *An Age of Crisis: Man and World in Eighteenth Century French Thought.* Baltimore: Johns Hopkins Press, 1959.

————, *Nature and Culture: Ethical Thought in the French Enlightenment.* Baltimore: Johns Hopkins Press, 1965.

GAY, PETER, *The Enlightenment: An Interpretation.* Two volumes; New York: Alfred A. Knopf, 1966, 1969.

HAMPSON, NORMAN, *A Cultural History of the Enlightenment.* New York: Pantheon Press, 1968.

HAZARD, PAUL, *European Thought in the Eighteenth Century: From Montesquieu to Lessing.* New York and Cleveland: Meridian Books, 1963; 1946.

KOCH, ADRIENNE, "Pragmatic Wisdom and the American Enlightenment," *William and Mary Quarterly,* 18, Ser. 3 (1961), pp. 313-19.

KRAUS, MICHAEL, *The Atlantic Civilization: Eighteenth-Century Origins.* Ithaca, N. Y.: Cornell University Press, 1949.

LOVEJOY, ARTHUR O., *The Great Chain of Being: A Study of the History of an Idea,* pp. 183-287. Cambridge, Mass.: Harvard University Press, 1936.

MAY, HENRY F., "The Problem of the American Enlightenment," *New Literary History,* 1 (1970), pp. 201-14.

NIKLAUS, ROBERT, "The Age of Enlightenment," in W. H. Barber, *et al.,* eds., *The Age of Enlightenment: Studies Presented to Theodore Besterman,* pp. 395-412. London and Edinburgh: Oliver & Boyd, 1967.

PARRINGTON, VERNON LOUIS, *Main Currents in American Thought, I: The Colonial Mind, 1620-1800.* New York: Harcourt, Brace, & Co., 1927.

PERSONS, STOW, *American Minds: A History of Ideas,* pp. 71-83. New York: Henry Holt & Co., 1958.

PLUMB, J. H., "Reason and Unreason in the Eighteenth Century: The English Experience," in J. H. Plumb and Vinton A. Dearing, eds., *Some Aspects of Eighteenth-Century England,* pp. 3-26. Los Angeles: William Andrews Clark Memorial Library, 1971.

RILEY, I. WOODBRIDGE, *American Philosophy: The Early Schools.* New York: Russell & Russell, Inc., 1907.

SCHNEIDER, HERBERT W., *A History of American Philosophy,* pp. 35-85. New York: Columbia University Press, 1946.

WILLEY, BASIL, *The Eighteenth Century Background: Studies on the Idea of Nature in the Thought of the Period.* London: Chatts & Windus, Ltd., 1940.

WRIGHT, LOUIS B., *The Cultural Life of the American Colonies.* New York and Evanston: Harper & Row, Inc., 1957.

PART I
EXPERIMENTAL RELIGION

Primary Works

BACON, FRANCIS, *Selected Writings,* Hugh G. Dick, ed. New York: Modern Library, 1955.

CHAUNCY, CHARLES, *Enthusiasm Described and Caution'd against.* Boston: J. Draper, 1742.

———, *Seasonable Thoughts on the State of Religion in New England.* Boston: Printed by Rogers & Fowle for Samuel Eliot of Cornhill, 1743.

COOPER, ANTHONY ASHLEY, Third Earl of Shaftesbury, *Characteristics of Men, Manners, Opinions, Times* (1711), John M. Robertson, ed. Indianapolis and New York: Bobbs-Merrill, Inc., 1964.

EDWARDS, JONATHAN, *"The Mind" of Jonathan Edwards: A Reconstructed Text,* Leon Howard, ed. Berkeley and Los Angeles: University of California Press, 1963.

———, *The Nature of True Virtue* (1765). Ann Arbor: University of Michigan Press, 1960.

———, *Representative Selections,* Clarence H. Faust and Thomas H. Johnson, eds. New York: Hill & Wang, 1962; 1935.

———, *The Works of Jonathan Edwards,* John E. Smith, ed. New Haven and London: Yale University Press, 1957-

HOPKINS, SAMUEL, *An Inquiry into the Nature of True Holiness* (1773). In *The Works of Samuel Hopkins, D.D.* Three volumes; Boston: Doctrinal Tracts & Book Society, 1852. III.

HUME, DAVID, *Dialogues Concerning Natural Religion,* Henry D. Aiken, ed. New York: Hafner Publishing Co., 1948; originally published, 1779.

———, *A Treatise of Human Nature: Being an Attempt to Introduce the Experimental Method of Reasoning into Moral Subjects* (1739), L. A. Selby-Bigge, ed. Oxford: Oxford University Press, 1896.

LOCKE, JOHN, *An Essay Concerning Human Understanding* (1690), Alexander Campbell Fraser, ed. Two volumes; New York: Dover Publications, Inc., 1959; 1894.

———, *On the Reasonableness of Christianity as Delivered in the Scriptures,*

George W. Ewing, ed. Chicago: Henry Regnery Company, 1965; first published, 1695.

MAYHEW, JONATHAN, *Seven Sermons . . . Preached at a Lecture in the West Meeting-House in Boston . . . 1748*. London: John Noon, 1750.

Secondary Works

BUSHMAN, RICHARD L., *From Puritan to Yankee: Character and the Social Order in Connecticut, 1690-1765*. Cambridge, Mass.: Harvard University Press, 1967.

———, "Jonathan Edwards as Great Man: Identity, Conversion, and Leadership in the Great Awakening," *Soundings*, 52 (1969), pp. 15-46.

CARSE, JAMES, *Jonathan Edwards and the Visibility of God*. New York: Charles Scribner's Sons, 1967.

CHERRY, CONRAD, *The Theology of Jonathan Edwards: A Reappraisal*. New York: Doubleday, Anchor Books, 1966.

DELATTRE, ROLAND, *Beauty and Sensibility in the Thought of Jonathon Edwards: An Essay in Aesthetics and Theological Ethics*. New Haven and London: Yale University Press, 1968.

FLEW, ANTHONY, *Hume's Philosophy of Belief*. London: Oxford University Press, 1961.

FOSTER, FRANK HUGH, *A Genetic History of the New England Theology*. Chicago: University of Chicago Press, 1907.

GAUSTAD, EDWIN SCOTT, *The Great Awakening in New England*. Chicago: Quadrangle Books, 1957.

HAROUTUNIAN, JOSEPH, *Piety versus Moralism: The Passing of the New England Theology*. New York: Harper & Row, Inc., 1970; 1932.

HEIMERT, ALAN, *Religion and the American Mind: From the Great Awakening to the Revolution*. Cambridge, Mass.: Harvard University Press, 1966.

HOWELL, SAMUEL WILBUR, *Eighteenth-Century British Logic*. Princeton: Princeton University Press, 1971.

MCLOUGHLIN, WILLIAM G., *New England Dissent; 1630-1833: The Baptists and the Separation of Church and State*. Two volumes; Cambridge, Mass.: Harvard University Press, 1971.

MILLER, PERRY, *Jonathan Edwards*. New York: Meridian Books, 1959; 1949.

SHEA, DANIEL B., JR., *Spiritual Autobiography in Early America*, pp. 187-208. Princeton: Princeton University Press, 1968.

SMITH, JOHN E., *Introduction to Jonathan Edwards, A Treatise Concerning Religious Affections* (1746). *The Works of Jonathan Edwards*, III, pp. 1-89. New Haven and London: Yale University Press, 1956.

SMITH, NORMAN KEMP, *The Philosophy of David Hume*. London: Macmillan, 1941.

WINSLOW, OLA ELIZABETH, *Jonathan Edwards, 1703-1758: A Biography*. New York: Macmillan, 1940.

WRIGHT, CONRAD, *The Beginnings of Unitarianism in America*. Boston: Beacon Press, 1955.

YOLTON, JOHN W., ed., *John Locke: Problems and Perspectives. A Collection of New Essays*. Cambridge: Cambridge University Press, 1969.

PART II
EXPERIMENTAL MORALITY

Primary Works

DEMOS, JOHN, ed., *Remarkable Providences, 1600-1760*. New York: George Braziller, 1972.

FRANKLIN, BENJAMIN, *A Benjamin Franklin Reader*, Nathan G. Goodman, ed. New York: Thomas Y. Crowell Company, 1971; 1945.

———, *Benjamin Franklin: Representative Selections*, Chester E. Jorgenson and Frank Luther Mott, eds. New York: Hill & Wang, 1962; 1936.

———, *The Papers of Benjamin Franklin*, Leonard W. Labere, ed. New Haven and London: Yale University Press, 1959-

———, *The Writings of Benjamin Franklin*, Albert Henry Smyth, ed. Ten volumes; New York and London, Macmillan, 1907.

GAY, PETER, ed., *Deism: An Anthology*. Princeton, N. J.: Princeton University Press, 1968.

HUME, DAVID, *Dialogues Concerning Natural Religion*, Henry D. Aiken, ed. New York: Hafner Publishing Co., 1948; originally published, 1779.

HUTCHESON, FRANCIS, *Essay on the Nature and Conduct of the Passions with Illustrations upon the Moral Sense*. New York: Garland Publications, 1971; 1725.

———, *Inquiry into the Original of Our Ideas of Beauty and Virtue*. New York: Garland Publications, 1971; 1725.

LOCKE, JOHN, *Of the Conduct of the Understanding*, Francis W. Garforth, ed. New York: Teachers College Press, Columbia University, 1966; originally published in 1706.

———, *On the Reasonableness of Christianity as Delivered in the Scriptures*, George W. Ewing, ed. Chicago: Henry Regnery Company, 1965; first published, 1695.

———, *Some Thoughts Concerning Education*, Francis W. Garforth, ed.

Woodbury, N. Y.: Barron's Educational Series, Inc., 1964; originally published, 1693.

SELBY-BIGGE, L. A., ed., *British Moralists: Being Selections from Writers Principally of the Eighteenth Century.* Two volumes in one; Indianapolis and New York: Bobbs-Merrill Co., Inc., 1964; originally published, 1897.

Secondary Works

ALDRIDGE, ALFRED OWEN, *Benjamin Franklin and Nature's God.* Durham, N.C.: Duke University Press, 1967.

———, "Benjamin Franklin and the *Philosophes*," *Studies on Voltaire and the Eighteenth Century*, Vol. 24 (1963), pp. 43-65.

———. *Benjamin Franklin: Philosopher and Man.* Philadelphia and New York: J. B. Lippincott Co., 1956.

———, *Franklin and His French Contemporaries.* New York: New York University Press, 1957.

BELJAME, ALEXANDRE, *Men of Letters and the English Public in the Eighteenth Century, 1660-1744*, ed. Bonamy Dobrée, trans. E. O. Lorimore. London: Kegan Paul, Trench, Trubner & Co., Ltd., 1948; original French edition, 1881.

BRIDENBAUGH, CARL, *Cities in Revolt: Urban Life in America, 1743-1776.* New York: G. P. Putnam's Sons, Capricorn Books, 1964; 1955.

BRIDENBAUGH, CARL and JESSICA, *Rebels and Gentlemen: Philadelphia in the Age of Franklin.* London, Oxford, New York: Oxford University Press, 1962; 1942.

COHEN, BERNARD I., *Benjamin Franklin: His Contribution to the American Tradition.* Indianapolis and New York: Viking Press, 1953.

———, *Franklin and Newton: An Inquiry into Speculative Newtonian Experimental Science and Franklin's Work in Electricity as an Example Thereof.* Philadelphia: American Philosophical Society, 1956.

CONKIN, PAUL K., "Benjamin Franklin: Science and Morals" in *Puritans and Pragmatists: Eight Eminent American Thinkers*, pp. 73-108. New York and Toronto: Dodd, Mead & Co., 1968.

CONNER, PAUL W., *Poor Richard's Politicks: Benjamin Franklin and His New American Order.* London, Oxford, New York: Oxford University Press, 1965.

CREMIN, LAWRENCE A., *American Education: The Colonial Experience, 1607-1783.* New York, Evanston, London: Harper & Row, Inc., 1970.

FAY, BERNARD, *Franklin, the Apostle of Modern Times.* Boston: Little, Brown & Co., 1929.

GRANGER, BRUCE INGHAM, *Benjamin Franklin: An American Man of Letters.* Ithaca, New York: Cornell University Press, 1964.

HANS, NICOLAS, *New Trends in Education in the Eighteenth Century.* London: Routledge & Kegan Paul, Ltd., 1951.

———, "UNESCO of the Eighteenth Century: *La Loge des Neuf Soeurs* and Its Venerable Master, Benjamin Franklin," American Philosophical Society, *Proceedings,* 97 (1953), pp. 513-24.

HOFSTADTER, RICHARD, *America at 1750: A Social Portrait.* New York: Alfred A. Knopf, 1971.

HURLBUTT, ROBERT H., *Hume, Newton, and the Design Argument.* Lincoln, Nebr.: University of Nebraska Press, 1965.

LARRABEE, HAROLD A., "Poor Richard in an Age of Plenty," *Harper's Magazine.* 212 (1956), pp. 64-68.

LAWRENCE, D. H., *Studies in Classic American Literature,* pp. 13-31. New York: Viking Press, 1923.

LEVIN, DAVID, "The Autobiography of Benjamin Franklin: Puritan Experimenter in Life and Art," *Yale Review,* 53 (1963), pp. 258-75.

LUCAS, F. L., *The Art of Living: Four Eighteenth-Century Minds.* London: Cassell & Co., 1959.

MEYER, GLADYS E., *Free Trade in Ideas: Aspects of American Liberalism Illustrated in Franklin's Philadelphia Career.* Morningside Heights, N. Y.: King's Crown Press, 1941.

NYE, RUSSEL B., *American Literary History, 1607-1830.* New York: Alfred A. Knopf, 1970.

SPILLER, ROBERT E., "Benjamin Franklin on the Art of Being Human," American Philosophical Society, *Proceedings,* 100 (1956), pp. 304-15.

STEPHEN, LESLIE, *History of English Thought in the Eighteenth Century.* Two volumes. New York and Burlingame: Harcourt, Brace & World, Inc., 1962; first published 1878.

STOURZH, GERALD, "Reason and Power in Benjamin Franklin's Political Thought," *American Political Science Review,* 47 (1953), pp. 1092-1115.

VAN DOREN, CARL, *Benjamin Franklin.* New York: Viking Press, 1938.

VOITLE, ROBERT, "The Reason of the Enlightenment," *Studies on Voltaire and the Eighteenth Century,"* 27 (1963), pp. 1735-74.

WESTFALL, RICHARD, *Science and Religion in Seventeenth-Century England.* New Haven: Yale University Press, 1958.

PART III
EXPERIMENTAL POLITICS

Primary Works

ADAMS, JOHN, *Diary and Autobiography of John Adams*, L. H. Butterfield, ed. Four volumes; Cambridge, Mass.: Harvard University Press, 1961.

————, *The Political Writings of John Adams: Representative Selections*, George A. Peek, Jr., ed. Indianapolis and New York: Bobbs-Merrill Co., Inc., 1954.

————, *The Works of John Adams*, Charles Francis Adams, ed. Ten volumes; Boston: Little, Brown & Co., 1850-1856.

————, and JEFFERSON, THOMAS, *The Adams-Jefferson Letters*, Lester J. Cappon, ed. Two volumes; New York: Simon & Schuster, 1959.

————, and RUSH, BENJAMIN, *The Spur of Fame: Dialogues between John Adams and Benjamin Rush, 1805-1813.* John A. Schutz and Douglass Adair, ed. San Marino, Calif., The Huntington Library, 1966.

————, and WATERHOUSE, BENJAMIN, *Statesman and Friend: Correspondence of John Adams with Benjamin Waterhouse, 1784-1822*, Worthington Chauncy Ford, ed. Boston: Little, Brown & Co., 1927.

BAILYN, BERNARD, ed., *Pamphlets of the American Revolution.* Two volumes; Cambridge, Mass.: Harvard University Press, 1965.

HAMILTON, ALEXANDER; JAY, JOHN; and MADISON, JAMES, *The Federalist: A Commentary on the Constitution of the United States*, Edward Mead Earle, ed. New York: Modern Library, 1937.

HUME, DAVID, *Essays, Moral, Political, and Literary*, T. H. Green and T. H. Grose, eds. Two volumes; London: Oxford University Press, 1882.

JEFFERSON, THOMAS, *The Commonplace Book of Thomas Jefferson: A Repertory of His Ideas on Government*, Gilbert Chinard, ed. Baltimore: Johns Hopkins Press, 1926.

————, *The Life and Selected Writings of Thomas Jefferson.* Adrienne Koch and William Peden, eds. New York: Modern Library, 1944.

————, *The Literary Bible of Thomas Jefferson: His Commonplace Book of Philosophers and Poets*, Gilbert Chinard, ed. Baltimore: Johns Hopkins Press, 1928.

————, *The Papers of Thomas Jefferson*, Julian Boyd, ed. Princeton, N. J.: Princeton University Press, 1950-

————, *The Writings of Thomas Jefferson*, Andrew A. Lipscomb and Albert Ellery Bergh, eds. Twenty volumes; Washington, D.C.: Taylor and Maury, 1905.

KOCH, ADRIENNE, ed., *The American Enlightenment: The Shaping of the American Experiment and a Free Society.* New York: George Braziller, 1965.

LOCKE, JOHN, *Two Treatises of Government*, Thomas I. Cook, ed. New York: Hafner Publishing Company, 1947; originally published in 1690.

MADISON, JAMES, *The Mind of the Founder: Sources of the Political Thought of James Madison*, Marvin Meyers, ed. Indianapolis and New York: Bobbs-Merrill, 1973.

———, *The Papers of James Madison*, William T. Hutchinson and William M. W. Rachel, eds. Chicago and London: University of Chicago Press, 1962-1973.

———, *The Writings of James Madison*, Gaillard Hunt, ed. Nine volumes; New York: G. P. Putnam's Sons, 1900-1910.

PAINE, THOMAS, *The Writings of Thomas Paine*, Moncure D. Conway, ed. Four volumes; New York: G. P. Putnam's Sons, 1894-1896.

PRICE, RICHARD, *Observations on the Importance of the American Revolution, and the Means of Making It a Benefit to the World.* Boston: Powar & Willis, 1784.

ROUSSEAU, JEAN-JACQUES, *The Social Contract*, trans. by Maurice Cranston. Baltimore: Penguin Books, 1968; first published in French in 1762.

SECONDAT, CHARLES, Baron de Montesquieu, *The Spirit of the Laws*, trans. by Thomas Nugent. New York and London: Hafner Publishing Co., 1949; original French edition, 1748.

THORNTON, JOHN WINGATE, *The Pulpit of the American Revolution.* New York: De Capo Press, 1970; 1860.

WILSON, JAMES, *The Works of James Wilson*, Robert Green McCloskey, ed. Two volumes; Cambridge, Mass.: Harvard University Press, 1967.

Secondary Works

ADAIR, DOUGLASS, *Fame and the Founding Fathers, Essays by Douglas Adair*, Trevor Colbourn, ed. New York: W. W. Norton & Co., 1974.

———, " 'That Politics May Be Reduced to a Science': David Hume, James Madison, and the Tenth *Federalist*," *Huntington Library Quarterly*, 20 (1957), pp. 343-60.

ARENDT, HANNAH, *On Revolution.* New York: Viking Press, 1963.

BAILYN, BERNARD, *The Ideological Origins of the American Revolution.* Cambridge, Mass.: Harvard University Press, 1967.

BECKER, CARL L., *The Declaration of Independence: A Study in the History of Political Ideas.* New York: Alfred A. Knopf, 1922.

BENSON, G. RANDOLPH, *Thomas Jefferson as Social Scientist.* Rutherford, Madison, Teaneck, N. J.: Fairleigh Dickinson University Press, 1971.

BINGER, CARL, *Thomas Jefferson: A Well-Tempered Mind.* New York: W. W. Norton & Co., 1970.

BOORSTIN, DANIEL J., *The Genius of American Politics.* Chicago: University of Chicago Press, 1953.

————, *The Lost World of Thomas Jefferson.* Boston: Beacon Press, 1960; 1948.

BRIDENBAUGH, CARL, *Mitre and Sceptre: Transatlantic Faiths, Ideas, Personalities, and Politics, 1689-1775.* New York: Oxford University Press, 1962.

BURNS, EDWARD MCNALL, *James Madison: Philosopher of the Constitution.* New Brunswick, N. J.: Rutgers University Press, 1938.

BURY, J. B., *The Idea of Progress: An Inquiry into Its Origins and Growth.* London: Macmillan, 1928.

COBBAN, ALFRED, "The Enlightenment and the French Revolution," pp. 305-15. *Aspects of the Eighteenth Century,* Earl R. Wasserman, ed. Baltimore: Johns Hopkins Press, 1965.

COLBOURN, TREVOR H., *The Lamp of Experience: Whig History and the Intellectual Origins of the American Revolution.* Chapel Hill, N. C.: University of North Carolina Press, 1965.

DAVIS, HERBERT, "The Augustan Conception of History," pp. 213-29, *Reason and Imagination: Studies in the History of Ideas, 1600-1800,* J. A. Mazzeo, ed. New York: Columbia University Press, 1962.

DAVIS, RICHARD BEALE, *Intellectual Life in Jefferson's Virginia, 1790-1830.* Chapel Hill, N. C.: University of North Carolina Press, 1964.

DIAMOND, MARTIN, "Democracy and *The Federalist*: A Reconsideration of the Framers' Intent," *American Political Science Review,* 53 (1959), pp. 53-68.

DIETZE, GOTTFRIED, *The Federalist: A Classic on Federalism and Free Government.* Baltimore: Johns Hopkins University Press, 1960.

DUNN, JOHN, *The Political Thought of John Locke: An Historical Account of the Argument of the "Two Treatises of Government."* Cambridge: Cambridge University Press, 1969.

————, "The Politics of Locke in England and America in the Eighteenth Century," pp. 45-80, *John Locke: Problems and Perspectives. A Collection of New Essays,* John W. Yolton, ed. Cambridge: Cambridge University Press, 1969.

ECHEVERRIA, DURAND, *Mirage in the West: A History of the French Image of American Society to 1815.* Princeton, N. J.: Princeton University Press, 1957.

FAY, BERNARD, *The Revolutionary Spirit in France and America: A Study of Moral and Intellectual Relations between France and the United States at the End of the Eighteenth Century,* trans. by Ramon Guthrie, New York: Harcourt, Brace & Co., 1927.

GAY, PETER, "The Enlightenment in the History of Political Theory," *Political Science Quarterly,* 69 (1954), pp. 374-89.

———, *The Enlightenment, II: An Interpretation. The Science of Freedom.* New York: Alfred A. Knopf, 1969.

GREENE, EVARTS B., *The Revolutionary Generation, 1763-1790.* New York: Macmillan, 1943.

GUMMERE, RICHARD M., *The American Colonial Mind and the Classical Tradition: Essays in Comparative Culture.* Cambridge, Mass.: Harvard University Press, 1963.

HANDLER, EDWARD, *America and Europe in the Political Thought of John Adams.* Cambridge, Mass.: Harvard University Press, 1964.

HARTZ, LOUIS, "American Political Thought and the Revolution," *American Political Science Review,* 46 (1952), pp. 321-42.

HOWE, JOHN R., JR., *The Changing Political Thought of John Adams.* Princeton, N. J.: Princeton University Press, 1966.

HOWELL, WILBUR SAMUEL, "The Declaration of Independence and Eighteenth-Century Logic," *William and Mary Quarterly,* 18, Ser. 3 (1961), pp. 463-84.

JONES, HOWARD MUMFORD, *America and French Culture, 1750-1848.* Chapel Hill, N. C.: University of North Carolina Press, 1927.

———, *The Pursuit of Happiness.* Cambridge, Mass.: Harvard University Press, 1953.

JORDAN, WINTHROP D., *White over Black: American Attitudes toward the Negro, 1550-1812.* Chapel Hill, N. C.: University of North Carolina Press, 1968.

KETCHAM, RALPH L., "James Madison and the Nature of Man," *Journal of the History of Ideas,* 19 (1958), pp. 62-76.

KOCH, ADRIENNE, "The Contest of Democracy and Aristocracy in the American Enlightenment," *Studies on Voltaire and the Eighteenth Century,* 26 (1963), pp. 999-1018.

———, *The Philosophy of Thomas Jefferson.* New York: Columbia University Press, 1943.

— — —, *Power, Morals, and the Founding Fathers: Essays in the Interpretation of the American Enlightenment.* Ithaca, N. Y.: Cornell University Press, 1961.

LEDER, LAWRENCE H., *Liberty and Authority: Early American Political Ideology, 1689-1764.* Chicago: Quadrangle Press, 1968.

LEHMANN, KARL, *Thomas Jefferson: American Humanist.* Chicago and London: University of Chicago Press, 1965; 1947.

LOVEJOY, ARTHUR O., *Reflections on Human Nature.* Baltimore: Johns Hopkins Press, 1961.

LYND, STAUGHTON, *Intellectual Origins of American Radicalism.* New York: Pantheon Books, 1968.

MAIER, PAULINE, *From Resistance to Revolution: Colonial Radicals and the Development of American Opposition to Britain, 1765-1775.* New York: Alfred A. Knopf, 1972.

MALONE, DUMAS, *Jefferson and the Ordeal of Liberty.* Boston: Little, Brown, & Co., 1962.

———, *Jefferson and the Rights of Man.* Boston: Little, Brown, & Co., 1951.

———, *Jefferson the Virginian.* Boston: Little, Brown & Co., 1948.

MARTIN, EDWIN T., *Thomas Jefferson: Scientist.* New York: Collier Books, 1961; 1952.

MILLER, JOHN C., *The Federalist Era, 1789-1801.* New York: Harper & Row, 1960.

MORRIS, RICHARD B., *The American Revolution Reconsidered.* New York: Harper & Row, Inc., 1967.

MULLETT, CHARLES F., "Classical Influences on the American Revolution," *The Classical Journal,* 35 (1939), pp. 92-104.

PALMER, R. R., *The Age of the Democratic Revolution.* Two volumes; Princeton, N. J.: Princeton University Press, 1959, 1964.

———, "The American Revolution," in C. Vann Woodward, ed., *The Comparative Approach to American History,* pp. 47-61. New York and London: Basic Books, 1968.

———, "The Dubious Democrat: Thomas Jefferson in Bourbon France," *Political Science Quarterly,* 72 (1957), pp. 388-404.

PETERSON, MERRILL D., *Thomas Jefferson and the New Nation: A Biography.* New York: Oxford University Press, 1970.

PLAMENATZ, JOHN, *Man and Society: Political and Social Theory.* Two volumes; New York and San Francisco: McGraw-Hill Co. Inc., 1963.

READ, CONYERS, ed., *The Constitution Reconsidered.* New York: Columbia University Press, 1938.

ROBBINS, CAROLINE, "Algernon Sidney's *Discourses Concerning Government*: Textbook of Revolution," *William and Mary Quarterly,* 4, Ser. 3 (1947), pp. 267-96.

———, *Eighteenth Century Commonwealth.* Cambridge, Mass.: Harvard University Press, 1959.

———, " 'When It Is that Colonies May Turn Independent': An Analysis of the Environment and Politics of Francis Hutcheson," *William and Mary Quarterly,* 11, Ser. 3 (1954), pp. 214-51.

SCANLAN, JAMES P., "*The Federalist* and Human Nature," *Review of Politics,* 21 (1959), pp. 657-77.

SMELSER, MARSHALL, "The Federalist Era as an Age of Passion," *American Quarterly,* 10 (1958), pp. 391-419.

SPURLIN, PAUL MERRILL, *Montesquieu in America, 1760-1801.* Baton Rouge: Louisiana State University Press, 1940.

———, *Rousseau in America, 1760-1809.* University, Ala.: University of Alabama, 1969.

TATE, THAD W., "The Social Contract in America, 1774-1787," *William and Mary Quarterly,* 22, Ser. 3 (1965), pp. 375-91.

TYLER, MOSES COIT, *The Literary History of the American Revolution, 1763-1783.* Two volumes; New York and London: G. P. Putnam's Sons, 1897.

WOOD, GORDON, *The Creation of the American Republic, 1776-1787.* Chapel Hill, N. C.: University of North Carolina Press, 1969.

———, "Republicanism as a Revolutionary Ideology" (1967) in John R. Howe, Jr., ed., *The Role of Ideology in the American Revolution,* pp. 83-91. New York: Holt, Rinehart, & Winston, 1970.

———, Rhetoric and Reality in the American Revolution," *William and Mary Quarterly,* 23, Ser. 3 (1966), pp. 3-32.

WRIGHT, BENJAMIN F., JR., *American Interpretations of Natural Law.* Cambridge, Mass.: Harvard University Press, 1931.

PART IV
THE ENLIGHTENMENT AS AN AMERICAN INSTITUTION

Primary Works

BEATTIE, JAMES, *An Essay on the Nature and Immutability of Truth, in Opposition to Sophistry and Skepticism.* Edinburgh: Denhom & Dick, 1805; 1770.

BLAU, JOSEPH, ed., *American Philosophic Addresses, 1700-1900.* New York: Columbia University Press, 1946.

CHANNING, WILLIAM ELLERY, *Memoir of William Ellery Channing, with Extracts from His Correspondence and Manuscripts,* William Henry Channing, ed. Three volumes; Boston: William Crosby & H. P. Nichols, 1851; 1848.

———, *The Works of William Ellery Channing.* Boston: American Unitarian Association; 1903.

DENNIE, JOSEPH, *The Letters of Joseph Dennie,* Laura G. M. Pedder, ed. Orono, Maine: Maine University Press, 1936.

DWIGHT, TIMOTHY, *The Nature, and Danger, of Infidel Philosophy.* New Haven: G. Bunce, 1798.

PAINE, THOMAS, *The Age of Reason: Being an Investigation of True and of Fabulous Theology* (Two volumes, 1794, 1796). In *The Writings of Thomas Paine,* Moncure D. Conway, ed. Four volumes; New York: G. P. Putnam's Sons, 1894-1896, IV.

PALMER, ELIHU, *Principles of Nature; Or, a Development of the Moral Causes of Happiness and Misery among the Human Species.* London: R. Carlile, 1823; originally published, 1801.

REID, THOMAS, *Essays on the Active Powers of Man* (1788), Vol. II, *The Works of Thomas Reid, D.D.,* Sir William Hamilton, ed. Two volumes; Edinburgh: Maclachlam & Steward, 1863.

————, *An Inquiry into the Human Mind, on the Principles of Common Sense.* Second edition, corrected. London: A. Miller; Edinburgh: A. Kincaid and J. Bell, 1765; 1764.

RUSH, BENJAMIN, *Essays, Literary, Moral and Philosophical.* Philadelphia: Thomas & William Bradford, 1806.

————, *The Letters of Benjamin Rush,* Lyman H. Butterfield, ed. Two volumes; Princeton, N. J.: Prnceton University Press, 1948.

SCHNEIDER, LOUIS, ed., *The Scottish Moralists on Human Nature and Society.* Chicago and London: University of Chicago Press, 1967.

SIMPSON, LEWIS, ed., *The Federalist Literary Mind: Selections from The Monthly Anthology and Boston Review, 1803-1811.* Baton Rouge, La.: Louisiana State University Press, 1962.

STEWART, DUGALD, *The Philosophy of the Active and Moral Powers of Man* (1828), Vols. VI and VII, *The Collected Works of Dugald Stewart, Esq., F.R.S.S.,* Sir William Hamilton, ed. Edinburgh: Thomas Constable & Co.; Boston: Little, Brown & Co., 1855.

TOCQUEVILLE, DE, ALEXIS, *Democracy in America,* J. P. Mayer, ed., trans. by George Lawrence. Garden City, N. Y.: Anchor Books, 1969. Original French edition, two volumes, 1835, 1840.

WITHERSPOON, JOHN, *John Witherspoon Comes to America: A Documentary Account Based Largely on New Materials,* Lyman H. Butterfield, ed. Princeton, N. J.: Princeton University Press, 1953.

————, *Lectures on Moral Philosophy.* Princeton, N. J.: Princeton University Press, 1912; originally published, 1800.

WOOD, GORDON S., ed., *The Rising Glory of America, 1760-1820.* New York: George Braziller, 1971.

Secondary Works

ARIELI, YEHOSHUA, *Individualism and Nationalism in American Ideology.* Baltimore: Penguin Books, 1966; 1964.

BARKER, CHARLES A., *American Convictions: Cycles of Public Thought, 1600-1850.* Philadelphia and New York: J. B. Lippincott Co., 1970.

BARR, MARY MARGARET H., *Voltaire in America, 1744-1800.* Baltimore: Johns Hopkins Press, 1941.

BELLAH, ROBERT N., "Civil Religion in America," pp. 3-23, *Religion in America*, William G. McLoughlin and Robert N. Bellah, eds. Boston: Beacon Press, 1968.

BODO, JOHN R., *The Protestant Clergy and Public Issues, 1812-1848.* Princeton, N. J.: Princeton University Press, 1954.

BUEL, RICHARD, JR., *Securing the Revolution: Ideology in America Politics, 1789-1815.* Ithaca and London: Cornell University Press, 1972.

CHADWICK, JOHN WHITE, *William Ellery Channing: Minister of Religion.* Boston and New York: Houghton Mifflin Co., 1903.

CURTI, MERLE, "The Great Mr. Locke, America's Philosopher, 1783-1861," Huntington Library, *Bulletin*, Number 11 (1937), pp. 107-151.

EATON, CLEMENT, *Freedom of Thought in the Old South.* Durham, N. C.: Duke University Press, 1940.

EDGELL, DAVID P., *William Ellery Channing: An Intellectual Portrait.* Boston: Beacon Press, 1955.

FOSTER, CHARLES I., *An Errand of Mercy: The Evangelical United Front, 1790-1870.* Chapel Hill, N. C.: University of North Carolina Press, 1960.

FOX, DIXON RYAN and KROUT, JOHN A., *The Completion of Independence, 1790-1830.* New York and London: Macmillan, 1944.

HARTZ, LOUIS, *The Liberal Tradition in America.* New York: Harcourt, Brace & World, 1955.

HOWARD, LEON, *The Connecticut Wits.* Chicago: University of Chicago Press, 1942.

———, "The Late Eighteenth Century: An Age of Contradictions," pp. 51-89. *Transitions in American Literary History,* Harry Hayden Clark, ed. Durham, N. C.: Duke University Press, 1953.

HOWE, DANIEL WALKER, *The Unitarian Conscience: Harvard Moral Philosophy, 1805-1861.* Cambridge, Mass.: Harvard University Press, 1970.

KAMMEN, MICHAEL, *People of Paradox: An Inquiry Concerning the Origins of American Civilization.* New York: Alfred A. Knopf, 1972.

KERBER, LINDA K., *Federalists in Dissent: Imagery and Ideology in Jeffersonian America.* Ithaca and London: Cornell University Press, 1970.

KOCH, G. ADOLPH, *Religion of the American Enlightenment.* New York: Thomas Y. Crowell, 1968; first published, 1933.

LIPSET, SEYMOUR MARTIN, *The First New Nation: The United States in Historical and Comparative Perspective.* New York: Basic Books, 1963.

MCCOSH, JAMES, *The Scottish Philosophy, Biographical, Expository, Critical, from Hutcheson to Hamilton.* New York: Robert Carter & Brothers, 1875.

MCLOUGHLIN, WILLIAM G., "Pietism and the American Character," *American Quarterly,* 17 (1965), pp. 163-86.

MARTY, MARTIN E., *The Infidel: Freethought and American Religion*. Cleveland and New York: World Publishing Company, 1961.

MEAD, SIDNEY E., *The Lively Experiment: The Shaping of Christianity in America*. New York, Evanston, London: Harper & Row, 1963.

MEYER, D. H., *The Instructed Conscience: The Shaping of the American National Ethic*. Philadelphia: University of Pennsylvania Press, 1971.

MILLER, PERRY, "From Covenant to Revival," pp. 322-68. *The Shaping of American Religion*, James Ward Smith and A. Leland Jamison, eds. Princeton, N. J.: Princeton University Press, 1961.

————, *The Life of the Mind in America from the Revolution to the Civil War*. New York: Holt, Rinehart, & Winston, 1965.

MOREIS, HERBERT M., *Deism in Eighteenth Century America*. New York: Columbia University Press, 1934.

MORGAN, EDMUND S., "The American Revolution Considered as an Intellectual Movement," pp. 11-33, *Paths of American Thought*, Arthur M. Schlesinger and Morton White, eds. Boston: Houghton Mifflin Co., 1970; 1962.

NYE, RUSSEL B., *The Cultural Life of the New Nation, 1776-1830*. New York, Evanston, London: Harper & Row, Inc., 1960.

PERSONS, STOW, *American Minds: A History of Ideas*. New York: Henry Holt, 1958.

ROSSITER, CLINTON, *Seedtime of the Republic: The Origins of the American Tradition of Political Liberty*. New York: Harcourt, Brace & Co., 1953.

SCHMIDT, GEORGE P., *The Old Time College President*. New York: Columbia University Press, 1930.

SLOAN, DOUGLAS, *The American Enlightenment and the American College Ideal*. New York: Teachers College of Columbia University, 1971.

SONNE, NIELS H., *Liberal Kentucky, 1780-1823*. New York: Columbia University Press, 1939.

TALMON, J. L., *The Origins of Totalitarian Democracy*. Boston: Beacon, 1952.

WHITE, MORTON, *Science and Sentiment in America: Philosophical Thought from Jonathan Edwards to John Dewey*. New York: Oxford University Press, 1972.

INDEX

Abolitionists, 126
Academician, 185; as public intellectual, 187-88
Académie Royale des Sciences, 52
Accademia del Cimento, 52
Adams, Abigail, 110
Adams, Henry, 115, 136
Adams, James Truslow, 123
Adams, John, xii, xxvi, 51, 54, 99, 109, 110, 111, 113, 115, 119, 120, 129-48, 152, 154, 164, 172, 175, 184, 187, 191, 196, 203; on Age of Reason, xii, 146-48; on government, 151, 166; and human nature, 132-33, 135, 138-39, 140-42, 143, 148; moral philosophy, 132-33; on philosophes, 135, 137, 141, 144-45; political philosophy, 130-31, 133-39, 146 ff.; and preservation of national virtue, 166; and radical Whigs, 136-37; and society, 138-39, 142-46; theory of sovereignty, 138; as Yankee philosophe, 130
Adams, John Quincy, 179
Adams, Samuel, 110, 134

Addison, Joseph, xx, xxiii, 57, 72, 88
Age of Reason, xii, 146-48. *See also* Enlightenment
Age of Reason (Paine), 13, 173
Agrarianism, and preservation of public virtue, 165-66
Alembert, *See* D'Alembert
Allen, Ethan, xxiii, 173, 174
American Academy for the Advancement of Science, 51
American colonies: cities, 56-58, 59; institutions, 55-56; literature, 53-54, 60; rural population, 58-59; science, 50-51, 52, 60
American Enlightenment, vii, xi, xix-xxvii; and Adams, 129-48; and Channing, 201-8; containment of, 171-81; cultural provinciality, xix-xx, 50-60; democratic character of, xxiv, 171 ff., 208; and education, xxv, 90-92, 185-93, 196-98; and Edwards, 18-34; Evangelicalism, 35-45, 177, 180, 184; Franklin, 61-81; intellectualism, 171-81; and